PATRISTIC SOURCES AND CATHOLIC SOCIAL TEACHING

ANNUA NUNTIA LOVANIENSIA
LIX

Brian J. Matz

Patristic Sources and Catholic Social Teaching: a Forgotten Dimension

A Textual, Historical, and Rhetorical Analysis of
Patristic Source Citations in the Church's Social Documents

PEETERS
LEUVEN – PARIS – DUDLEY, MA
2008

A CIP record for this book is available from the Library of Congress.

For
Tony, Dee,
Gina, Rita, Lora, John Paul
and their extended families

My introduction to authentic, Catholic Christianity

Cover: The Holy Hierarchs: Saints Gregory the Theologian, John Chrysostom
and Basil the Great
(Greek; 19th century; 125 × 73.5 cm).

© Uitgeverij Peeters, Bondgenotenlaan 153, B-3000 Leuven (Belgium)
ISBN 978-90-429-2029-3
D/2008/0602/28

Contents

Foreword VII
Acknowledgments VIII
List of Tables IX
List of Abbreviations X

General Introduction

Object of the Study 3
Organization of the Study 13

Analysis of the Patristic Source Citations

Rerum Novarum (1891) 16
Quadragesimo anno (1931) 22
Mater et magistra (1961) 25
Pacem in terris (1963) 28
Dignitatis humanae (1965) 35
Gaudium et spes (1965) 41
Populorum progressio (1967) 57
Evangelii nuntiandi (1975) 60
Puebla Documents (CELAM III, 1979) 74
Familiaris consortio (1981) 76
The Challenge of Peace (USCCB, 1983) 83
Economic Justice for All (USCCB, 1986) 88
Sollicitudo rei socialis (1987) 90
Centesimus annus (1991) 96
Santo Domingo Documents (CELAM IV, 1992) 98
Compendium of Catholic Social Thought (2004) 101
Deus caritas est (2005) 121

Reflection

Summary of the Study's Findings 142
A New Vision for CST 151

Bibliography 155

Foreword

As with any historical study, written documents do not always tell the whole story. There are people and events lying behind the texts that inspired the written words. Sometimes these people and events are from the distant past, whose legacies linger one way or another. This is no less true in reading the documents of Catholic social teaching. The documents emerged within their own particular, historical contexts, and they even invite their readers to consider the writings of earlier authorities in matters of social teaching, including the scriptures and the writings of Church fathers and of scholastics. Thankfully, scholars past and present have filled many gaps in the story with studies on the historical contexts in which the documents were written. However, there are still gaps to be filled in terms of the influence on the documents from people and events in the distant past. This study, it is hoped, contributes towards filling that gap as it evaluates how Catholic social teaching has employed patristic sources in its arguments.

On the one hand, this study was a process of reverse engineering, thinking the thoughts of the document's drafters after them and after their own time and culture. I have surmised what lay behind the use of patristic sources and what pedagogical or rhetorical function these sources play in the social documents. I trust the reader will agree that I was charitable in my estimation of how each patristic text fits the larger framework of the documents, particularly when this was not clear in the documents themselves. As well, I trust the reader will agree that I have done so with proper sensitivity to the aims of the documents themselves. Nevertheless, it will be clear to the reader that this study was prepared by one whose sympathies lie more with the patristic texts than they do with the Church's social documents. Put another way, my respect and appreciation for the documents remains unchanged; I merely express at various points a wish that the documents had let the patristic texts speak more fully.

Brian Matz
November 2006

Acknowledgments

It is with pleasure that I acknowledge the contributions of those who made it possible for me to bring this work to a completion. On behalf of the research center with which I am affiliated, the Centre for Catholic Social Thought at the K. U. Leuven, thanks must first and foremost go to the Fund for Scientific Research of Flanders. They provided a multi-year grant to support a research agenda, of which this book represents a part. Prof. Dr. Johan Verstraeten, director of the Centre, and Prof. Dr. Johan Leemans, of Universität Erfurt, have been my guides in this research agenda, and have read critically and carefully this book's early manuscripts. Lucrèce de Becker is my colleague at the Centre and has provided incalculable assistance to me in navigating the halls of the K. U. Leuven during my research time. Thanks are due to the staff of the Maurits Sabbe Library of the Faculty of Theology. They have brought together resources in the fields of patristics and ethics that are matched by few other institutions in the world. As well, I thank the ILL staff of the K. U. Leuven's central library for their acquisitions of obscure articles and texts on my behalf. I am grateful also for the cooperation of Patricia Killen O'Connell at the Pacific Lutheran University, who provided me access to her institution's resources during an extended visit to the Puget Sound in December 2005 at which some of the work for this book was prepared. Finally, I thank my wife, who has supported my work for years, but most especially through her tireless oversight and care of our family while in Leuven.

List of Tables

Table 1: CST Documents and their Patristic Sources – Summary   4

Table 2: Density of Patristic Source Citations in CST   5

Table 3: Patristic Sources in CST (Sorted by CST Document) .   6

Table 4: Patristic Sources in CST (Sorted by Patristic Source) ..   9

Table 5: Rhetorical Function of the Patristic Sources   146

Table 6: Frequency of Rhetorical Function according to Citation Category   149

Table 7: Frequency of Rhetorical Function according to CST Document   150

List of Abbreviations
Reference Works and Series

AAS	Acta Apostolicae Sedis
ACW	Ancient Christian Writers: The Works of the Fathers in Translation
ANF	The Ante-Nicene Fathers series
ASS	Acta Sanctae Sedis
CCSG	Corpus Christianorum Series Graeca
CCSL	Corpus Christianorum Series Latina
CPG	Corpus Christianorum Clavis Patrum Graecorum, five volumes and supplement
CSEL	Corpus Scriptorum Ecclesiasticorum Latinorum
CSLP	Corpus Scriptorum Latinorum Paravianum
CST:DocHer	Catholic Social Thought: The Documentary Heritage (eds. David J. O'Brien and Thomas A. Shannon)
CWS	Classics of Western Spirituality: A Library of the Great Spiritual Masters
FOTC	The Fathers of the Church
FP	Florilegium patristicum
GCS	Die griechischen christlichen Schriftsteller der ersten Jahrhunderte
LCL	Loeb Classical Library
LSJ	A Greek-English Lexicon with Revised Supplement, eds. Henry G. Liddell and Robert Scott, with rev. by Henry S. Jones
MGH	Monumenta Germaniae historica
NPNF	Nicene and Post-Nicene Fathers, in two series
PG	Patrologia Graeca, ed. J. P. Migne
PL	Patrologia Latina, ed. J. P. Migne
PTS	Patristiche Texte und Studien
RSV	Revised Standard Version of the Bible
SC	Sources Chrétiennes
Tanner I/II	Decrees of the Ecumenical Councils, 2 vols.
WSA	The Works of Saint Augustine: A Translation for the 21st Century

List of Abbreviations
Encyclicals

RN	Rerum Novarum (1891)
QA	Quadragesimo anno (1931)
MM	Mater et magistra (1961)
PT	Pacem in terris (1963)
DH	Dignitatis humanae (1965)
GS	Gaudium et spes (1965)
PP	Populorum progressio (1967)
Medellin	CELAM, Medellin Documents (1969)
OA	Octogesima adveniens (1971)
IM	Iustitia in mundo (1971)
EN	Evangelii nuntiandi (1975)
Puebla	CELAM, Puebla Documents (1979)
LE	Laborem exercens (1981)
FC	Familiaris consortio (1981)
ChP	The Challenge of Peace (1983)
EJA	Economic Justice for All (1986)
SRS	Sollicitudo rei socialis (1987)
CA	Centesimus annus (1991)
SDomingo	CELAM, Santo Domingo Documents (1992)
ComCST	Compendium of CST (2004)
DCE	Deus caritas est (2005)

I

General Introduction

The post-Enlightenment world has not always looked with great appreciation upon institutions that draw their inspiration from pre-Enlightenment historical events. Christian churches draw their share of the criticism for linking contemporary beliefs to the reality and significance of events in the distant past. These events, biblical and post-biblical, shape Christian expressions of faith. One such faith expression is the Catholic Church's social teaching, generally thought to encompass a set of documents that have emerged out of the Vatican and certain regional bishops' conferences since the late nineteenth century (hereafter referred to as CST documents).[1] This study examines these documents with an interest in the attention they pay to at least one aspect of the Church's historical roots, the patristic era.

The book's title suggests patristic sources are a forgotten dimension in Catholic social teaching. What this means is that patristic sources have largely been overlooked in the construction of CST documents. This is not to say they are absent, for more than a hundred patristic sources may be found in the documents. Rather, there are two problems

---

1. This phrase, "Catholic social teaching" is used in a technical sense, with the definition provided above, and is in contrast with "Catholic social thought." This latter phrase refers to the official texts *plus* the unofficial activities that take place in parishes, lay institutes, and Catholic worker movements, among other places. These unofficial activities not only engage in the work of alleviating injustice and caring for the marginalized, they also exhort the hierarchy to rethink continually its commitment to those people groups.

For a listing of documents that comprise CST, the reader is invited to consider David J. O'Brien and Thomas A. Shannon, *Catholic Social Thought: The Documentary Heritage* (Maryknoll, NY: Orbis Books, 1992); Kenneth Himes, ed., *Modern Catholic Social Teaching: Commentaries and Interpretations* (Washington, D.C.: Georgetown University Press, 2005). Of course, it is the case social teaching existed prior to the late nineteenth century, and the interested reader of these earlier sources is directed to the oft-cited book, Michael Schuck, *That They Be One: The Social Teaching of the Papal Encyclicals, 1740-1989* (Washington, D.C.: Georgetown University Press, 1991). This present study has limited itself to the so-called modern CST documents for the simple reason they comprise a body of literature that is a particular focus of study for many scholars of CST. There is no reason why a study such as this could not also be carried out for the pre-modern CST documents.

this study will explore. The first is that the citations of patristic sources one finds in the documents often do not reflect the full force of the arguments present in the patristic sources themselves. The CST documents often incorporate a part but not the whole of the argument from the original source, a move which oftentimes withholds from the reader important theological or practical extensions of the CST document's argument. The second problem is a lack of correlation between the quantity of patristic texts on socio-ethical themes and the texts selected for inclusion in the CST documents. There are many patristic texts on socio-ethical themes, but they are largely absent from the collection of patristic sources identified by this study.

The patristic era, encompassing at least the second through seventh centuries, is generally regarded as a time when the Church formulated its theology, narrowed its canon, and solidified its place in the social, cultural, and political contexts of the day. Theologically, the Church Fathers elucidated both Christianity's understanding of God as a trinity of coequal, consubstantial, and coeternal persons and its understanding of Christ as one person possessing in full both a divine and a human nature. These theologies were the foundation for additional considerations, including anthropology, ecclesiology, and eschatology.

Important with regard to the CST documents in this study are these expanded theological reflections. For instance, the CST document *Centesimus annus* (1991) argued, "The guiding principle of ... all of the church's social doctrine, is a correct view of the human person and of his unique value."[2] *CA* goes on to point out that a human person's unique value may be traced directly back to the *imago Dei* given to man at the creation of the world. God gave to man this *imago Dei* as a consequence of foreknowing that the Son of God would one day incarnate himself as a human. In other words, Catholic social teaching is built upon a notion of human dignity. This dignity is rooted in the gift of God to each person, a gift which is an outworking of the mutual love existing amongst the persons of the Trinity. Therefore, Christ would eventually redeem what had always been and will continue to be creatures in his own image. To the extent that the patristic world had correctly articulated the doctrine of the Trinity, of Christ and his two natures, of man and his need for redemption, and the Church's responsibility to pass along these truths to every new generation, then the CST documents owe an incalculable debt to its theological acumen.

---

2. *CA* 11; cf. CST:DocHer, 447.

It is precisely because of this theological debt that this study considers what might be the actual role played by patristic sources in the CST documents. An examination of the CST documents yielded a list of 110 patristic source citations. The study focused on how those sources function with respect to the larger context in which they are found in the CST documents. As well, the study assesses what is the theological or practical contribution of these historical sources to the arguments of the CST documents. Perhaps CST's debt to patristic theology will be matched by its qualitative use of patristic texts.

Object of the Study

This study focused its attention on a collection of modern CST documents. Table 1 below is a list of the CST documents that were included in this study. Although followers of CST may differ on one or another of the documents included in the list below, this study limits itself to major encyclicals from the Vatican, relevant documents from Vatican II, and significant pastoral letters emerging from regional bishops' conferences. To that end, this study was guided in its selection by the documents found in David J. O'Brien's and Thomas A. Shannon's book, *Catholic Social Thought: The Documentary Heritage*, and those commented upon in the volume edited by Kenneth Himes and others, *Modern Catholic Social Teaching: Commentaries and Interpretations*.[3] Looking to the table, the name of the CST document is given first, followed by a shorthand designation for it. This shorthand designation will be used throughout the rest of this study. The third column identifies how many patristic source citations may be found in that document, and the final three columns break down that number in accordance with how those sources are presented in the body of the document. One category is the direct quotations of patristic sources in the CST documents. The quotations may or may not be accompanied by the patristic author's name or the name of the text from which the quotation comes. Quotations are generally associated with a footnote that supplies this data. A second category is the general references to patristic source material in the body of the CST document. One common example is, "The Church Fathers say…" Such references may or may not be accompanied by a footnote to indicate what the drafter or drafters of the CST document had in

3. See above n. 1.

mind. A third category is footnote-only references to patristic sources, where, were it not for the presence of a footnote, the body of the CST document gives no indication a patristic source is behind its thought. Four of the CST documents examined cited no patristic sources. They are included in this list to let the reader know the extent of the study's search, but no further analysis as to their contents is given in the study.

Table 1: CST Documents and their Patristic Sources – Summary

CST Text	Text Abbrev.	Total Number Patristic Sources	Quotations	References	Footnotes
Rerum novarum (1891)	RN	2	2		
Quadragesimo anno (1931)	QA	2	1	1	
Mater et magistra (1961)	MM	3	2	1	
Pacem in terris (1963)	PT	3	3		
Dignitatis humanae (1965)	DH	8		8	
Gaudium et spes (1965)	GS	18	1	6	11
Populorum progressio (1967)	PP	2	1	1	
Medellin Documents (1969)	Medellin	0			
Octogesima adveniens (1971)	OA	0			
Iustitia in mundo (1971)	IM	0			
Evangelii nuntiandi (1975)	EN	15	6	3	6
Puebla Documents (1979)	Puebla	2		2	
Laborem exercens (1981)	LE	0			
Familiaris consortio (1981)	FC	4	3	1	
The Challenge of Peace (1983)	ChP	5	3	1	1
Economic Justice for All (1986)	EJA	2	1	1	
Sollicitudo rei socialis (1987)	SRS	6		6	
Centesimus annus (1991)	CA	1	1		
Santo Domingo Doc.s (1992)	SDomingo	2		1	1
Compendium of CST (2004)	ComCST	19	5	5	9
Deus caritas est (2005)	DCE	16	6	9	1
TOTALS		110	35	46	29

Table 1 makes clear an imbalance exists in the number of patristic sources cited across the CST documents. Of the 110 citations, sixty-eight (62%) are found in just four documents. It is not the case that these four documents are the longest; indeed, *DCE* is among the shortest and it has the third highest number of patristic source citations. The following table demonstrates this, for it shows the total number of words in each CST document, including footnotes, and the total number of those words used for the patristic source citations. *DCE* has the highest concentration of patristic source citations; nearly 8% of its total word count is devoted to patristic source material. In sum, there is very little correlation between the size of a CST document and the density of its patristic citations. The same is true with respect to the average word count for each patristic citation in the CST documents. *ChP* cites only five patristic sources, but, on average, each one is accorded generous space in the text. *GS*, by contrast, has the second highest number of patristic citations, but, on average, accords each one very little space in the text. Again, no significant correlation exists between average word counts for the citations and either the size of the texts or the number of sources.

Table 2: Density of Patristic Source Citations in the CST Documents

CST Text	Total Word Count (Latin)[4]	Word Count for Patristic Citations	Density of Citations (%)	Total Number Patristic Citations	Avg Words per Citation
RN	10,385	77	0.74%	2	38.5
QA	15,133	63	0.42%	2	31.5
MM	18,606	56	0.30%	3	18.7
PT	12,505	115	0.92%	3	38.3
DH	4,084	137	3.35%	8	17.1
GS	27,357	368	1.34%	18	20.4
PP	11,478	126	1.10%	2	63.0
EN	17,181	358	2.08%	15	23.9
Puebla	–	–	–	–	–
FC	27,642	239	0.86%	4	59.7
ChP	40,909	549	1.34%	5	109.8
EJA	56,929	152	0.27%	2	76.0
SRS	19,760	232	1.17%	6	38.7
CA	18,374	57	0.31%	1	57.0
SDomingo	–	–	–	–	–
ComCST	129,238	1,097	0.85%	19	57.7
DCE	12,934	1,030	7.96%	16	64.4
TOTALS	422,515	4,656	1.10%	106	43.9

4. The numbers shown in this and the next column are close approximations and are included here for the sake of the density calculation. The numbers in the first column were determined by applying Mirosoft Word's "Word Count" tool to the document's original language text (i.e., Latin for most documents). This study makes no affirmation this computer tool is exact in its calculation. The word counts in the second column were prepared by me.

A listing of the 110 patristic source citations follows in the next two tables. Table 3 orders the citations in accordance with the place in the CST documents at which they are found. Table 4 orders the citations by patristic author. The final column in each table indicates what type of citation it is, a quotation (Q), a general reference (R), or a footnote-only reference (F). For two reasons these tables supersede all previous listings of patristic source material in the CST documents, including even the official footnotes of the documents themselves. The first reason is that the official footnotes of the CST documents do not always indicate every time a patristic reference is made in the main text. General references to "the Church Fathers," for example, are not footnoted and so may be easily overlooked by the individual who scours only the footnotes for patristic source material instead of reading the documents in their entirety. A second reason is that, in several cases, the CST documents give incorrect or incomplete references for the patristic sources they are citing. For example, consider number 104 in the list below. The CST document mentioned Gregory's name and gave some indication of his contribution, but it nowhere mentioned the text by Gregory to which it was referring. This study has tracked down the proper references for each patristic source citation and included them in the tables below.

Table 3: Patristic Sources in the CST Documents
(Sorted by CST Document)

Source No.[5]	CST Text	*AAS* Vol: Pg[6]	Patristic Source	Patristic Text	Citation Type[7]
1	RN 19	ASS 23:652	Gregory the Great	*Homily on the Gospel* 9.7	Q
2	RN 24	ASS 23:655	Tertullian	*Apology* 39	Q
3	QA 16	23:181	Ambrose	*On the Passing of Satyrus* I.44	Q
4	QA 50	23:194	"Church Fathers"		R
5	MM 119	53:430	Gregory the Great	*Homily on the Gospel* 9.7	Q

5. This column assigns a unique number to each patristic source. The records of patristic sources in the tables that follow are tied to this number.

6. This column gives the location (volume:page) of the patristic source in the *Acta Apostolicae Sedis* (AAS). In the case of RN, reference is to the *Acta Sanctae Sedis* (ASS). The designation "n/a" is assigned to those patristic source references where the official document was composed in a language other than Latin.

7. This column indicates how the patristic source is presented in the CST document.

Q = a direct quotation from the patristic source is given in the body of the CST document;

R = a general reference to the patristic source is given in the body of the CST document;

F = a footnote-only reference to the patristic source is given in the CST document.

Source No.	CST Text	AAS Vol: Pg	Patristic Source	Patristic Text	Citation Type
6	MM 214	53:452	Augustine	*Confessions* I.1	Q
7	MM 235	53:456	"Ascetical tradition"		R
8	PT 46	55:269	John Chrysostom	*Comm. on Rom., Hom. XXIII* 13.1	Q
9	PT 92	55:282	Augustine	*City of God* 4.4	Q
10	PT 165	55:302	Augustine	*Sermon LIIIA* 12	Q
11	DH 10	58:936	Lactantius	*Divine Institutions* V.19	R
12	DH 10	58:936	Ambrose	*Letter to the Emp. Valentinian* 21	R
13	DH 10	58:936	Augustine	*Against the Letters of Petilian* II.83	R
14	DH 10	58:936	Augustine	*Letter* 23	R
15	DH 10	58:963	Augustine	*Letter* 34	R
16	DH 10	58:963	Augustine	*Letter* 35	R
17	DH 10	58:936	Gregory the Great	*Letter to Virgil and Theodore*	R
18	DH 10	58:936	Gregory the Great	*Letter to John of Constantinople*	R
19	GS 21	58:1042	Augustine	*Confessions* I.1	Q
20	GS 22	58:1042	Tertullian	*The Resurrection of the Body* 6	F
21	GS 22	58:1042	Council – Const. II	*Canon* 7	F
22	GS 22	58:1042	Council – Const. III		F
23	GS 22	58:1042	Council – Chalcedon		F
24	GS 22	58:1042	Council – Const. III		F
25	GS 39	58:1056	Irenaeus (Lyon)	*Against Heresies* V.36	F
26	GS 43	58:1064	Ambrose	*On Virginity* Ch. 8, Art. 48	F
27	GS 44	58:1065	Justin Martyr	*Dialogue with Trypho* Ch. 110	F
28	GS 44	58:1065	Tertullian	*Apology* 50.13	F
29	GS 48	58:1068	Augustine	*On the Good of Marriage* 2-5, 23-24	F
30	GS 57	58:1078	Irenaeus (Lyon)	*Against Heresies* III.1.2	F
31	GS 69	58:1091	Basil (Caesarea)	*Homily VII* 2	R
32	GS 69	58:1091	Lactantius	*Divine Institutions* V.5	R
33	GS 69	58:1091	Augustine	*On John* Ev. Tr. 50, Art. 6	R
34	GS 69	58:1091	Augustine	*Expositions on the Psalms* 147	R
35	GS 69	58:1091	Gregory the Great	*Homily on the Gospel* 20.10-11	R
36	GS 69	58:1091	Gregory the Great	*Rules for Pastors* III.21	R
37	PP 23	67:268-69	Ambrose	*On Naboth* 12.53	Q
38	PP 23	67:269	"Church Fathers"		R
39	EN 15	68:15	Augustine	*Sermon XLVI, De Pastoribus,* 1-2	F
40	EN 16	68:16	Cyprian (Carthage)	*On the Unity of the Church* 14	F
41	EN 16	68:16	Augustine	*Expositions on the Psalms* 88, II.14	F
42	EN 16	68:16	John Chrysostom	*Homily on the Capture of Eutropius* 6	F
43	EN 21	68:20	Minucius Felix	*Octavius* 19 and 31	F
44	EN 21	68:20	Tertullian	*Apology* 39	F
45	EN 53	68:41	Justin Martyr	*Apol., Book I* 46.1-4	Q

Source No.	CST Text	*AAS* Vol: Pg	Patristic Source	Patristic Text	Citation Type
46	EN 53	68:41	Justin Martyr	*Apol., Book II* 7.1-4; 10.1-3; 13.3-4	Q
47	EN 53	68:41	Clement (Alex.)	*Stromata* I.19.91, 94	Q
48	EN 53	68:41	Eusebius (Caesarea)	*Preparation for the Gospel* I.1	Q
49	EN 59	68:50	Augustine	*Expositions on the Psalms* 44.23	Q
50	EN 61	68:51	Didache	*Didache* 9.1	R
51	EN 61	68:51	Gregory the Great	*Homily on the Gospel* 19.1	R
52	EN 67	68:56-57	Leo I	*Sermons* 69.3; 70.1-3; 94.3; 95.2	R
53	EN 71	68:60	John Chrysostom	*Homilies on Genesis* VI.2; VII.1	Q
54	Puebla II.1.1	n/a	"Church Councils"		R
55	Puebla II.2.4	n/a	"Church Fathers"		R
56	FC 6	74:88	Augustine	*City of God* 14.28	R
57	FC 13	74:94	Tertullian	*To His Wife* II.8.6-8	Q
58	FC 16	74:98	John Chrysostom	*On Virginity* 10	Q
59	FC 25	74:110	Ambrose	*Hexameron* V.7.19	Q
60	ChP 81	n/a	Augustine	*City of God* 4.15	R
61	ChP 112	n/a	Justin Martyr	*Dialogue with Trypho* Ch. 110	Q
62	ChP 112	n/a	Justin Martyr	*Apol., Book I* 14 and 39	F
63	ChP 113	n/a	Cyprian (Carthage)	*Letter to Cornelius* 60.2	Q
64	ChP 114	n/a	Sulpicius Severus	*Life of St. Martin* 4.3	Q
65	EJA II.34	n/a	Cyprian (Carthage)	*On Works and Almsgiving* 25	Q
66	EJA II.57	n/a	"Church Fathers"		R
67	SRS 31	80.1:555	Basil (Caesarea)	*Longer Rules* Q. 37, 1-2	R
68	SRS 31	80.1:555	Theodoret (Cyrus)	*Concerning Providence* Or. 7	R
69	SRS 31	80.1:555	Augustine	*City of God* 19.17	R
70	SRS 31	80.1:555	John Chrysostom	*On the Gospel of St. Matthew* 50.3-4	R
71	SRS 31	80.1:555	Ambrose	*On the Work of Ministry* II, 28.136-40	R
72	SRS 31	80.1:555	Possidius	*Life of St. Augustine* 24	R
73	CA 3	83.2:795	Irenaeus (Lyon)	*Against Heresies* I.10.1 and III.4.1	Q
74	SDomingo I.1.9	n/a	Epistle to Diognetus	*Epistle to Diognetus* 8	F
75	SDomingo II.1.4.3	n/a	Council – Const. I	Nicene-Constantinopolitan Creed	R
76	ComCST 53	n/a	"Church Fathers"		F
77	ComCST 87	n/a	"Church Fathers"		R
78	ComCST 114	n/a	Augustine	*Confessions* I.1	Q
79	ComCST 135	n/a	Gregory (Nyssa)	*Life of Moses* 2.2-3	F
80	ComCST 142	n/a	Augustine	*Confessions* II.4.9	F
81	ComCST 184	n/a	Gregory the Great	*Rules for Pastors* III.21	Q
82	ComCST 265	n/a	John Chrysostom	*Homilies on Acts* 35.3	F
83	ComCST 265	n/a	Basil (Caesarea)	*Longer Rules* Q. 42	F
84	ComCST 265	n/a	Athanasius (Alex.)	*Life of Antony* 3	F
85	ComCST 265	n/a	Ambrose	*On the Death of Valentius* 62	R

Source No.	CST Text	AAS Vol: Pg	Patristic Source	Patristic Text	Citation Type
86	ComCST 266	n/a	Irenaeus (Lyon)	*Against Heresies* V.32.2	F
87	ComCST 266	n/a	Theodoret (Cyrus)	*Concerning Providence* Ors. 5-7	F
88	ComCST 328	n/a	"Church Fathers"		R
89	ComCST 329	n/a	Hermas	*The Shepherd* III.1	F
90	ComCST 329	n/a	Clement (Alex.)	*Homily, Quis dives salvetur* 13	Q
91	ComCST 329	n/a	John Chrysostom	*21 Homilies "On the Statues"* 2.6-8	R
92	ComCST 329	n/a	Basil (Caesarea)	*Homily VII* 5	Q
93	ComCST 329	n/a	Gregory the Great	*Rules for Pastors* III.21	R
94	ComCST 582	n/a	John Chrysostom	*Homily on Perfect Love* 1.2	Q
95	DCE 7		"Church Fathers"		R
96	DCE 7		Gregory the Great	*Rules for Pastors* II.5	Q
97	DCE 9		Ps. Dionysius	*Divine Names* IV.12-14	F
98	DCE 17		Augustine	*Confessions* III.6.11	Q
99	DCE 19		Augustine	*On the Trinity* VIII.8.12	Q
100	DCE 22		Justin Martyr	*Apology, Book I* 67	R
101	DCE 22		Tertullian	*Apology* 39.7	R
102	DCE 22		Ignatius of Antioch	*Letter to the Romans*	Q
103	DCE 23		4-6th centuries Egypt		R
104	DCE 23		Gregory the Great	*Letter to John of Italy*	R
105	DCE 23		Ambrose	*On the Work of Ministry* II.28.140-43	R
106	DCE 24		Julian the Apostate	*Letter 83*	R
107	DCE 28		Augustine	*City of God* IV.4	Q
108	DCE 38		Augustine	*Sermon LII* 16	Q
109	DCE 40		Sulpicius Severus	*Life of St. Martin* 3.1-3	R
110	DCE 40		Antony/Early monastics		R

Table 4: Patristic Sources in the CST Documents
(Sorted by Patristic Source)

Source No.	Patristic Source	Patristic Text	CST Text	AAS Vol #: Pg	Citation Type
103	4-6th centuries Egypt		DCE 23		R
59	Ambrose	*Hexameron* V.7.19	FC 25	74:110	Q
12	Ambrose	*Letter to the Emperor Valentinian* 21	DH 10	58:936	R
37	Ambrose	*On Naboth* 12.53	PP 23	67:268-69	Q
3	Ambrose	*On the Passing of Satyrus* I.44	QA 16	23:181	Q
26	Ambrose	*On Virginity* Ch. 8, Art. 48	GS 43	58:1064	F
71	Ambrose	*On the Work of Ministry* II, 28.136-40	SRS 31	80.1:555	R
105	Ambrose	*On the Work of Ministry* II.28.140-43	DCE 23		R
85	Ambrose	*On the Death of Valentinus* 62	ComCST 265	n/a	R

Source No.	Patristic Source	Patristic Text	CST Text	AAS Vol #: Pg	Citation Type
110	Antony/early monastics		DCE 40		R
7	"Ascetical tradition"		MM 235	53:456	R
84	Athanasius (Alex.)	*Life of Antony* 3	ComCST 265	n/a	F
13	Augustine	*Against the Letters of Petilian* II.83	DH 10	58:936	R
6	Augustine	*Confessions* I.1	MM 214	53:452	Q
19	Augustine	*Confessions* I.1	GS 21	58:1042	Q
78	Augustine	*Confessions* I.1	ComCST 114	n/a	Q
80	Augustine	*Confessions* II.4.9	ComCST 142	n/a	F
98	Augustine	*Confessions* III.6.11	DCE 17		Q
60	Augustine	*City of God* 4.15	ChP 81	n/a	R
9	Augustine	*City of God* 4.4	PT 92	55:282	Q
107	Augustine	*City of God* 4.4	DCE 28		Q
56	Augustine	*City of God* 14.28	FC 6	74:88	R
69	Augustine	*City of God* 19.17	SRS 31	80.1:555	R
14	Augustine	*Letter* 23, 34, 35	DH 10	58:936	R
15	Augustine	*Letter* 34	DH 10	58:936	R
16	Augustine	*Letter* 35	DH 10	58:936	R
29	Augustine	*On the Good of Marriage* 2-5, 23-24	GS 48	58:1068	F
33	Augustine	*On John Ev. Tr.* 50, Art. 6	GS 69	58:1091	R
99	Augustine	*On the Trinity* VIII.8.12	DCE 19		Q
49	Augustine	*Expositions on the Psalms* 44.23	EN 59	68:50	Q
41	Augustine	*Expositions on the Psalms* 88, II.14	EN 16	68:16	F
34	Augustine	*Expositions on the Psalms* 147	GS 69	58:1091	R
39	Augustine	*Sermon XLVI, De Pastoribus*, 1-2	EN 15	68:15	F
108	Augustine	*Sermon LII* 16	DCE 38		Q
10	Augustine	*Sermon LIIIA* 12	PT 165	55:302	Q
31	Basil (Caesarea)	*Homily VII* 2	GS 69	58:1091	R
92	Basil (Caesarea)	*Homily VII* 5	ComCST 329	n/a	Q
67	Basil (Caesarea)	*Longer Rules* Q. 37, 1-2	SRS 31	80.1:555	R
83	Basil (Caesarea)	*Longer Rules* Q. 42	ComCST 265	n/a	F
54	"Church Councils"		Puebla II.1.1	n/a	R
4	"Church Fathers"		QA 50	23:194	R
38	"Church Fathers"		PP 23	67:269	R
55	"Church Fathers"		Puebla II.2.4	n/a	R
66	"Church Fathers"		EJA II.57	n/a	R
76	"Church Fathers"		ComCST 53	n/a	F
77	"Church Fathers"		ComCST 87	n/a	R
88	"Church Fathers"		ComCST 328	n/a	R
95	"Church Fathers"		DCE 7		R
47	Clement (Alex.)	*Stromata* I.19.91, 94	EN 53	68:41	Q

Source No.	Patristic Source	Patristic Text	CST Text	AAS Vol #: Pg	Citation Type
90	Clement (Alex.)	*Homily, Quis dives salvetur* 13	ComCST 329	n/a	Q
75	Council – Const. I	*Nicene-Constantinopolitan Creed*	SDomingo II.1.4.3	n/a	R
21	Council – Const. II	*Canon 7*	GS 22	58:1042	F
22	Council – Const. III		GS 22	58:1042	F
23	Council – Chalcedon		GS 22	58:1042	F
24	Council – Const. III		GS 22	58:1042	F
63	Cyprian (Carthage)	*Letter to Cornelius* 60.2	ChP 113	n/a	Q
40	Cyprian (Carthage)	*On the Unity of the Church* 14	EN 16	68:16	F
65	Cyprian (Carthage)	*On Works and Almsgiving* 25	EJA II.34	n/a	Q
50	Didache	*Didache* 9.1	EN 61	68:51	R
48	Eusebius (Caesarea)	*Preparation for the Gospel* I.1	EN 53	68:41	Q
74	Epistle to Diognetus	*Epistle to Diognetus* 8	SDomingo I.1.9	n/a	F
79	Gregory (Nyssa)	*Life of Moses* 2.2-3	ComCST 135	n/a	F
1	Gregory the Great	*Homily on the Gospel* 9.7	RN 19	ASS 23:652	Q
5	Gregory the Great	*Homily on the Gospel* 9.7	MM 119	53:430	Q
51	Gregory the Great	*Homily on the Gospel* 19.1	EN 61	68:51	R
35	Gregory the Great	*Homily on the Gospel* 20.10-11	GS 69	58:1091	R
18	Gregory the Great	*Letter to John of Constantinople*	DH 10	58:936	R
104	Gregory the Great	*Letter to John of Italy*	DCE 23		R
17	Gregory the Great	*Letter to Virgil and Theodore*	DH 10	58:936	R
96	Gregory the Great	*Rules for Pastors* II.5	DCE 7		Q
36	Gregory the Great	*Rules for Pastors* III.21	GS 69	58:1091	R
81	Gregory the Great	*Rules for Pastors* III.21	ComCST 184	n/a	Q
93	Gregory the Great	*Rules for Pastors* III.21	ComCST 329	n/a	R
89	Hermas	*The Shepherd* III.1	ComCST 329	n/a	F
102	Ignatius of Antioch	*Letter to the Romans*	DCE 22		Q
73	Irenaeus (Lyon)	*Against Heresies* I.10.1 and III.4.1	CA 3	83.2:795	Q
30	Irenaeus (Lyon)	*Against Heresies* III.1.2	GS 57	58:1078	F
86	Irenaeus (Lyon)	*Against Heresies* V.32.2	ComCST 266	n/a	F
25	Irenaeus (Lyon)	*Against Heresies* V.36	GS 39	58:1056	F
91	John Chrysostom	*21 Homilies "On the Statues"* 2.6-8	ComCST 329	n/a	R
8	John Chrysostom	*Comm. on Rom., Hom. XXIII* 13.1	PT 46	55:269	Q
82	John Chrysostom	*Homilies on Acts* 35.3	ComCST 265	n/a	F
53	John Chrysostom	*Homilies on Genesis* VI.2; VII.1	EN 71	68:60	Q
42	John Chrysostom	*Homily on the Capture of Eutropius* 6	EN 16	68:16	F
94	John Chrysostom	*Homily on Perfect Love* 1.2	ComCST 582	n/a	Q
70	John Chrysostom	*On the Gospel of St. Matthew* 50.3-4	SRS 31	80.1:555	R
58	John Chrysostom	*On Virginity* 10	FC 16	74:98	Q
106	Julian the Apostate	*Letter 83*	DCE 24		R
62	Justin Martyr	*Apology, Book I* 14 and 39	ChP 112	n/a	F

Source No.	Patristic Source	Patristic Text	CST Text	AAS Vol #: Pg	Citation Type
45	Justin Martyr	*Apology, Book I* 46.1-4	EN 53	68:41	Q
100	Justin Martyr	*Apology, Book I* 67	DCE 22		R
46	Justin Martyr	*Apology, Book II* 7.1-4; 10.1-3; 13.3-4	EN 53	68:41	Q
27	Justin Martyr	*Dialogue with Trypho* Ch. 110	GS 44	58:1065	F
61	Justin Martyr	*Dialogue with Trypho* Ch. 110	ChP 112	n/a	Q
32	Lactantius	*Divine Institutions* V.5	GS 69	58:1091	R
11	Lactantius	*Divine Institutions* V.19	DH 10	58:936	R
52	Leo I	*Sermons* 69.3; 70.1-3; 94.3; 95.2	EN 67	68:56-57	R
43	Minucius Felix	*Octavius* 19 and 31	EN 21	68:20	F
72	Possidius	*Life of St. Augustine* 24	SRS 31	80.1:555	R
97	Ps. Dionysius	*Divine Names* IV.12-14	DCE 9		F
109	Sulpicius Severus	*Life of St. Martin* 3.1-3	DCE 40		R
64	Sulpicius Severus	*Life of St. Martin* 4.3	ChP 114	n/a	Q
2	Tertullian	*Apology* 39	RN 24	ASS 23:655	Q
44	Tertullian	*Apology* 39	EN 21	68:20	F
101	Tertullian	*Apology* 39.7	DCE 22		R
28	Tertullian	*Apology* 50.13	GS 44	58:1065	F
20	Tertullian	*The Resurrection of the Body* 6	GS 22	58:1042	F
57	Tertullian	*To His Wife* II.8.6-8	FC 13	74:94	Q
68	Theodoret (Cyrus)	*Concerning Providence* Or. 7	SRS 31	80.1:555	R
87	Theodoret (Cyrus)	*Concerning Providence* Ors. 5-7	ComCST 266	n/a	F

As noted above, Table 4 organizes the 110 citations by the name of the patristic source. From this table it is clear an imbalance exists between Greek and Latin patristic sources. Of the 110 citations, eighty-six allow for such a distinction to be made.[8] Of the eighty-six, twenty-two are Greek sources (26%), sixty-four are Latin sources (74%). Despite an imbalance in the number of citations, the number of authors cited is relatively more balanced. From the Latin side, eleven authors are cited; from the Greek side, ten are cited. What this means is that some Latin authors are cited with greater frequency than others. Indeed, some of the same patristic texts are cited multiple times (e.g., Augustine's *City of God*). This may be

8. The excluded items are numbered 4, 7, 21, 22, 23, 24, 25, 30, 38, 50, 54, 55, 66, 73, 74, 75, 76, 77, 86, 88, 89, 95, 103, and 106. Didache and Shepherd of Hermas are early texts and had a significant influence in both the Greek and Latin speaking worlds. Similarly, Irenaeus of Lyon wrote in Greek, yet his influence extended both to Latin and Greek Fathers. Julian the Apostate is excluded for he was not a Christian source, even though he was an emperor in the East.

evidence that the drafters of CST documents often relied on earlier CST documents for their identification of patristic sources.

Organization of the Study

Having listed the CST documents included in this study, and having identified all the patristic source citations included in these documents, it remains to explain the process by which the study will proceed with its investigation of these historical sources. This is not a study of themes or of theologies in the CST documents, nor is it a study of the cultural and historical forces at work in the arguments made by those who drafted them. Were it any of these, this study should proceed by grouping the CST documents according to some scheme (e.g., pre-Vatican II and post-Vatican II). As it is, this study is interested in the rhetorical function of patristic sources in the CST documents. In that regard, each document stands on its own as a rhetorical *tour de force*. It seemed best, then, to organize the study along chronological lines – and that merely for the sake of convenience. The study begins its analysis of each CST document with brief introductory comments of an historical or thematic nature. It then continues with the textual, historical, and rhetorical analysis of each patristic source citation in the document. Finally, summary reflections on the use of patristic sources in the document are given before proceeding to the next CST document.

The reader will soon recognize several patterns in the analytical portion of the study. One important pattern is how it examines quotations of patristic sources in the CST documents. The study includes within its analysis of such citations the Latin text and English translation of the CST document pertaining to the quotation. In addition, the study supplies the original language text of the patristic source from the edition of that text cited in the CST document's footnotes or, if such a citation is missing, then from the critical edition that was most recently available at the time the CST document was promulgated. More often than not, the CST documents cite Migne's PG or PL text as its source for the patristic quotation. Even when the quotation is from a Greek patristic source, e.g., John Chrysostom, the CST document always relies on the Latin translation of the Greek text that is found in Migne's PG.

Another important pattern is how this study identifies the source texts for each of the patristic citations. The name of the patristic source and its location in the CST document are usually given in the first sentence of a new paragraph. A footnote affixed to the patristic source at this point will then direct the reader of this study to the books where that particular patristic source may be found. If the patristic source can be found in one of Migne's PG or PL volumes, then that citation is first. Although dated, the PG and PL are still widely-available and may be the only resource to which some readers of this study will have access. Following the citation of PG or PL, the study will then indicate where the patristic source may be found in modern, critical editions (including the series Corpus Christianorum, Sources Chrétiennes, and Fontes Christiani, among others).[9] All attempts were made to include the most recently published edition and any others found in the major series, but such notes are not intended to be an exhaustive list. Finally, after reference is given to the critical editions, this study provides a reference to the most recent English translation of the patristic source that appears in a major series (e.g., Fathers of the Church series or the Ancient Christian Writers series) or that may be found in a book specifically devoted to that text or author.

One final pattern is the analytical process followed by this study. As noted above, this study initiates its examination of each patristic source with an identification of the patristic text and its location in the CST document. If the patristic source is quoted in the CST document, then a linguistic comparison is made between the original wording of the patristic source and the wording of it found in the CST document. Following that, a comparison is made between the two contexts, both of the original patristic text and of the CST document, and with an interest in both the historical and literary contexts. Similarities and differences between the two contexts are explained. Finally, examination is made of the rhetorical function of the patristic source in the CST document. If the full force of the argument in the original patristic text is not reflected in the CST document, or if the CST document employs the patristic text for a different purpose than would otherwise have been expected, then such points are explained.

9. Identification of these sources was made possible by use of the following sources: Maurits Geerard, ed., *Patres Antenicaeni*, CPG, 1 (Turnhout: Brepols, 1983); id., *Ab Athanasio ad Chrysostomum*, CPG, 2 (Turnhout: Brepols, 1974); id., *A Cyrillo Alexandrino ad Iohannem Damascenum*, CPG, 3 (Turnhout: Brepols, 1979); Maurits Geerard et al., *Supplementum*, CPG (Turnhout: Brepols, 1998); Adalbert Keller, *Translationes Patristicae Graecae et Latinae: Bibliographie der Übersetzungen altchristlicher Quellen*, two volumes (Stuttgart: Hiersemann, 1997-2004). Finally, to identify recently published sources, a search was conducted using WorldCat and other book catalogues.

The final part of the book reflects on the use of patristic sources across the twenty-one CST documents that comprised this study. Several points of a summary nature are examined first, including a fuller explanation of what it means for the patristic sources to be a "forgotten dimension" to CST. Following that, the study concludes with some suggestions for what might be a new way forward for the inclusion of patristic sources in CST documents of the future.

II

Analysis of the Patristic Source Citations

Rerum novarum (1891)

The first in this series of CST documents, *RN* is given this pride of place for having broken new ground in the Church's willingness to presume upon its moral authority to expose the economic injustices rampant in the late nineteenth century. *RN* opened a new path for the Church's witness to an increasingly secular, or at least pluralistic, world. Social injustice would not be rectified by government intervention alone; there must be a moral component in teaching people to think and to act differently. In furtherance of its estimable goals, *RN* drew upon two patristic sources, one at *RN* 19 and the other at *RN* 24.

Examination of the patristic source material in *RN* was undertaken in two studies published in 1997, one by Jean-Marie Salamito and the other by Françoise Monfrin.[1] Salamito's article concluded that patristic ideas were more influential than any particular patristic text or author. Salamito argued *RN*'s drafters were hardly aware of particular patristic texts relying instead, most likely, on a qualitatively poor sourcebook.[2] A corrolary study by Monfrin evaluated the linguistic choices made by the drafters of this CST document.[3] Monfrin concluded that the document's drafters were favorably disposed to classical Latin and that they took it upon themselves to reword quotations of biblical and historical sources to fit their particular disposition. The present study confirms their findings, at least with respect to the use of patristic sources in *Rerum novarum*, as the following analysis will demonstrate.

---

1. Jean-Marie Salamito, "*Rerum novarum*, une encyclique néo-scolastique? La question sociale ou le déclin de la communauté," in *Rerum Novarum: Écriture, contenu et réception d'une encyclique: Actes du colloque international organisé par l'École française de Rome et le Greco n 2 du CNRS (Rome, 18-20 avril 1991)* (Rome: École française de Rome, 1997) 187-206.

2. Salamito, "*Rerum novarum*, une encyclique néo-scolastique?," 196.

3. Françoise Monfrin, "Pauvreté et richesse: Le lexique latin de l'encyclique: inspiration classique ou inspiration patristique?," in *Rerum Novarum: Écriture, contenu et réception d'une encyclique* (Rome: École française de Rome, 1997) 133-186.

Two patristic sources are employed in the construction of this CST document. The first is a quotation from Gregory the Great's *Homily on the Gospel* 9.7.[4] At the time of *RN*, it was natural for those who drafted the encyclical to rely on the PL edition for Gregory's text. Since 1891, at least two critical editions of Gregory's *Homilies* have been published. Below are the Latin texts of the patristic source and of *RN* and the English translation of *RN*.

Hom. 9.7[5]	*RN* 19[6]	*RN* 19[7]
Habens ergo intellectum curet omnino ne taceat, habens rerum affluentiam vigilet ne a misericordiae largitate torpescat, habens artem qua regitur magnopere studeat ut usum atque utilitatem illius cum proximo partiatur, ...	Habens ergo talentum, curet omnino ne taceat: habens rerum affluentiam, vigilet ne a misericordiae largitate torpescat: habens artem qua regitur, magnopere studeat ut usum atque utilitatem illius cum proximo partiatur.	He that hath a talent, let him see that he hideth not; he that hath abundance, let him arouse himself to mercy and generosity; he that hath art and skill, let him do his best to share the use and utility thereof with his neighbour.

There is one substantive difference between the PL edition of *Hom.* 9.7 and the Latin text in the CST document. This is found in the first line of the quotation, *Habens ergo intellectum/talentum*. Ought we read here, "he who has understanding," or "he who has a talent/quantity of money"? Incidentally, the most recent critical edition of *Hom.* 9.7 reads, *Habens igitur intellectum*, although its apparatus does not indicate an awareness of alternative readings. The evidence that *intellectum* is to be preferred to *talentum* is based on the fact that a parallel sentence is found earlier in *Hom.* 9.7. It reads, *Alius nec internorum intelligentiam, nec rerum affluentiam accepit*, ... On the other hand, the larger context is concerned with the right use of one's *talenti*. Whatever "talent" one possesses – be it spiritual wisdom (*internorum intelligentiam*), excess of physical goods, or trade skills – the only proper course of action is to share that talent with those who do not possess it. By substituting *talentum* for *intellectum*, the

4. PL 76.1109; the critical editions are Gregory the Great, *Homiliae in evangelia*, ed. Michael Fiedrowicz, Fontes Christiani 28, part 1 (Freiburg: Herder Press, 1997) 160-162; id., *Homiliae in evangelia*, ed. Raymond Étaix, CCSL 141 (Turnhout: Brepols, 1999) 63-64. ET: David Hurst, *Gregory the Great: Forty Gospel Homilies*, Cistercian Studies Series 123 (Kalamazoo, MI: Cistercian Publications, 1990) 132.

5. PL 76.1109.

6. ASS 23, 652. Cf. also Pope Leo XIII, *L'Enciclica Rerum novarum: testo autentico e redazioni preparatorie dai documenti originali*, ed. Giovanni Antonazzi (Rome: Storia e letteratura, 1957) 117 lines 780-783.

7. CST:DocHer, 23.

CST document has acknowledged its awareness of the larger context, but it has changed the meaning of the quotation. In the CST document, *talentum* has now become something to stand alongside *rerum affluentiam* and *artem*, instead of being a broader term of which *intellectum, rerum affluentiam* and *artem* are three examples.

That said, a complication remains. There is a bait-and-switch in the text. The quotation from Gregory is at the end of *RN* 19. The first two-thirds of *RN* 19 are expressly concerned with the problem of excess riches. The biblical texts brought to bear on the issue all relate to the redistribution of one's excess wealth through almsgiving. This is the bait in the text. The switch comes in one transitional sentence that appears just after this lengthy focus on money and immediately before the quotation from Gregory.

> Thus to sum up what has been said: – Whoever has received from the divine bounty a large share of blessings, whether they be external and corporal, or gifts of the mind, has received them for the purpose of using them for perfecting his own nature, and, at the same time, that he may employ them, as the minister of God's Providence, for the benefit of others.[8]

That this is a switch in the argument of *RN* 19 is clear on account of the fact that nowhere prior in the text is the claim made that excess wealth meant anything other than money. For the document then to say, "Thus, to sum up what has been said," and connect it with excesses other than money is inappropriate, rhetorically. It is an attempt to include in a summary what was not said in the main body of the argument.

One of two things is taking place here. On the one hand, it is possible the CST document employed this bait-and-switch tactic consciously. In that case, the quotation from Gregory is a rhetorical ornament to what the drafters presumed to be the established argument of the text. Alternatively, the bait-and-switch was not done consciously. In such a case, the quote from Gregory was in the mind of the drafters prior to drafting this part of the CST document, and so it was necessary for the drafters to make the switch that they do in order to fit the argument from Gregory that they already had in mind. Under such a scenario, one wishes the drafters had been clearer earlier in the encyclical about the extended meanings for excess wealth they apparently had in mind.

---

8. CST:DocHer, 23.

A case can be made that the first of these two options is preferred. The case depends, remarkably enough, on the fact that the drafters modified Gregory's quote in the first place. The original language of Gregory's quote (*intellectum*) actually supports better the argument of the summary sentence quoted above by making *intellectum* parallel to "internal blessings." However, by substituting *talentum* for *intellectum*, the quotation is a rhetorical ornament that also summarizes the argument of *RN* 19 in its entirety. That is to say, *RN* 19 begins with a concern about excess riches, attempts to switch to a concern about excesses of many forms, and then affirms this switch with a quote from Gregory that argues *both* for a concern about excess money (*talentum*) and other things (*rerum affluentiam* and *artem*).

Thus, the bait-and-switch was conscious on the part of the CST document's drafters. To fit this wider argument about excesses of all kinds, Gregory's quotation had to be modified. It could then serve as a nice rhetorical ornament that also summarized the argument of *RN* 19 as a whole.

The second patristic source in this CST document is a quotation from *Apology* 39 by Tertullian.[9] It may be found in *RN* 24.

Apol. 39[10]	*RN* 24[11]	*RN* 24[12]
Haec quasi deposita pietatis sunt. Nam inde non epulis … dispensatur, sed egenis alendis humandisque, et pueris ac puellis re ac parentibus destitutis, jamque domesticis senibus, item naufragis.	deposita pietatis *nuncupat Tertullianus, quod scilicet insumerentur* egenis alendis humandisque, et pueris ac puellis re ac parentibus destitutis inque domesticis senibus, item naufragis.	Tertullian calls these contributions …"deposits of piety," because, to cite his words, they were employed "in feeding the needy, in burying them, in the support of boys and girls destitute of means and deprived of their parents, in the care of the aged, and in the relief of the shipwrecked."

9. PL 1.470; the critical editions are Tertullian, *Opera, Pars I: Opera Catholica, Adversus Marcionem*, ed. Eligius Dekkers, Janus G. P. Borleffs and R. Willems, CCSL 1 (Turnhout: Brepols, 1954) 150-153; id., *Apologeticum*, ed. Heinrich Hoppe, CSEL 69 (Vienna: Tempsky, 1939) 91-95. ET: Emily Joseph Daly, *Tertullian: Apologetical Works*, FOTC 10 (Washington, D.C.: Catholic Univ. of America Press, 1950) 98-102.

10. PL 1.470.

11. ASS 23, 655. Cf. also Pope Leo XIII, *L'Enciclica Rerum novarum*, 125 lines 940-943.

12. CST:DocHer, 25.

The citation from *Apology* 39 in the CST document conflates two of Tertullian's sentences. In the first sentence, Tertullian stated simply that monetary gifts by Christians to their churches are to be called "deposits of piety." The second sentence began with a disclaimer that the money was not used for frivolous purposes ("The money therefrom is spent not for banquets or drinking parties or good-for-nothing eating houses, but for...").[13] On the contrary, Tertullian described the good purposes for which the money was used (feeding the needy, etc.). Thus, the CST document has merged the phrase "deposits of piety" from one sentence with Tertullian's list of purposes for which those monetary contributions are expended in a second sentence.

The larger context for the quote from Tertullian's *Apology* 39 explains the rationale for monetary offerings by Christians. The contributions are for the charitable purposes of the Christian churches. Tertullian emphasized the gifts are voluntary, given with some sort of regularity, and that they are never an initiation fee. They are, in brief, "deposits of piety," in that the phrase both points to the piety of the giver and the pious purposes for which the money will be used.

The CST document has preserved much the same context. Much as Tertullian's *Apology* had the aim of defending Christianity from its Roman critics, so too *RN* is lifting up the Church as a model of charity as a way of quelling the attacks of its enemies. It claims the Church has, throughout her history, been a champion for relief of the poor. It recalls the biblical testimony from Acts 2 where it is recorded that the earliest Christians shared their food and possessions with one another, and from Acts 1 where it is explained that the office of deacon was established by Christians strictly for the purpose of administering the Church's charitable work. As well, the CST document referred to the Apostle Paul's collection of funds from the Christians in Asia Minor and elsewhere for the poorer Christians in Jerusalem (cf. 2 Cor 8:1-5). Following these illustrations is the quotation from Tertullian.

One might expect that Tertullian's text is placed here as further proof that post-New Testament era Christians continued what the New Testament era Christians had begun; however, this is not the case. Instead, the quotation from Tertullian serves two other purposes in the CST document. First, it gives greater clarity to what is Christian charity. Consider

---

13. Tertullian, *Apology* 39, ed. Dekkers, Borleffs and Willems, *Opera Catholica*, CCSL 1, 151; transl. Daly, *Apologetical Works*, FOTC 10, 99: Quippe non epulis inde nec potaculic nec ingratis uoratrinis dispensatur, sed....

how the quotation is introduced, "Tertullian calls *these* contributions, given voluntarily by Christians in their assemblies, 'deposits of piety'." The near demonstrative, these, refers to the whole discussion of Christian relief for the poor that preceded the Tertullian quote. Thus, while the larger contexts of this part of *RN* and Tertullian's treatise are both apologetic, the quote from Tertullian itself is not employed as evidence of Christian charity among early Christians; instead, it is a definition of that charity.

The second function of the Tertullian quote in the CST document is not revealed until later in the paragraph that follows the quotation. It is written there, "At the present day there are many who, *like the heathen of old*, blame and condemn the Church for this beautiful charity." Nowhere prior to this sentence in the CST document does one find a discussion of how the "heathen of old" despised Christians for their charity. However, as mentioned above, this is precisely the context into which Tertullian wrote his *Apology*. Apparently, the quotation from Tertullian in the previous paragraph was supposed to remind the reader of that earlier setting, and this would then set the stage for the CST document to claim that the Church's present struggle with its despisers is nothing new. Those who drafted the CST document recognized the connection, but since they did not provide the historical context for the Tertullian quote earlier, it was incumbent upon the reader to know that context and draw the relevant connection.

The two patristic source citations in *RN* represent less than 1% of the encyclical's total word count, and yet it has been shown here that *RN* placed upon them a heavy rhetorical burden in their respective contexts. The citation of Gregory the Great was supposed to make clear to the reader that a person's excess wealth meant more than simply his or her financial resources. One's wealth also includes talents, arts, and skills. The citation of Tertullian was obliged both to provide concrete examples of charity and to remind *RN*'s readers that there once was a day when Christians were despised for their charity, the latter of which itself presumed a certain knowledge of that history on the part of the reader. Both patristic citations support *RN*'s central message; the citations are not frivolous or incidental in that regard. However, the more than 99% of the document that did not contain patristic sources would perhaps have been better served had it shared its rhetorical burdens with a greater quantity of such sources.

Quadragesimo anno (1931)

This CST document is perhaps best known for its attempt to carve out a middle path between economic liberalism and socialism. It is divided into 148 sections in the English edition, two sections of which incorporate a reference to a patristic source. The first patristic reference is a quotation from Ambrose in *QA* 16, and the second is a general reference to "the Fathers of the Church" in *QA* 50. Taking them in turn, the relevant texts for the quotation of Ambrose's *On the Passing of His Brother Satyrus* I.44[14] follow.

On … Satyrus I.44[15]	*QA* 16[16]	*QA* 16[17]
Nullum referenda gratia maius esse officium.	Nullum referenda gratia maius esse officium.	No duty is more urgent than that of returning thanks.

Textually, *QA* relied on PL and did so without emendation. However, the footnote does not indicate this reliance, and the reader is left to wonder what might be different had *QA* looked instead to the Fontes patristicum edition that had been available for over a decade hence.[18] The FP editor substitutes the PL's substantival participle and corresponding adjective *referenda gratia* with the prepositional phrase *ad referendam gratiam*.[19] FP's reading suggests a purposeful element to Ambrose's text.[20]

14. PL 16.1304-05; the critical edition is Ambrose, *Opera. Pars VII. Explanatio symboli, De sacramentis, De mysteriis, De paenitentia, De excessu fratris, De obitu Valentiniani, De obitu Theodosii*, ed. Otto Faller, CSEL 73 (Vienna: F. Tempsky, 1955) 233. ET: John J. Sullivan and Martin R. P. McGuire, "On the Passing of His Brother Satyrus," in *Funeral Orations by Saint Gregory Nazianzen and Saint Ambrose*, FOTC 22 (Washington, D.C.: Catholic University of America Press, 1953) 181.

15. PL 16.1304.

16. AAS, vol. 23, 181.

17. CST:DocHer, 45.

18. Ambrose, *De obitu Satyri fratris laudatio funebris*, ed. Paulus B. Albers, FP 15 (Bonn: Sumptibus Petri Hanstein, 1921) 38. This critical edition updated Carolus Schenkl, *Ambrosiana scritti varii publicati nel XV centenario della morte di Sant Ambrogio* (Milan: L. F. Cogliati, 1897). Albers examined anew the manuscripts identified by Schenkl and added to that apparatus additional materials then at his disposal. "All the same codices were inspected, the variant readings were recorded with the highest diligence, and they were added to the whole, in order that a true critical edition was made properly available." (Ipse codices omnes inspexit et summa diligentia variantes lectiones adnotavit omniaque adiunxit, ut editionem vere ut aiunt criticam, publici iuris faceret. Albers, 9).

19. Faller's critical edition for CSEL agrees with the PL reading, although the apparatus points the reader to a family of manuscripts, identified as Z, which have *ad referendam gratiam*. Faller is not inclined to accept the reading of Z for, in his view, this family of manuscripts exhibits common lacunas and many scribal conjectures (Faller, 92*-93*).

20. Cf. P. G. W. Glare, ed., *Oxford Latin Dictionary* (Oxford: Clarendon Press, 1982), s.v. "ad" G.42-46, p. 34.

Thus, two readings are possible: (1) according to FP, Ambrose said, "no duty is better for the purpose of giving thanks," or (2) according to PL, he said, "no duty is better than giving thanks." If QA had followed the FP text, then it would have been incumbent on the reader to know, from the wider context of Ambrose's text, what is the duty in order to understand why that duty held a purposeful element of giving thanks. By following the PL reading, QA has been able to maintain the emphasis on "giving thanks" in suggesting such is a duty of all persons.

Irrespective of the FP text's variant reading, an awareness of Ambrose's wider context brings us to a contextual difference between Ambrose's text and the CST document. The CST document cites only the final clause of a lengthy Latin sentence in Ambrose's text. The full sentence from which the quotation comes is,

> In short, he was first rescued from the waves and brought ashore. He was fully conscious of his debt to the Protector to whom he had entrusted himself, and at once, when he had either rescued the rest of his servants or found that this had been done, without concern for his goods or regret for his losses, he sought out a church of God to return thanks for his deliverance and to be fully initiated in the eternal Mysteries. *For he declared that no greater duty was incumbent upon him for returning thanks.*[21]

This quotation itself is found within a context of Satyrus' decision to receive baptism in the face of a near-death experience at sea. In Satyrus' mind, giving thanks for God's miraculous deliverance entailed nothing less than receipt of baptism and participation in the eucharist. The duty to which Ambrose is referring is Satyrus' decision to receive the sacraments, and thus there is nothing greater than participation in these as a way of giving thanks to God. The quotation in QA can provide this understanding when read within the wider context of the Satyrus panegyric, but it does not *demand* an awareness of it. It has meaning as a stand-alone sentence, and thus may be more easily extracted and placed into a new context.

Indeed, QA places the Ambrose passage in a very different context. In the CST document, one is called to give thanks neither for miraculous deliverance nor by acceptance of the sacraments, but is here asked to

---

21. Ambrose, *On the Passing of ... Satyrus*, I.44, ed. Faller, *Sancti Ambrosii opera*, CSEL 73, 233; transl. Sullivan and McGuire, *Funeral Orations by Saint Gregory Nazianzen and Saint Ambrose*, FOTC 22, 181: denique primus servatus ex undis et in portum terrenae stationis evectus praesulum suum, cui se crediderat, recognovit, statimque, ubi etiam ceteros servulos suos vel ipse liberavit vel liberatos conperit, neglegens facultatum nec amissa desiderans dei ecclesiam requisivit, ut ageret gratias liberatus et mysteria aeterna cognosceret, pronuntians nullum referenda gratia maius esse officium.

give thanks to God for the benefits brought to the world on account of the promulgation of *RN* by Pope Leo XIII. The only connection between the two contexts is that God is the recipient of thanks in both; the cause for thanksgiving in each, however, is quite different. That this is the case suggests the Ambrose quote had been extracted from its original context merely for ornamental purposes. The life of Satyrus is of no consequence for the overall purposes of the CST document. As this study progresses, it will be clear that such ornamental use of the patristic sources is not an isolated incident.

The second citation of a patristic source is a general reference to "the Fathers of the Church" in *QA* 50, which reads,

> At the same time a man's superfluous income is not left entirely to his own discretion. We speak of that portion of his income which he does not need in order to live as becomes his station. On the contrary, the grave obligations of charity, beneficence and liberality which rest upon the wealthy are constantly insisted upon in telling words by Holy Scripture and the Fathers of the Church.[22]

The CST document provides no footnote marker to explain its reference to Scripture or to the Fathers. Rhetorically, this is an appeal to authorities, the knowledge of which is presumed of the reader by those who drafted the document. The context of the reference is the behaviour of the wealthy. The wealthy are defined here as those with superfluous income, or income that exceeds what is needed to live in accordance with one's station. The secondary literature on this point has already emphasized the medieval character of such a definition.[23] Indeed, in the section that follows, a reference is made to Thomas Aquinas for how a wealthy person may best dispense with his or her superfluous income. In this section, at least, the wealthy are charged with the obligation to be charitable. For the Fathers of the Church, the drafters could have in mind a variety of texts that make such a point, including: Basil the Great's *Homily* 7, Ambrose's *On Naboth*, or Gregory the Great's *Homily on the Gospel* 9.[24]

---

22. *QA* 50 (AAS, vol. 23, 194; transl. in CST:DocHer, 53): Neque omnimodo hominis arbitrio reditus eius liberi relinquuntur; ii scilicet quibus ad vitam convenienter atque decore sustentandam non eget: quin immo gravissimo divites teneri praecepto eleemosynae, beneficentiae, magnificentiae exercendae, Sacra Scriptura Sanctique Ecclesiae Patres apertissimis verbis assidue denuntiant.

23. Albino Barrera, *Modern Catholic Social Documents and Political Economy* (Washington, D.C.: Georgetown University Press, 2001) 227-244.

24. The commentary on *QA* prepared by Oswald von Nell-Breuning, *Reorganization of Social Economy: The Social Encyclical Developed and Explained*, transl. Bernard W. Dempsey (New York: Bruce Publishing Co., 1936) 114-115, makes no mention of any Church Fathers. We should not be surprised at this, perhaps, since both Von Nell-

The two patristic source citations in *QA* are rather unremarkable. The first was extracted from its original context in order to serve a different purpose; the second is too general a reference in appealing to unnamed authorities to be helpful. These two citations comprise less than half of one percent of the overall word count for the citation, and so it is clear that the drafters of *QA* thought little of the role patristic sources could play in articulating a socio-ethical vision for the Church.

Mater et magistra (1961)

Promulgated in 1961, *MM* focused on the growing interdependencies of people in the world. It recognized a growing role for the State in confronting the abuses of economic and labor systems. These abuses were then on such a global scale that they had eclipsed the power of any one individual or labor organization to prevent them. Within this document, three references are made to patristic sources.

The first patristic source is in *MM* 119. It is a quotation from Gregory the Great's *Homily on the Gospel* 9.7 that is embedded within a quotation of *RN* 19.[25] Below is the PL edition of Gregory's text, alongside the Latin and English texts of the quotation in *MM* 119.

Hom. 9.7	*MM* 119	*MM* 119[26]
Habens ergo intellectum curet omnino ne taceat, habens rerum affluentiam vigilet ne a misericordiae largitate torpescat, habens artem qua regitur magnopere studeat ut usum atque utilitatem illius cum proximo partiatur, …	Habens ergo talentum, curet omnino ne taceat: habens rerum affluentiam, vigilet ne a misericordiae largitate torpescat: habens artem qua regitur, magnopere studeat, ut usum atque utilitatem illius cum proximo partiatur.	He who has a talent [says St. Gregory the Great], let him take care that he hides it not;[27] he who has abundance, let him arouse himself to mercy and generosity; he who has skill in managing affairs, let him make special effort to share the use and utility thereof with his neighbor.

Breuning, who also drafted *QA*, and the English translator of the commentary were economists and not theologians or church historians.

25. See above, 17.

26. CST:DocHer, 103.

27. The translation of "he hides it not" for *ne taceat* is somewhat strange. A more literal translation would be, "He who has a talent, let him take care that *he does not keep silent about it*." True, "he hides it not" could pass as a dynamic equivalent to "he does not keep silent about it." It seems the English translation has forced here an allusion to the Gospel passage where Jesus tells the parable of the talents and refers to one who hid his talent in the ground. However, the Vulgate records this person as saying to the giver of the talents, *et abscondi talentum tuum in terra* (Mt 25:25).

Discussion of the textual and translational issues for this quotation may be found in the earlier discussion of this quotation from Gregory in *RN*. It is worth noting, though, that the earlier problem of bait and switch is not so prominent here. This is because the context is about private property rights, and "property" is here defined as whatever "supply of goods" is in one's personal possession.[28] With that as a backdrop, the subsequent quotation of *RN*, including the quotation from Gregory's homily, supports and elaborates on the breadth with which one ought to understand the "goods" God gives to human persons. That said, the ornamental function of the patristic quotation remains in this context.

The second patristic reference in *MM* is to Augustine of Hippo and is a quotation from his *Confessions* I.1.[29] *MM* relies here on the PL edition, although the footnote does not indicate this, and despite the fact the CSEL critical edition had been available since 1896.

Conf. I.1[30]	*MM* 214[31]	*MM* 214[32]
… fecisti nos ad te, et inquietum est cor nostrum, donec requiescat in te.	Fecisti nos ad te, Domine; et inquietum est cor nostrum, donec requiescat in te.	Thou hast made us for Thyself, O Lord, and our hearts are restless until they rest in Thee.

The one striking difference between the PL and *MM* texts is the addition of the word *Domine* in the latter. *Domine* is the referent for *te*, according to the two prior sentences in Augustine's text. However, having excerpted this quotation from its context, it was important that the CST document supply the referent for the sake of clarity. One may wish here for at least some indication that this has been done. *MM* provides no indication that *Domine* is supplied for the sake of clarity, whereas when *GS* later uses this same text, it separates *Domine* out from the Augustine quotation and, thus, is more faithful to the PL edition it is citing.

The original context for this quotation from Augustine's *Confessions* declares that, because God created humans for his own sake, it is the yearning of the human soul to praise the creator God. In fact, there is no rest for the human soul until it has found that which it has sought.

28. CST:DocHer, 103.
29. PL 32.661; the critical editions are Augustine, *Confessionum libri XIII*, ed. Lucas Verheijen, CCSL 27 (Turnhout: Brepols, 1990) 1; id., *Confessionum libri tredecim*, ed. Pius Knoll, CSEL 33 (Vienna: F. Tempsky, 1896) 1. ET: Henry Chadwick, *Aurelius Augustinus: Confessions* (Oxford: Oxford University Press, 1991) 3.
30. PL 32.661.
31. AAS 53, 430.
32. CST:DocHer, 119.

MM incorporates the quotation as a rhetorical ornament for its own construction of the same argument. *MM* challenges the modern assumption that the idea of the soul's proclivity for connecting with its divine creator is "adventitious or imaginary" and "altogether inconsistent with the spirit of our age and the progress of civilization."[33] *MM* argues that man's proclivity towards religion is proof enough of God's role in the creation of humanity. The quotation from Augustine merely substantiates that such a claim is not uncharacteristic of Christian doctrine, but it does not expand or explain the argument any further.

The third patristic source to which *MM* refers is found in *MM* 235. There, the CST document finds support for its claim that Christians ought to be models of self-denial in "the ascetical tradition handed down to us."[34] This is one of the general references to a patristic source and has no accompanying footnote indicating to what the CST document's drafters are referring. In Christian antiquity, the ascetical tradition began in earnest with Athanasius's *Vita Antonii*.[35] From that point, many sampled the ascetic life by retreating to deserts, caves, wilderness regions, mountains, or other lonely places. By the late fourth century, the steady stream of temporary ascetics even prompted some churchman like Gregory Nazianzus to warn his flock, out of a concern for their health, not to take too literally the example of Jesus that he fasted for forty days in the wilderness. "And indeed he [i.e., Jesus] fasted for forty days – for He was God – but we are measuring it [i.e., our fasting] by our power, even if zeal induces some to recklessness and to go beyond their power."[36] The Christian ascetics of late antiquity were, indeed, models of self-denial. A regulated form of their life passed to later centuries from various books of monastic rules, prepared by the likes of Benedict of Nursia.[37] Likely, the audience for *MM* had some awareness

33. *MM* 214; CST:DocHer, 119. Utpote cum a nostrorum indole dierum et a procedente hominum civili cultu omnino discrepet.

34. *MM* 235 (AAS 53, 456; transl. in CST:DocHer, 121): et nobis traditam asceseos disciplinam postulare.

35. PG 26.837-976; the critical edition is Athanasius of Alexandria, *Vie d'Antoine*, ed. Gerhardus J. M. Bartelink, SC 400 (Paris: Éditions du Cerf, 1994). ET: Robert C. Gregg, *Athanasius: The Life of Antony and the Letter to Marcellinus*, CWS (New York, NY: Paulist Press, 1980).

36. Gregory Nazianzen, *Oration* 40.30, ed. Claudio Moreschini, *Discours 38-41*, SC 358 (Paris: Les Éditions du Cerf, 1990) 266; (transl. is my own): Καὶ ὁ μὲν νηστεύει τεσσαράκοντα ἡμέρας – Θεὸς γὰρ ἦν – , ἡμεῖς δὲ τῇ δυνάμει τοῦτο συνεμετρήσαμεν, εἰ καί τινας ἄττειν ὁ ζῆλος πείθει καὶ ὑπὲρ δύναμιν.

37. For a recent translation of Benedict's Rule, see ed. Patrick Barry, *Saint Benedict's Rule* (York: Ampleforth Abbey, 1997). Also important to Christians in later centuries was

of what asceticism in late antiquity was, even if that audience did not know the historical details of the tradition. However, one wonders how helpful the example of self denial in the early ascetics was to that audience. Perhaps concrete examples of self denial in mid-twentieth century persons, especially non ascetics, would have been more helpful.

In concert with the two earlier CST documents, *MM* breaks no new ground here in its use of patristic source citations. The first two found in this document function ornamentally and the third as an appeal to authority. Little space is accorded each citation, and the three citations combined represent less than half of a percent of the overall word count for the document. Like *QA*, the drafters of *MM* thought little of the role patristic sources could play in developing a contemporary social ethic.

Pacem in terris (1963)

Following *MM* by only two years, the encyclical *PT* provides greater clarity to the problems associated with economic globalization. Solidarity is no longer between and amongst individual persons or labor organizations, but it also must be fostered between and amongst states. Organizations with a global impact must take greater responsibility to foster this solidarity and protect against the exploitation of one people group for the benefit of another.

In furtherance of its aims, the drafters of *PT* incorporated three patristic sources into the document. All three are quotations, one from John Chrysostom and the remaining two from Augustine. The first

---

Basil of Caesarea's longer and shorter rules; cf. M. Monica Wagner, *Basil. Ascetical Works*, FOTC 9 (Washington, D.C.: Catholic University of America, 1950). However, Basil's "rules" were not necessarily rules for monastic communities but for all Christians interested in deeper, spiritual living; cf. Augustine Holmes, *A Life Pleasing to God: The Spirituality of the Rules of St. Basil*, Cistercian Studies 189 (Kalamazoo, MI: Cistercian Publications, 2000).

General studies of asceticism in late antiquity abound, among which include Elizabeth Clark, *Reading Renunciation: Asceticism and Scripture in Early Christianity* (Princeton, NJ: Princeton University Press, 1999); Susanna Elm, *"Virgins of God": The Making of Asceticism in Early Christianity*, Oxford Classical Monographs (Oxford: Clarendon, 1996); Graham Gould, *The Desert Fathers on Monastic Community*, Oxford Early Christian Studies (Oxford: Clarendon, 1993); William Harmless, *Desert Christians: An Introduction to the Literature of Early Monasticism* (New York: Oxford University Press, 2004); Philip Rousseau, *Pachomius: The Making of a Community in Fourth-Century Egypt*, The Transformation of the Classical Heritage 6 (Berkeley, CA: University of California Press, 1985).

appears in *PT* 46 and is the quotation from Chrysostom's *Commentary on Romans, Homily XXIII,*[38] where the focus is on Romans 13:1. Below is the Greek text and Latin translation from the PG edition, followed by the Latin text of the CST document and its English translation.

Hom. XXIII[39]

Quid dicis? omnisne princeps a Deo ordinates est? Non hoc dico, inquit: neque enim de singulis principibus mihi nunc sermo est, sed de re ipsa. Nam quod principatus sint, et quod alii imperent, alii subjecti sint, neque omnia casu ac temere ferantur, populis quasi fluctibus hinc et inde circumactis, divinae esse sapientiae dico.

PT 46[40]

Quid dicis? Omnisne princeps a Deo ordinates est? Non hoc dico, inquit: neque enim de singulis principibus mihi nunc sermo est, sed de re ipsa. Nam quod principatus sint, et quod alii imperent, alii subiecti sint, neque omnia casu ac temere ferantur, divinae esse sapientiae dico.

PT 46[41]

What are you saying? Is every ruler appointed by God? I do not say that, he replies, for I am not dealing now with individual rulers, but with authority itself. What I say is, that it is the divine wisdom and not mere chance, that has ordained that there should be government, that some should command and others obey.

Hom. XXIII

Τί λέγεις; πᾶς οὖν ἄρχων
ὑπὸ τοῦ Θεοῦ κεχειρο-
τόνηται; Οὐ τοῦτο λέγω,
φησίν· οὐδὲ γὰρ περὶ τῶν
καθ' ἕκαστον ἀρχόντων ὁ
λόγος μοι νῦν, ἀλλὰ περὶ
αὐτοῦ τοῦ πράγματος. Τὸ
γὰρ ἀρχὰς εἶναι, καὶ τοὺς
μὲν ἄρχειν, τοὺς δὲ ἄρχεσθαι,
καὶ μηδὲ ἁπλῶς καὶ ἀνέδην
ἅπαντα φέρεσθαι, ὥσπερ
κυμάτων τῇδε κἀκεῖσε τῶν
δήμων περιαγομένων, τῆς
τοῦ Θεοῦ σοφίας ἔργον
εἶναί φημι.

Hom. XXIII (my translation)

What do you say? Is not, therefore, every ruler appointed by God? "I do not say that," he says; for to me the saying is not about particular rulers, but about the same practicalities. For, I say, it is a work of the wisdom of God that there are to be authorities. On the one hand, some are to rule, while, on the other hand, some are to be ruled, and are not to be moving about freely either in one way or every way, people led here and there like waves.

38. PG 60.615; no critical edition exists. ET: J. B. Morris and W. H. Simcox, "The Homilies of St. John Chrysostom on the Epistle of St. Paul to the Romans," in *Saint Chrysostom: Homilies on the Acts of the Apostles and the Epistle to the Romans*, NPNF I.11 (Edinburgh: T&T Clark, 1877) 511.

39. PG 60.615-16.

40. AAS 55, 269.

41. CST:DocHer, 138.

The *PT* footnote for the quotation from Chrysostom's text directs the reader to the Latin translation of the passage in Migne's PG edition. However, there are two differences between the Latin translation in the PG edition and the quotation in *PT* that make clear the reliance was not total. One difference is orthographic. *PT* substitutes the "j" in *subjecti* with "i." This conforms to the orthography of the rest of the encyclical, and suggests the willingness of its drafters to modify the earlier Latin text to suit its own standards. Besides, the Latin text in the PG is only a translation and not the original. Perhaps one ought not to expect the document to slavishly follow an older orthography.

The second difference is the exclusion from the encyclical of Chrysostom's phrase, *populis quasi fluctibus hinc et inde circumactis* (ὥσπερ κυμάτων τῇδε κἀκεῖσε τῶν δήμων περιαγομένων), which is translated above, "the people being led around here and there like waves." In light of its larger context, Chrysostom argued that people are less inclined to feel tossed about "like waves" when they are being led in a consistent direction by their rulers. The missing phrase modifies the previous phrase, which, in turn, modifies the one before that. Thus, it may be argued that the exclusion of this last phrase from *PT* is of little consequence since the main point had already been established earlier in the text. Still, there is no indication of this elision in the CST document. I suspect, in fact, that what has happened here is a simple, scribal error known as *parablepsis*. The drafter of the CST document, in copying the Latin translation from the PG, actually lost his place in the text after *ferantur*, and resumed with *divinae*. This is possible because of how the text actually appears in the PG edition. The word *divinae* is placed almost directly under and following *ferantur*. Removal of the phrase does not alter the meaning, so there is nothing to gain by hiding the fact that the text has been elided. *Parablepsis* is possible, but one cannot be certain.

It is the case that the Latin text of every encyclical is the only official version, but it stands to reason that most of the English-speaking world will rely on the approved English translation for their reading of the encyclical. Thus, it is worth noting that the English translation of the Chrysostom quote in *PT* is consistent neither with the Latin text nor the Greek text. I am concerned here with the wording of the *PT* phrase, "What I say is, that it is the divine wisdom *and not mere chance*, that..." The phrase *and not mere chance* is not found in the Latin or Greek texts. Ostensibly, it is correlated with the encyclical's Latin text, *neque omnia casu ac temere ferantur*. Since the encyclical had elided the intervening phrase, it is possible to see how the English translator believed the phrase was modifying *divinae sapientiae*, but surely the translator was confused as to how best to render the phrase; thus, his or her dynamic approach to translation is evident here.

Having evaluated the textual differences between the Latin, Greek, and English texts, attention now turns to the different contexts, that of Chrysostom's homily and of the encyclical, in which the quotation is found. In the former context, the quotation supports the broader point that God has established the various structures of power that exist in society, but that God does not go about establishing particular expressions of those structures. That is to say, God is responsible for establishing the concept of government and that some people are to rule and others are to be ruled; however, God is not responsible for the establishment of particular rulers and of the particular ways in which rulers carry out their governing functions. Similarly, Chrysostom argues, God has ordained the concept of marriage between a man and a woman, but God did not determine that a particular man is to be married to a particular woman. The broad outline of power structures and of marriage are from God, but the particular details are left to human conscience. According to Chrysostom, so long as the governing powers do not subvert religion, then religious people are to be subject to those power structures.

In the encyclical, the quotation from Chrysostom follows the quotation of the New Testament passage, Romans 13:1, which it is interpreting. Both quotations support the preceding claim in the encyclical that all legitimate authorities in the world derive their authority from God. That having been said, the quotation from Chrysostom functions as more than mere rhetorical ornament. It is supplementary evidence from the Christian tradition explaining why the encyclical maintains the position it does. Another point to be made is that, compared to the patristic source quotations of earlier encyclicals, this quotation is the first we encounter that has been given some literary context. The words immediately preceding the quotation are, "These words of St. Paul are explained thus by St. John Chrysostom: …"[42] The reader is left to wonder who is St. John Chrysostom and when did he make these comments, but at least the reader of the encyclical is aware of the homiletic or commentary nature of the quotation.

A second patristic source quotation may be found in *PT* 92. It is a quotation from Augustine's *City of God* 4.4.[43] Although *PT* relied on the

42. CST:DocHer, 138.

43. PL 41.115; the critical editions are Augustine, *De civitate Dei, Pars I: Libri I-XII*, ed. Emmanuel Hoffmann, CSEL 40, part 1 (Vienna: F. Tempsky, 1899) 166; id., *De civitate*

Latin text of the PL, it could just as easily have cited either one of the two critical editions then available for this patristic text. The Latin text for this quotation is the same in the PL and both critical editions. Below are the relevant texts for the quotation.

City of God 4.4[44]	*PT* 92[45]	*PT* 92[46]
Remota itaque justitia, quid sunt regna, nisi magna latrocinia?	Remota iustitia, quid sunt regna nisi magna latrocinia?	What are kingdoms without justice but large bands of robbers?

The Latin texts of the PL and the CST document have one important difference. The word *itaque* ("thus, therefore") is absent in *PT* 92. It is noteworthy this quotation from Augustine is the first sentence of Book IV.4. The conjunctive *itaque* merges the argument of IV.3 with what will be developed further in IV.4. That the CST document removed *itaque* from the quotation signals a decision on the part of its drafters that the quotation was not to be understood either within its original, Augustinian context or to function as a further development of the CST document's own argument. It is a quotation capable of standing on its own.

That having been said, the contexts both of the CST document and the *City of God* IV.3-4 are concerned with transnational justice. They differ, however, with respect to the development of that context. In the former, it is argued states rightfully ought to pursue their own development and seek out goods that foster sustainability; however, such development ought not to harm other nations in the process. Thus, how a state treats its neighboring states, and even how it treats its own minority groups (cf. *PT* 94-97), are part of the calculus for justice. In the latter context, *City of God* IV.3-4, Augustine first explained that discontent with one's own resources is to blame for interpersonal, interfamilial, and transnational conflicts. At this point, it is possible to envision a connection between national discontent or greed (Augustine's text) and the unjust treatment of other states (CST text). However, at the end of IV.3 Augustine argues that good rulers have become good because they receive from God the good gifts of rulership. It is in the exercise of these

---

Dei, Libri I-X, ed. Bernardus Dombart and Alphonsus Kalb, CCSL 47 (Turnhout: Brepols, 1955) 101. ET: R. W. Dyson, *Augustine: The City of God Against the Pagans*, Cambridge Texts in the History of Political Thought (Cambridge: Cambridge University Press, 1998) 147-148.

44. PL 41.115.
45. AAS 55, 282.
46. CST:DocHer, 146.

good gifts from God that true happiness comes to their land and subjects. Only the exercise of rule by bad rulers (i.e., those who do not exercise the good gifts of God) yields injustice. The quotation above found at the beginning of IV.4 furthers the argument about bad rulers. States led by bad rulers are little more than bands of robbers. They are discontent with their own resources and greedy for the goods of others.

Having abandoned the conjunction *itaque*, the CST document sidestepped Augustine's larger context of divine gifts for rulers and his theology of contentment that is defined by what God has allowed states to possess by virtue of what is available on their own land. Instead, the CST document connects directly the actions of unjust states with the activities of robbers. By the same token, Augustine's argument for contentment that states should utilize their existing land to meet their existing needs well suited his agrarian-based economic setting. Yet by the mid-twentieth century, states required technology and forms of capital that were not easily obtainable only from land. It had become necessary for states to trade sometimes just to meet basic necessities. The CST document, then, does not miss the larger point Augustine has made, but perhaps Augustine would have wished his theological underpinnings had not been so easily set aside.

The third and final patristic source citation in *PT* is another quotation from Augustine, from his *Sermon 53A* 12, and is in *PT* 165.[47] The relevant Latin text of Augustine's sermon and the Latin and English texts for the quotation from the encyclical are presented below.

Sermon 53A 12[48]	*PT* 165[49]	*PT* 165[50]
Vult autem mens tua idonea esse vincere libidines tuas?	Vult autem mens tua idonea esse vincere libidines tuas?	Does your soul desire to overcome your lower inclinations?

47. The footnote in *PT* directs the reader simply to a page number in a volume on sermons not included in the Maurist edition (thus, it is not found in the PL). The volume is Augustine, *Sancti Augustini sermones post Maurinos reperti. Probatae dumtaxat auctoritatis nunc primum disquisiti, in unum collecti et codicum fide instaurati studio et diligentia*, Miscellanea Agostiniana: Testi e studi pubblicati a cura dell'ordine eremitano di S. Agostino nel XV centenario dalla morte del santo dottore, vol. 1, ed. Germain Morin (Rome: Tipografia Poliglotta Vaticana, 1930) 633.

The sermon is identified in this volume as Morin 11, and it is equivalent to what is identified as Sermon 53A. Cf. Hubertus R. Drobner, *Augustinus von Hippo: Sermones ad populum*, Supplements to Vigiliae Christianae (Leiden: Brill, 2000) 161 and 202. ET: Edmund Hill, *Augustine: Sermones III (51-94) on the New Testament*, WSA (Brooklyn, NY: New City Press, 1991) 82-83.

48. Augustine, *Sancti Augustini sermones post Maurinos reperti*, 633.

49. AAS 55, 302.

50. CST:DocHer, 146.

Subdatur maiori, et vincet inferiorem; et erit pax in te vera, certa, ordinatissima. Qui est ordo pacis huius? Deus imperat menti, mens carni: nihil ordinatius.	Subdatur maiori et vincet inferiorem: et erit pax in te: vera, certa, ordinatissima. Qui est ordo pacis huius? Deus imperat menti: mens carni: nihil ordinatius.	Let it be subject to Him Who is on high and it will conquer the lower self: there will be peace in you; true, secure and well-ordered ordered peace. In what does that order consist? God commands the soul; the soul commands the body; and there is nothing more orderly than this.

The few differences between the two Latin texts concern only punctuation, and the differences do not lend themselves to a substantial variation in meaning. With respect to the two contexts, *PT* situated the quotation at the end of its claim that social and economic justice is really about the establishment of peace between and amongst persons, Catholics and non-Catholics alike, at the transnational and interpersonal levels. Moreover, such peace begins within the mind of each individual. When a person's ambitions are ordered towards God, then those ambitions will not cause a person to seek the goods of others and otherwise disrupt that person's desire to make peace. Rhetorically, *PT* cited Augustine at the end of this argument chain to explain in practical terms how a person is internally ordered towards peace. He or she submits to God and receives peace from God in return. By comparison, Augustine too has situated this same point about the need for internal peacemaking as a starting point for interpersonal peace. It is one part of a larger homily in which Augustine exposits the eight beatitudes taught by Jesus (cf. Mt 5).[51] One final observation is that the English translation of the encyclical translated *mens* as "spirit" and not "mind." While Augustine generally considered *anima* and *mens* to refer to the same thing, *mens* is a bit more technical than *anima*. The *anima* is what is joined to a body to make a person what he or she is.[52] *Mens* refers to a triad (memory, understanding, and love) that enables a person to direct himself or herself towards the Trinity of persons in the Godhead.[53] Understandably, the English translation of the encyclical had neither the time nor the inclination to explain these technical matters, nor to engage in a discourse about Augustine's understanding of the human person. The quotation needed to stand on

51. Consider also that, in Augustine's *On the Trinity* XV.12.21, he argued that the mind directed toward God is the ultimate beatitude.

52. Sheri Katz, "Person," in *Augustine Through the Ages: An Encyclopedia*, ed. Allan D. Fitzgerald (Grand Rapids, MI: Eerdmans, 1999) 647-650.

53. Cf. Wayne J. Hankey, "Mind," in *Augustine Through the Ages*, 563-567; and Roland J. Teske, "Soul," in *ibid.*, 807-812.

its own, and the translation of *mens* as "spirit" sufficiently captured the sense of Augustine's argument for the sake of an English audience in the twentieth century.

Two of the three patristic source citations in *PT* were noted for having made some change to the patristic author's own language, and two of the three citations revealed a willingness on the part of the encyclical's English translator(s) to apply a rather dynamic translation technique. On the other hand, each patristic citation did further the argument of the encyclical theologically or in practical terms. Still, given the encyclical's substantial length, the socio-ethical teachings of the patristic world arguably played little role in the development of *PT*.

Dignitatis humanae (1965)

The last of the Vatican II documents approved, *DH* charted a new course for Catholics in the world. *DH* supplanted the long-held position that "error has no rights" with an embrace of religious freedom within the context of civil government. What may be considered a thesis statement for the document is also the place where eight patristic sources are identified in a footnote. *DH* 10 begins,

> It is one of the major tenets of Catholic doctrine that man's response to God in faith must be free. Therefore, no one is to be forced to embrace the Christian faith against his own will. This doctrine is contained in the word of God and it was constantly proclaimed by the Fathers of the Church.[54]

According to this passage in *DH*, the idea that faith be free is supported in at least two sources, the scriptures and the Church Fathers. However, following this passage, *DH* does not elaborate on what is the contribution from the Church Fathers. The patristic sources are abandoned to this one footnote. For this reason, the eight patristic sources function rhetorically as appeals to historical authorities. Yet, as the following discussion will make clear, the patristic authorities do offer strong support to *DH*'s position; what is more, they offer practical suggestions for how to protect freedom for faith. Considering the fact that

---

54. *DH* 10 (AAS 58, 936; transl. in "Religious Freedom," *The Documents of Vatican II*, ed. Walter M. Abbott [New York, NY: America Press, 1966] 689): Caput est ex praecipuis doctrinae catholicae, in verbo Dei contentum et a Patribus constanter praedicatum, hominem debere Deo voluntarie respondere credendo; invitum proinde neminem esse cogendum ad amplectendam fidem.

some in the Catholic Church believed *DH* had turned its back on earlier teachings (i.e., error has no rights), *DH* could have blunted those
criticisms by elaborating on the contribution of these patristic sources.
It is expected the following analysis will fill some of that void.

The first of the eight patristic sources is Lactantius' *Divine Institutes*
V.19.[55] The *Divine Institutes* was likely prepared by Lactantius during his
days of service as rhetor to the emperor Diocletian.[56] Book V follows
four previous books that take aim at the false teachings and errors of the
pagan religions. In Books V and VI, Lactantius elaborates on the truth
and virtues of Christianity and of Christians, in general. This particular
section of *Divine Institutes*, V.19, challenges the leaders of the false religions to win over their Christian opponents with arguments, reason,
and logic instead of with tortures, executions, and persecutions. Lactantius writes, "Let them come out into the open ... and let them invite us
to a meeting and encourage us to adopt cults of gods; ... There is no
need for violence and brutality: worship cannot be forced; it is something to be achieved by talk rather than blows, so that there is free will
in it."[57] Lactantius goes on to argue that his pagan opponents will not
act in this way is because theirs is a religion built on lies, myths and
ridiculous rituals. With respect to the argument of *DH*, the citation of
Lactantius is interesting for much the same reason as will be shown for
its citation of the other patristic sources. *DH* has looked back to dis-
cover an unpleasant world when Christianity was the persecuted religion, and it has looked ahead and imagined the possibility that such a
state of persecution might one day return. In Lactantius *DH* finds a
Christian who asked merely for the right for Christians to be heard in
the public square; indeed, Lactantius similarly asked his opponents to
share their religious convictions in that same public square. Lactantius
was convinced the truth of Christianity would shine through the pagan
morass, but all he wanted at the time of writing the *Divine Institutes* was

55. PL 6.614, 616; the critical editions are Lactantius, *Opera omnia, Pars I: Divinae
institutiones et epitome divinarum institutionum*, ed. Samuel Brandt, CSEL 19 (Prague:
F. Tempsky, 1890) 463-65; id., *Institutions divines*, ed. Pierre Monat, SC 204 (Paris: Édi-
tions du Cerf, 1973) 228-240. ET: Anthony Bowen and Peter Garnsey, *Lactantius:
Divine Institutes*, Translated Texts for Historians 40 (Liverpool: Liverpool University
Press, 2003) 319-323.

56. Bowen and Garnsey, *Lactantius. Divine Institutes*, 2-3.

57. Lactantius, *Divine Institutes* V.19.10-11 (ed. Monat, *Institutions divines*, SC 204, 232;
transl. Bowen and Garnsey, *Lactantius: Divine Institutes*, 320): Procedant in medium ...
conuocent nos ad contionem, cohortentur ad suscipiendos cultus deorum, ... Non est opus
ui et iniuria, quia religio cogi non potest, uerbis potius quam verberibus res agenda est, ut
sit uoluntas.

the freedom to be heard and the freedom of will to believe as he saw fit. To the extent *DH* can win a similar concession from the world's citizens, it has protected Christianity as much as it has protected the world's other religions. Truth, not tortures, may then be the judge of religious truth.

Following Lactantius is a citation of Ambrose's *Letter 21, To the Emperor Valentinian.*[58] Whereas Lactantius appealed to his pagan rivals for a sharing of the public stage, Ambrose, to put it metaphorically, requests that a separate stage remain for Christians to debate their own faith. The difference between the two writers is due to their differing contexts; Lactantius wrote during a time of Christian persecution, Ambrose during a time of state sponsorship of Christianity. The context of this particular letter, however, is one in which the emperor Valentinian has directed Ambrose to recognize the selection of bishops being made by the *homoian* bishop Auxentius. Ambrose chastises Valentinian for meddling into the affairs of a religion with which he has no connection via baptism and, what is more, for overstepping his place as a lay person in telling a bishop what to do about matters of faith. Ambrose writes, "Are we so bent down with flattery as to forget our priestly privileges and think that we should entrust to others that which God has given to us?"[59] In sum, Ambrose understood state sponsorship left the Church at the mercy of whimsical policies by ever-changing emperors. Thus, *DH* could draw from Ambrose a lesson on the need for church independence, much as it drew from Lactantius a lesson about the need for church freedom.

Next in this footnote is a citation of several texts from Augustine. First among them is Augustine's *Contra litteras Petiliani* II.83.[60] Then follows three letters, numbered 23, 34, and 35.[61] In the former, Petilian

58. PL 16.1005; the critical edition is Ambrose, *Opera, Pars X: Epistula et Acta, Tome III: Epistularum liber decimus, Epistulae extra collectionem, Gesta concili Aquileiensis*, ed. Michaela Zelzer, CSEL 82 (Vienna: Tempsky, 1982) 74-81; ET: Mary Melchior Beyenka, *Ambrose: Letters*, FOTC 26 (Washington D.C.: Catholic University of America Press, 1954) 52-56.

59. Ambrose, *Letter 21* (ed. Zelzer, *Opera*, CSEL, 75; transl. Beyenka, *Letters*, FOTC 26, 52): Ita ergo quadam adulatione curvamur, ut sacerdotalis iuris simus immemores et quod deus donavit mihi hoc ipse aliis putem esse credendum?

60. PL 43.315; the critical edition is Augustine, *Scripta contra Donatistas, Pars II: Contra litteras Petiliani libri tres, Epistula ad Catholicos de secta Donatistarum, Contra Cresconium libri quattuor*, ed. Michael Petschenig, CSEL 52 (Vienna: F. Tempsky, 1909) 112. ET: J. R. King, "Answer to Letters of Petilian, Bishop of Cirta," in *St. Augustin: The Writings Against the Manichaeans and Against the Donatists*, rev. by C. D. Hartranft, NPNF I.4 (Edinburgh: T. & T. Clark, 1887) 572.

61. The Latin text of the *Letters* 23, 34, and 35 may be found in PL 33.98, 132, and 135, respectively; the critical editions for the letters are Augustine, *Epistulae I-LV*, ed.

blamed the Catholics for compelling, by force of law, some among the Donatists to "do good," which is to say join the Catholics. According to Petilian, it is contrary to the conscience of his fellow Donatists to compel belief from others. In response, Augustine claimed no one has been compelled to embrace faith against his will; rather, the laws of which Petilian speaks were intended to curb evil. Augustine then goes through a litany of complaints about the Donatists' abuse of power in the cities in which they were dominant. The laws that have been written to curb their authority should not be construed as a compulsion to Catholic faith, but to a cessation of such abuses. Interestingly, with respect to the argument of *DH*, Augustine balances a fine line here. He embraces the government's right to enact laws that restrict the behavior of schismatic religious groups while, at the same time, refuses to advocate for laws that proscribe particular religious beliefs. This comes very close to the pre-Vatican II position that "error has no rights." Likewise, in his letters cited in *DH*'s footnote, Augustine balances this line. Letters 23, 34 and 35 were all written early in his priesthood,[62] and all concerned the Donatist controversy. In Letter 23, Augustine informed the Donatist bishop, Maximinus, that he will confront the problem of re-baptism by Donatists within his own community at Hippo only after a military contingent then in the town departs. Augustine offered this course of action in order to demonstrate his desire to settle the schism outside the presence of judicial authorities, and leave the matter instead to the judgments of people's own will.

> I will do it [i.e., read the letters exchanged between Augustine and Maximinus on the issue of re-baptism] after the departure of the army in order that all who hear us may understand that it is not part of my purpose that people be forced against their will into communion with anyone, but that the truth may become known to those who seek it most peacefully.[63]

Somewhat differently, in Letter 34 Augustine is frustrated by the fact that he must appeal to a judicial representative (the letter is addressed to

Klaus D. Daur, CCSL 31 (Turnhout: Brepols, 2004) 61-67, 124-129. ET: Roland Teske, *Augustine: Letters 1-99*, WSA 2, part 1 (New York: Newman Press, 2001) 63-68, 118-123; Wilfrid Parsons, *Augustine: Letters 1-82*, FOTC 12 (Washington D.C.: Catholic University of America Press, 1951) 58-65, 131-137.

62. Teske, *Augustine: Letters 1-99*, 63, 118, 121, provides a date range for the three letters, respectively. A range of 391-395 is given for *Letter* 23, 395-396 for *Letter* 34, and 396-397 for *Letter* 35.

63. Augustine, *Letter* 23.7 (ed. Daur, *Epistulae I-LV*, CCSL 31, 66-67; transl. Teske, *Letters 1-99*, WSA 2.1, 67): sed post abscessum militis, ut omnes qui nos audiunt intelligant non hoc esse propositi mei, ut inuiti homines ad cuiusquam communionem cogantur, sed ut quietissime quaerentibus ueritas innotescat.

Eusebius, a Roman official in Hippo) in order to mediate the dispute with the Donatist bishop Proculeian. "I am not trying to force anyone involuntarily into the Catholic communion, but to reveal the plain truth to all who are in error."[64] Augustine is not happy that the Donatists have spurned his earlier attempts to "reveal the plain truth," thus his appeal to Eusebius for intervention. I am surprised to find this cited in *DH*, for Augustine is not representing here a view of religious freedom in which people are allowed *not* to listen to the teaching of Christianity. Augustine is not in a situation like Lactantius, where his views have no opportunity to be heard; on the contrary, the Donatists are well aware of the complaints about them by Augustine and other Catholics. The Donatists simply do not want to listen to the Catholics anymore. How different than the other two letters, then, is Letter 35 in which we read Augustine's defense of the right for people to convert to the Donatist side. In the case of a woman who converted to the Donatists against her Catholic father's wish, Augustine intervenes on behalf of the woman to stop her father's verbal and physical assaults. "I had refused that the woman, whose mind had been corrupted, should be taken back unless she were willing and desired by free choice what is better."[65] All told, the three letters by Augustine and his response to Petilian are a composite picture that *DH* would like its readers to appreciate. To Augustine, the government is obliged to ensure equal access for religious views in the public square. Similarly, the government is obliged to enact laws that curb the behavior of groups that infringe on the rights of others. To Augustine, this meant ensuring that the Donatists did not have the right *not* to hear the Catholics. And yet, once the government has done these things, it must then step back and let individual conscience decide what is and is not true. Belief simply could not be compelled.

Finally, the reference at *DH* 10 cites two letters from Gregory the Great, *To Bishops Virgil and Theodore*[66] and *To Bishop John of Constantinople*.[67]

---

64. Augustine, *Letter* 34.1 (ed. Daur, *Epistulae I-LV*, CCSL 31, 124; transl. Teske, *Letters 1-99*, WSA 2.1, 118): me id agere ut ad communionem catholicam quisquam cogatur inuitus, sed ut omnibus errantibus aperta ueritas declaretur.

65. Augustine, *Letter* 35.4 (ed. Daur, *Epistulae I-LV*, CCSL 31, 129; transl. Teske, *Letters 1-99*, WSA 2.1, 123): ego feminam corruptae mentis nisi uolentem et libero arbitrio meliora deligentem suscipi noluissem.

66. This letter is numbered 47 in Register 1 of PL 77.510-511. It is numbered 45 in Register 1 of the critical editions, including Gregory the Great, *Registrum epistularum libri I-VII*, ed. Dag Norberg, CCSL 140 (Turnhout: Brepols, 1982) 59; id., *Registre des lettres, Livres I et II*, ed. Pierre Minard, SC 370 (Paris: Éditions du Cerf, 1991) 226-228. ET: James Barmby, "The Book of Pastoral Rule and Selected Epistles," in *Leo the Great. Gregory the Great*, NPNF II.12 (Edinburgh: T. & T. Clark, 1895) 93.

67. This letter is numbered 53 in Register 3 of PL 77.649. It is numbered 52 in Register 3 of the critical editions, including Gregory the Great, *Registrum epistularum*

In the first letter, Gregory asks these two bishops from Gaul (Virgil from Arles, Theodore from Marseilles) about a report he received from travelers to Rome from their region. The report was that some Jews had been forcibly baptized in the churches of Gaul. Gregory rebukes this behavior with the words,

> Now, I consider the intention in such cases to be worthy of praise, and allow that it proceeds from the love of our Lord ... [But], when any one is brought to the font of baptism, not by the sweetness of preaching, but by compulsion, he returns to his former superstition, and dies the worse from having been born again.[68]

Previous, failed attempts to convert Jews in Gaul were due to poor preaching, a fact which must not be remedied with judicial force. Gregory echoes what, by now, seems like a refrain in these patristic sources, and that is the firm belief that Christianity, if preached well, will be received as the truth by its hearers. The second letter is rather inward-focused, in that Gregory complains to John of Constantinople about the physical beating in his church of some men, including at least one cleric, for false teaching. The men charged with false teaching appealed to Gregory who, in this letter to John, rebukes him for having allowed a punishment that is contrary to canonical rules. Gregory writes, "For we have been made shepherds, not persecutors. And the excellent preacher says, *Argue, beseech, rebuke, with all longsuffering and doctrine* [2 Tim 4:2]. But new and unheard of is this preaching, which exacts faith by blows."[69] Here again, Gregory is concerned that conversion come by preaching rather than by force, especially so in this case in which the "convert" is an ordained priest who has strayed into false teaching. Like Augustine with the Donatists, so convinced is Gregory about the power of Scripture that it can redirect to truth even those who already find it authoritative and yet have read it in a different manner.

---

libri I-VII, CCSL 140, 197-99. ET: Barmby, "The Book of Pastoral Rule and Selected Epistles," 135-136.

68. Gregory the Great, *Letter I.45* (ed. Norberg, *Registrum epistularum libri I-VII*, CCSL 140, 59; transl. Barmby, "The Book of Pastoral Rule and Selected Epistles," 93): Nam intentum quidem huiuscemodi et laude dignum censeo et de Domini nostri descendere dilectione profiteor ... Dum enim quispiam ad baptismatis fontem non praedicationis suauitate sed necessitate peruenerit, ad pristinam superstitionem remeans inde deterius moritur, unde renatus esse uidebatur.

69. Gregory the Great, *Letter III.52* (ed. Norberg, *Registrum epistularum libri I-VII*, CCSL 140, 199; transl. Barmby, "The Book of Pastoral Rule and Selected Epistles," 136): Pastores etenim facti sumus, non persecutores. Et egregius Praedicator dicit: *Argue, obsecra, increpa, cum omni patientia et doctrina*. Noua uero atque inaudita est ista praedicatio, quae verberibus exigit fidem.

Christianity in the post-Constantinian period did not enjoy an exclusive claim to the hearts and minds of the Greco-Roman populace. Christianity had been a minority religion prior to the fourth century and had to continue combating the pagan religions and, increasingly, schismatic Christians in the centuries that followed. The four patristic authors – all Latin – identified in this reference and accompanying footnote at *DH* 10 draw the CST document's readers back to this earlier time when Christianity had to compete with other groups for attention. Although orthodox Christians may have had, from time to time, access to the political power-brokers and could have relied upon them for enforcement of their wishes, none of the patristic authors identified here advocated doing so. Augustine expressly rejected the presence of the army and only asked for assistance from the Roman officials to guarantee his voice is heard. Lactantius, too, had only wanted a public square that welcomed all religious voices. Common to all four is an appreciation for the power of the spoken (preaching) and the written (Scripture) word. No political authority could compete with that. This was the message *DH* wanted to send.

Gaudium et spes (1965)

One of the more prominent documents of Vatican II, *GS* recognized the Church must be interacting with the people of the world who either dislike the Church or who do not participate in it. It further argued the Church should be engaged in the worlds of science, technology, politics, economics, and workers' rights. While it retains earlier notions of universal moral norms that are safeguarded by the Church and others of good will, it recognized that each culture needs to adopt its own ways of living justly. *GS* incorporated into its arguments the largest pool of patristic sources – eighteen in all – compared with the other CST documents in this study. Among this collection is one quotation, six general references, and eleven footnote-only references.

The first patristic reference in *GS* is a repeat of the quotation from Augustine's *Confessions* I.1 as can be found in *MM* 214.[70] Again, I include the PL edition of Augustine's text alongside the Latin and English texts of the CST document.

70. See above, 26-27.

Conf. I.1[71]	*GS* 21[72]	*GS* 21[73]
… fecisti nos ad te, et inquietum est cor nostrum, donec requiescat in te.	"Fecisti nos ad te," Domine, "et inquietum est cor nostrum, donec requiescat in te."	"Thou hast made us for Thyself," O Lord, "and our hearts are restless until they rest in Thee."

In the earlier discussion of this quotation of *MM* 214, the textual difference with respect to the word *Domine* was discussed. It was pointed out there, but deserves remembering here, that the *GS* document takes greater care in alerting the reader to the insertion of *Domine*. Also above, the context of the quotation within Augustine's *Confessions* was elaborated, highlighting its ornamental role within the *MM* encyclical. Similarly, one may understand the rhetorical role of the *Conf.* I.1 quotation in *GS*. It is even more clearly so in this context, since the quotation is included without attribution to its author. This removes even the limited power of arguing from an authority, for, unless the reader bothered to check the footnotes, he or she would not be aware that the author was Augustine. Either the document's drafters intended the quotation to be understood by only a limited audience of readers aware of Augustine's text, or, more likely, it was determined that the quotation was important solely for ornamental purposes. The language of the quotation fits well the language and argument of the paragraph which it concludes; moreover, and like the *MM* passage composed earlier, the quotation does not expand or explain the argument of the *GS* passage. While *GS* is more careful than *MM* with the patristic quote, in view of its concern to more faithfully translate the Latin, it too incorporated the quotation within a rhetorical framework of ornamental speech.

Turning now to a series of footnote-only references of patristic sources, we examine first those that appear in three footnotes at *GS* 22. Five such references are found in this section under three different footnotes. The first of these occurs near the end of the sentence, "For Adam, the first man, was a figure of him who was to come, namely, Christ the Lord."[74] The footnote directs the reader to consider Romans 5:14 and Tertullian's *The Resurrection of the Body* 6[75] as supporting this claim. The footnote

71. PL 32:661.

72. AAS 58, 1042.

73. CST:DocHer, 178.

74. *GS* 22 (AAS 58, 1042; transl. in Tanner II, 1081): *Adam enim, primus homo, erat figura futuri, scilicet Christi domini.* The footnote appears after *futuri*.

75. PL 2.802 (848); the critical editions are Tertullian, *Opera, Pars III*, ed. Aemilii Kroymann, CSEL 47 (Vienna: F. Tempsky, 1906) 33; id., *Opera, Pars II: Opera monastica*, ed. Aloïs Gerlo, CCSL 2 (Turnhout: Brepols, 1954) 928 (971). ET: Ernest Evans, *Tertullian's Treatise on the Resurrection* (London: SPCK, 1960).

quotes the relevant portion from Tertullian's text, so we are in a position here to evaluate it much as any other patristic source quotation that appears in the body of the CST document.

De carnis resurr. 6[76]	*GS* 22[77]	*GS* 22[78]
Quodcumque enim limus exprimebatur, Christus cogitabatur homo futurus.	Quodcumque enim limus exprimebatur, Christus cogitabatur homo futurus.	For in all the shape given to the clay, Christ was intended as the man who was to be.

The quotation from Tertullian is, as with nearly all the patristic quotations, taken directly from the PL edition, although the CST footnote here includes a reference to the CSEL critical edition completed in 1906. By Vatican II, the CCSL critical edition had been available for nearly a decade, and still yet another critical edition with an accompanying English translation, both by Ernest Evans, was published in 1960. It is curious these more recent critical editions had been overlooked in favor of the CSEL edition. Still, the Latin texts are the same for this quotation in all the editions, excepting minor punctuation differences shared by the PL and the CST document. Textual issues aside, the CST document fairly judges the context of Tertullian's treatise. Both express the dignity of humans in terms of their connection to Christ, who is the ultimate end of God's creative work with Adam. *GS* explains that meaning for human life is found only when a person discovers that Christ is her or his ideal. Somewhat differently, Tertullian argued that the dignity of the Son guided the work of the Father in creating humans as he did. It is the dignity of the pre-Incarnate Son, then, that is generously applied to the creation of humans. It is a wonder that the CST document did not incorporate this text from Tertullian in the body of its own document, in view of the rich extension Tertullian's text provides to its anthropology.

The next three patristic sources in *GS* 22 are grouped together in one footnote. They are citations from three councils, Chalcedon, Constantinople II, and Constantinople III.[79] The relevant footnote texts are below.

76. PL 2.802.
77. AAS 58, 1042.
78. Tanner II, 1081 n. 20.
79. At the council at Chalcedon (held in 451), the patristic debate over Christ's divine and human natures was settled by a compromise that said one person, Jesus, possessed two natures simultaneously. The Second Council of Constantinople (held in 553) both confirmed the Church's rejection of Nestorianism by posthumously excommunicating three of his supposed adherents (Theodore of Mopsuestia, Theodoret of Cyrus, and Ibas of Edessa) and affirmed that neither one of Jesus' two natures were diluted as

Chalcedon[80]	*GS* 22[81]	*GS* 22[82]
in duabus naturis inconfuse, immutabiliter, indivise, inseparabiliter agnoscendum	in duabus naturis inconfuse, immutabiliter, indivise, inseparabiliter agnoscendum	must be acknowledged in two natures, without confusion or change, without division or separation.
Const. II Canon 7[83] neque Deo Verbo in carnis naturam transmutato, neque carne in Verbi naturam transducta.	*GS* 22 Neque Deo Verbo in carnis naturam transmutato, neque carne in Verbi naturam transducta.	*GS* 22 With neither God the Word being changed into the nature of human flesh, nor the human flesh transformed into the nature of the Word.
Const. III[84] Quemadmodum enim sanctissima atque immaculata animata eius caro deificata non est perempta, sed in proprio sui statu et ratione permansit	*GS* 22 Quemadmodum enim sanctissima atque immaculata animata eius caro deificata non est perempta (θεωθεῖσα οὐκ ἀνηρέθη), sed in proprio sui statu et ratione permansit	*GS* 22 For, just as his most holy and blameless animate flesh was not destroyed in being made divine (θεωθεῖσα οὐκ ἀνηρέθη), but remained in its own limit and category

These three patristic source quotations are a footnote to the point of the main CST text which reads, "Since human nature as he assumed it was not annulled, by that very fact it has been raised up to a divine dignity in our respect too."[85] The conciliar voices affirm what is the traditional teaching of the Church regarding Christ's two natures united in one person.[86] The humanity of Christ was not annulled at any point in

a result of their inseparable union. Finally, the Third Council of Constantinople (held from 680-681) confirmed that each of Jesus' two natures preserved their own, respective wills. That in Jesus there were two wills and not one protected from confusion and preserved, in the minds of the council's attendees, the one-person, two-nature Christology of the previous councils. For further reading, cf. Norman P. Tanner, *The Councils of the Church: A Short History* (New York, NY: Crossroad, 2002); Leo D. Davis, *The First Seven Ecumenical Councils (325-787): Their History and Theology*, Theology and Life 21 (Wilmington, DE: Glazier, 1987).

80. Heinrich Denzinger and Peter Hünermann, eds., *Enchiridion symbolorum, definitionem et declarationum de rebus fidei et morum* (Bologna: Dehoniana, 2001) §302.

81. The three quotations in this column are in AAS 58, 1042.

82. The three quotations in this column are in Tanner II, 1082 n. 22.

83. Denzinger-Hünermann, §428.

84. Denzinger-Hünermann, §556.

85. *GS* 22 (AAS 58, 1042; transl. in CST:DocHer, 178-179): Cum in Eo natura humana assumpta, non perempta sit, eo ipso etiam in nobis ad sublimem dignitatem evecta est. The footnote marker is after "assumpta."

86. Interestingly, no excerpts from the third ecumenical council (at Ephesus, 431) are incorporated into this footnote. This council resolved, to some extent, the debate between

Jesus' life; on the contrary, divinity was added to humanity at the Incarnation and the two were inseparable thenceforth. It is at points such as this in the CST documents that the attentive reader is aware how much patristic theology undergirds Catholic social ethics. It is by no means overt; these conciliar documents are relegated to a footnote and it is not stated in the main text that an historical tradition marks Catholic teaching on this point. More than likely, the conciliar texts were included here because of their inherent authority in buttressing these theological claims.

The third footnote in *GS* 22 that incorporates a patristic source follows immediately after the previous one and is another citation from Constantinople III. The footnote comes at the end of this phrase, "He [i.e., Christ] worked with human hands, he thought with a human mind, acted by human choice, ..."[87] The Latin text of the council's statement, and the Latin and English texts from the footnote of the CST document are here provided.

Const. III[88]	*GS* 22[89]	*GS* 22[90]
ita et humana eius voluntas deificata non est perempta.	ita et humana eius voluntas deificata non est perempta.	so his human will as well was not destroyed by being made divine.

The text of this quotation from Constantinople III follows immediately after the text that was cited in the previous footnote. Having cited the texts in this order, the CST document is substantiating its own Christologically-driven anthropology by the progression of these Christological ideas in the history of the Church. CST's anthropology

Cyril of Alexandria and Nestorius on the two natures of Christ. Cyril had argued the one person of Jesus possessed a fully divine and a fully human nature, and that those natures were inseparable. Thus, to say Mary was the mother of Jesus is to say the same thing as Mary is the mother of God. Nestorius, on the other hand, argued that Jesus bore the *Logos* but was not inseparably united to it. To him, Mary was the *Christotokos* or the *anthropotokos*, but not *theotokos*. Nestorius was anathematized at the council, but the issue did not go away. Supporters of Cyril and Nestorius continued their fight up to the Council of Chalcedon. There, a middle ground was forged, and it was concluded things should be said of Jesus in accordance with one or another of his natures. Thus, e.g., Mary is the mother of God in accordance with Jesus' human nature. As well, Jesus performed miracles in accordance with his divine nature.

87. *GS* 22 (AAS 58, 1042; transl. in CST:DocHer, 179): Humanis manibus opus fecit, humana mente cogitavit, humana voluntate egit,...

88. Denzinger-Hünermann, §556.

89. AAS 58, 1042.

90. Tanner II, 1082 n. 23.

is driven by a concern to connect the dignity of every person to the dignity of the Son of God. This is a dignity that was made manifest in the union of divinity with humanity at the Incarnation. By Christ's preservation of two distinct natures within himself, and by correlation, the Church's preservation of that faith statement, each person realizes his or her own dignity when he or she conforms to Christlikeness in daily life and is eventually united for eternity with the divine creator. Interestingly, this Christologically-driven anthropology not only grants dignity to each person, but it also confers dignity on human works that elevate the humanity and self-awareness of others.

The next patristic source citation is a footnote in *GS* 39. It is a reference to Irenaeus's *Against Heresies* V.36.[91] In the context of the CST document, the footnote is intended to supplement the claim that the earth, in its present form and on account of its presumed deformity due to sin, will one day cease to exist. Instead, it will give way to a new created order where justice is uncompromised. The footnote first cites 1 Corinthians 7:31, the latter half of which reads, "For the form of this world is passing away" (RSV). Fortunately, Irenaeus provides the explanation of what exactly is the "form" that is passing away due to sin. He wrote,

> 'The *fashion* of the world passeth away'; that is, those things among which transgression has occurred, since man has grown old in them. And therefore this [present] fashion has been formed temporary, ... But when this [present] fashion [of things] passes away, and man has been renewed, and flourishes in an incorruptible state, so as to preclude the possibility of becoming old, [then] there shall be the new heaven and the new earth, in which the new man shall remain [continually], always holding fresh converse with God.[92] (bracketed words are in the English translation)

The form (or, fashion) that is passing away is those parts of the earth that have been corrupted by sin, seemingly through either the direct or

---

91. PG 7:1221-22; the critical editions are Irenaeus of Lyon, *Contre les hérésies*, ed. Adelin Rousseau, SC 153 (Paris: Éditions du Cerf, 1969) 452-454; id., *Adversus haereses*, ed. Norbert Brox, Fontes Christiani 8, part 5 (Freiburg: Herder, 2001) 268-270. ET: Alexander Roberts and James Donaldson, "Against Heresies," in *The Apostolic Fathers with Justin Martyr and Irenaeus*, ANF 1 (Edinburgh: T. & T. Clark, 1867) 566.

92. Irenaeus, *Against Heresies* V.36.1 (ed. Brox, Fontes Christiani 8.5, 268-270; transl. Roberts and Donaldson, "Against Heresies," 566): sed "figura transit mundi huius," hoc est in quibus transgressio facta est, quoniam veteratus est homo in ipsis. Et propter hoc figura haec temporalis facta est, ... Praetereunte autem figura hac et renovato homine et vigente ad incorruptelam ut non possit iam veterescere, "erit caelum novum et terra nova," in quibus novus perseverabit homo, semper nove confabulans Deo.

indirect activity of human persons on the earth. The reference to Irenaeus is important, then, to provide clarity to the eschatology of CST. This type of footnote is another example of how important is patristic theology to CST. In this case, the ideal of a just society is framed within the context of an eschatological world where human sin and the effects of human sin on the earth, the causes of injustice, are set aside in favor of a new and just created order. However, since only a reference to Irenaeus's text, and not the quotation above, was provided in the footnote, it is incumbent upon the reader of CST to study for themselves its underlying eschatology.

GS 43 incorporates into a footnote the next patristic source. It is a reference to Ambrose's *On Virginity* 8.48[93] in support of the CST document's main text which claims the Church has, across history, remained both faithful to Christ and a constant sign of salvation to the world.[94] This claim is made with the acknowledgment that it is also true some members of the Church have not modeled this witness in their own lives. With respect to *GS* 43, this is an important acknowledgement since the CST document offers the Church's own members to the world as both models for and advocates of virtue, justice, and charity. The Church wants the world to embrace its members and not discount their contribution based on the poor behavior of a minority. Ambrose's text *On Virginity* 8.48 makes a similar claim, although its value for the CST document is not in merely supporting its claim, but in offering a further ecclesiological reflection. Ambrose writes, "Not in herself, daughters, not in herself, I say, is the Church wounded, but in us. We must be careful, then, that no fall of ours becomes an injury for the Church; ..."[95] In this treatise otherwise devoted to a defense of women who choose virginity and a life of service to God, Ambrose makes a distinction between the Church and its adherents. As a thing in itself, the Church upholds a particular way of life (Ambrose here calls his audience to wear the same mantle of patience and prudence as did Christ and the Apostles). He admits it is possible for particular adherents to act discordantly, and the

---

93. PL 16:278; the critical edition is Ambrose, *De virginitate liber unus*, ed. Egnatius Cazzaniga, CSLP (Turin: In Aedibus Io. Bapt. Paraviae et Sociorum, 1954) 22-23. ET: Daniel Callam, *Ambrose: On Virginity*, Peregrina Translations Series 7 (Toronto: Peregrina, 1980) 27.

94. Tanner II, 1098 n. 20.

95. Ambrose, *On Virginity* 8.48 (ed. Cazzaniga, *De virginitate liber unus*, CSLP 22; transl. Callam, *Ambrose: On Virginity*, Peregrina Translations Series 7, 27): Non in se, filiae; non, inquam, in se, filiae, sed in nobis Ecclesia vulneratur. Caveamus igitur ne lapsus noster vulnus Ecclesiae fiat; ...

Church will be injured in the process but not, as he says, in itself. This substance of the Church is separate from the individual adherents, and so is capable of offering its proper way of life anew to every generation of people. The Church's reputation, then, may be harmed by people who live discordantly, but its substance as a genuine witness to the proper life remains intact. Promulgated as it was during a council marking several shifts in the Church's own direction, GS's reliance on Ambrose's text here balances its desire to heal any divisions between both the Church and the world and the Church's own members and the world.

Justin Martyr and Tertullian are two patristic sources cited in a footnote at GS 44, at which place is an acknowledgment that whoever works for justice in the world, whether of the Church or not, contributes to the Church's own community. Even those who oppose the Church might nevertheless play a role in supporting it, as far as the Church itself is concerned, when such opposition leads to self-reflection and improvement. This is precisely the point of the last sentence at GS 44, which reads, "Indeed, the Church admits that she has greatly profited and still profits from the antagonism of those who oppose or persecute her."[96] The footnote at the end of this sentence calls upon the reader to consider two patristic quotations and a text in *Lumen gentium* (II.9). The relevant Latin and English texts for the two patristic quotations are below, first that from Justin Martyr's *Dialogue with Trypho* 110,[97] and then from Tertullian's *Apology* 50.13.[98]

Dialogue 110[99]	*GS* 44[100]	*GS* 44[101]
… sed, quanto magis talia nobis infliguntur, tanto plures alii fideles et pii per nomen Iesu fiunt.	… sed quanto magis talia nobis infliguntur, tanto plures alii fideles et pii per nomen Iesu fiunt.	… for the more such persecutions are are inflicted on us, the greater the number of others who become devout believers in the name of Jesus.

96. *GS* 44 (AAS 58, 1065; transl. in CST:DocHer, 194): Immo Ecclesia, ex ipsa oppositione eorum qui ei adversantur vel eam persequuntur, se multum profecisse et proficere posse fatetur.

97. PG 6.729; the critical edition is Justin Martyr, *Dialogus cum Tryphone*, ed. Miroslav Marcovich, PTS 47 (Berlin: Walter de Gruyter, 1997) 259. ET: Thomas B. Falls, *Writings of Saint Justin Martyr: The First Apology; The Second Apology; Dialogue with Trypho; Exhortation to the Greeks; Discourse to the Greeks; The Monarchy or the Rule of God*, FOTC 6 (Washington D.C.: Catholic University of America Press, 1977) 318.

98. PL 1.534; the critical editions are Tertullian, *Opera Catholica*, CCSL 1, 171; id., *Apologeticum*, CSEL 69, 120. ET: Daly, *Tertullian. Apologetical Works*, FOTC 10, 125.

99. The Latin text here and the Greek below it are from Justin Martyr, *Opera quae feruntur omnia, Tomi I, Pars I: Opera Iustini indubitata*, ed. Johan Karl Theodor von Otto, Corpus Apologeticorum Christianorum saeculi secundi (Jena: Fischer, 1876) 391-393, which is referenced as the source of the citation in the footnote of the CST document. PG 6.729 is also referenced in the footnote.

100. The texts in this column are found in AAS 58, 1065.

101. Tanner II, 1099 n. 23.

ἀλλ' ὅσῳπερ ἂν τοιαῦτά
τινα γίνηται, τοσούτῳ
μᾶλλον ἄλλοι πλείονες
πιστοὶ καὶ θεοσεβεῖς διὰ
τοῦ ὀνόματος τοῦ Ἰησοῦ
γίνονται.

Apology 50.13[102]	*GS* 44	*GS* 44
Etiam plures efficimur,	Etiam plures efficimur,	We become even more numerous
quoties metimur a vobis:	quoties metimur a vobis:	whenever you mow us down: for
semen est sanguis	semen est sanguis	the blood of Christians is a seed!
christianorum!	christianorum!	

The contexts of both patristic texts are quite different from the CST document's own context. As above, *GS* acknowledges the value to the Church of all people in the world, including the work of those otherwise opposed to it, since such people help the Church better understand society and make it possible for the Church to frame its message accordingly. On the other hand, the patristic texts acknowledge the value to the Church of those whose work is directly intended to undermine it. A Christian in the second century faced very physical consequences, for the Christian belief system was viewed as a threat to the cultural and political fabric of society. *GS* addressed a world where opposition had a more intellectually or politically dismissive character, where it was possible simply to avoid the Church while living within a pluralistic cultural and political framework. It is curious, then, that *GS* mixed these two contexts, though perhaps the drafters of the CST document were not concerned with the type of opposition that distinguishes the two contexts, but with the end result that they believed both shared. That is to say, just as martyrdom in the second century had the perceived effect of increasing the raw numbers of Christians and thereby improving the Church, so too the work of the Church's intellectual detractors in the mid-twentieth century improved it by clarifying its message and mission.

In *GS* 48 there is another footnote directing the reader to a patristic source, here to Augustine's text *On the Good of Marriage* 3-5, 24.[103] At the beginning of the second half of the document, that part devoted to an examination of particular social issues, *GS* 48 explains the Church's high view of marriage and the value of children in family

102. PL 1.534.
103. PL 40:375-76, 394; the critical edition is Augustine, *De fide et symbolo, de fide et operibus, de agone christiano, de continentia, de bono coniugali, de sancta virginitate*, ed. Iosephus Zycha, CSEL 41 (Vienna: F. Tempsky, 1900) 190-194, 218. ET: P. G. Walsh, *Augustine: De bono coniugali, De sancta virginitate*, Oxford Early Christian Texts (Oxford: Clarendon Press, 2001) 7-13, 45.

life. The footnote referencing Augustine's text is at the end of the clause, "It is God who is the author of marriage and its endowment with various values and purposes, ..."[104] In Augustine's text, one finds several expansions on these themes. On God being the author of marriage, Augustine proclaims in §2 of this treatise that it was the divine command to procreate that provided the framework for marriage after the Fall. Prior to the Fall, Augustine believed it was possible to envision a scenario whereby procreation took place without sexual intercourse, but the Fall necessitated a framework for procreation that protected against the commission of further sin, and this was the bond of marriage. It is this post-lapsarian framework that allows Augustine, in §3-5 and 24 to identify at least three goods associated with marriage. First, of course, is the begetting of children, which provides for the continuation of the human race and the channeling of marital love towards another being. A second good is the faith of chastity. Marriage makes provision for the human passions, which, left alone, would increase the commission of sins (namely, sexual immorality), and thereby is a help to humanity in the post-lapsarian era. What is more, this faith of chastity fosters a relationship of mutual devotion between a man and woman, which functions as a tutor for behavior within the larger society. A third and final good of marriage is that it is a sacrament, in that God has provided a special grace to marriage partners for living as they should within the bonds of marriage and so functions as a deterrent against the commission of sexual sins. The CST document does not explicate these goods itself, but relies on Augustine for this theology of marriage. It is clear, though, that this theology permeates the argument of *GS*. Following the footnote in *GS* 48, it is claimed that marriage contributes to the dignity and stability of society, that marriage exists for the procreation and education of children, and that marriage is mutually beneficial to the husband and wife. From these claims, some of which have broader appeal than just to the Church's own members, it is argued that political authorities ought to pursue policies that strengthen families, and encourage the healthy raising of children (cf. *GS* 52).

At *GS* 57 one encounters the next patristic source citation. It is a footnote reference to Irenaeus's *Against Heresies* III.11.8 and some related passages.[105] The context of the footnote in the CST document acknowledges

---

104. Tanner II, 1100.
105. PG 7.885-890; the critical editions are Irenaeus of Lyon, ed. Adelin Rousseau and Louis Doutreleau, *Contre les hérésies, Livre III*, SC 211 (Paris: Les Éditions du Cerf, 1974) 161-170; id., *Adversus Haereses*, ed. Norbert Brox, Fontes Christiani 8, part 3

that human progress in the scientific and humanities disciplines should raise the overall standard of humanity's commitment to truth, goodness, beauty, and justice. Furthermore, when this is combined with an impulse of divine grace (*impulsu gratiae*),[106] it is believed that human persons are led inexorably to an acknowledgement of Christ, and to a proper awareness of God's design for the world. "Under the influence of grace it [i.e., the human mind] is in a position to acknowledge the Word of God who, before becoming flesh to save all things and draw them together in himself, was already in the world as 'the true light that enlightens everyone' (Jn 1,9)."[107] The footnote reference to Irenaeus follows this quotation. To this context Irenaeus contributes a great deal from a theological perspective. In *Against Heresies* III.11.8, Irenaeus contends that the Word of God had made himself known to the patriarchs of the Genesis narrative by speaking to them directly, and that he gave the Law and priestly system to make himself known to those living in that later age. Then, in III.16.6, 21.10, and 22.3, Irenaeus confirms that the Word of God was not only responsible for the creation of Adam and all humans, but also that he had been continuously present to that creation prior to the Incarnation in anticipation of saving it. What is more, in III.11.8 and 16.6, Irenaeus explained the presence of Christ with the creation in terms of four dispensational arrangements, including: the pre-lapsarian period when creator and creature shared the greatest intimacy; from the fall of Adam until the demiurge; from the demiurge until the giving of the law; and from the law until the Incarnation. In sum, Irenaeus provides to the CST document a Christology whereby God's design for the world embraces the whole of human history. Christ is the Second Adam, yes, but that does not mean he is simply recapitulating only the acts of the *first Adam*, but of all the Adams', that is to say, all the men and women of history. Christ was present to all people prior to the Incarnation for the sake of salvation, and equally desires a closeness with all those who have been born since the Incarnation. As far as *GS* 57 is concerned, to the extent humanity receives from God an infusion of grace for such an understanding, it will bring to fullness humanity's search for truth.

(Freiburg: Herder, 1995) 108-114. ET: Roberts and Donaldson, "Against Heresies," 428-29. The related passages are *Adversus haereses* III.16.6, 21.10, and 22.3.

106. AAS 58, 1078.

107. *GS* 57 (AAS 58, 1078; transl. in Tanner II, 1108): Immo impulsu gratiae ad agnoscendum Dei Verbum disponitur, quod, antequam caro fieret adomnia salvanda et in Se recapitulanda, iam in mundo erat, tamquam "lux vera quae illuminat omnem hominem" (Io. 1, 9).

We turn, finally, to the last set of patristic source citations in this CST document. At *GS* 69, six patristic sources are identified in a footnote following this comment, "This was the view of the fathers and doctors of the church in teaching that we are obliged to support the poor, and not just from our surplus."[108] The footnote directs the reader first to Basil of Caesarea's *Homily VII* (*Destruam horrea mea*) 2, an exegesis of Luke 12:18.[109] The biblical text is the parable told by Jesus about the rich man who harvests a bountiful crop. Not knowing how to store such a large crop, the rich man decides to tear down his existing barns and build bigger ones. As a result, the man rejoices in his newfound security and comfort in life, but is unaware that God has decided to take his life that very night. Basil's treatment of the passage castigates the man for not thinking of giving away his excess to the poor. Rather than thinking only of himself and of his own security, he should have said instead, "I will fill the souls of the hungry, I will open the storehouses, and I will call out to all the ones in need."[110] Later, in §3, Basil entirely redefines wealth. "And if you marvel at things on account of the honor given by them, consider how much more profitable it is for glory to have been called the father of countless children, than to have countless coins in a purse."[111] Basil, then, contributes two elements to the argument of *GS* 69. First, he rebukes the wealthy, a group that surely must include any person that possesses more than he or she needs. Second, he substitutes as a definition of wealth the quality and quantity of one's relationship to other members of the human family for the traditional notion of the quantity and quality of one's possessions. Consequently, as far as Basil and, by extension, the CST document are concerned, no one is above the obligation to live justly alongside his or her fellow humans.

108. *GS* 69 (AAS 58, 1091; transl. in Tanner II, 1118): Ita Patres Doctoresque Ecclesiae senserunt, docentes ad pauperes sublevandos homines obligari, et quid., non tantum ex superfluis.

109. PG 31.263; the critical edition is Basil of Caesarea, *Homélies sur la richesse*, ed. Yves Courtonne, Collection d'études anciennes (Paris: Firm-Didot, 1935) 19-21. ET: Hieroschemamonk Janis (Berzins), "Homily on the Words of St. Luke's Gospel: 'I will pull down my barns and build larger ones' and on Avarice," *Orthodox Life* 42 (1992) 10-17, here 11; cf. also M. F. Toal, *The Sunday Sermons of the Great Fathers*, vol. 3 (Chicago, IL: Henry Regnery, 1959) 325-332.

110. Basil, *Hom.* VII.2 (ed. Courtonne, *Homélies sur la richesse*, 19; English translation is my own): Ἐμπλήσω τὰς ψυχὰς τῶν πεινώντων, ἀνοίξω τὰς ἀποθήκας, καὶ πάντας καλέσω τοὺς ἐνδεεῖς.

111. Basil, *Hom.* VII.3 (ed. Courtonne, *Homélies sur la richesse*, 21; English translation is my own): Εἰ δὲ θαυμάζεις τὰ χρήματα διὰ τὴν ἀπ' αὐτῶν τιμήν, σκόπει πόσῳ πρὸς δόξαν λυσιτελέστερον, μυρίων παίδων πατέρα προσαγορεύεσθαι, ἢ μυρίους ἔχειν στατῆρας ἐν βαλλαντίῳ.

The next patristic source in the footnote is Lactantius's *Divine Institutes* V.5.[112] Noted for his interaction with classical texts,[113] Lactantius here recalls the ancient poets who lamented the loss of justice in the world and recalled the days of Saturn when justice had been present. Lactantius also draws on the more recent philosophers who reminded their contemporaries that humans used to be content to live on less and to share the goods of the earth. From these reflections Lactantius reminds his own readers that God had created the earth and all its goods for the benefit of all humans, and so that humans might live their lives in common. "What was produced for all should not be denied to any."[114] Lest one conclude from his remarks that private property should be banned, Lactantius adds, "We are not to take these poet's words to mean that there was no private property at all in those days; they are rather a poetical image of people being so generous …"[115] With respect to the overall point of *GS*, then, Lactantius wants justice to return to earth, and perhaps its return will be hastened by a renewed vigor for generosity.

Following Lactantius is a citation of Augustine's *Commentary on John* 50.6.[116] Here Augustine comments on John 12:3, in which one finds the story of Mary annointing Jesus with costly perfume and wiping Jesus's feet with her hair. Augustine points out that the term for liquid ($\pi\iota\sigma\tau\acute{\iota}\varkappa\circ\varsigma$), referring to the ointment used by Mary, also means "faithful." Thus, Mary's spreading of the ointment on and care for Jesus is an act of faithfulness by Mary. So too is it an act of faithfulness whenever a Christian meets the need of another person (Augustine establishes this connection with a reference to Matthew 25:40). Mary meets Jesus's need for clean feet by washing his feet with her hair. To Augustine, hair is superfluous; thus, the giving of one's superfluities to meet the needs of

---

112. PL 6.565B; the critical editions are Lactantius, *Opera omnia, Pars I*, CSEL 19, 413-416; id., *Institutions divines*, SC 204, 150-154. ET: Bowen and Garnsey, *Lactantius. Divine Institutes*, 290-292.

113. Cf. R. M. Ogilvie, *The Library of Lactantius* (Oxford: Clarendon Press, 1978).

114. Lactantius, *Divine Institutes* V.5.6 (ed. Monat, *Institutions divines*, SC 204, 152; transl. Bowen and Garnsey, *Lactantius. Divine Institutes*, 291): nec ulli deesset quod omnibus nasceretur.

115. Lactantius, *Divine Institutes* V.5.7. (ed. Monat, *Institutions divines*, SC 204, 152; transl. Bowen and Garnsey, *Lactantius. Divine Institutes*, 291): Quod poetae dictum sic accipi oportet, non ut existimemus nihil omnino tum fuisse priuati, sed more poetico figuratum, ut intellegamus tam liberales fuisse homines.

116. PL 35.1760; the critical edition is Augustine, *Sancti Aurelii Augustini In Iohannis Evangelium, tractatus CXXIV*, ed. Radbodus Willems, CCSL 36 (Turnhout: Brepols, 1954) 435. ET: John W. Rettig, *Augustine. Tractates on the Gospel of John, 28-54*, FOTC 88 (Washington D.C.: Catholic University of America Press, 1993) 263-264.

another is an example of how a Christian may exercise faithfulness to Christ. Since Augustine does not overly concern himself here either with care for the poor or with the meaning of superfluous resources, the link between this passage from his *Commentary on John* 50.6 and *GS* is rather tenuous. To speak positively, one recognizes in this citation how CST documents do, at times, enrich the contexts of the patristic text by situating them within a new context.

Next, a citation of Augustine's *Exposition of the Psalms* 147.12[117] contributes to the CST document in two ways. Theologically, Augustine connects the giving of one's superfluity to meet the needs of another with works of mercy, works which align a person's life to the will of God. It is not the case that a person may presume upon these works of mercy for entrance into heaven, but Augustine does suggest that Scripture's exhortations to be merciful ought relieve any anxiety we might have about the receipt of that divine mercy in the afterlife. Practically speaking, Augustine extends the argument of the CST document by asking his hearers to take inventory of their goods, to determine what items are absolutely necessary for the continuation of God's work (including maintenance of the body, which is a creative work of God), and then to give the superfluous items away to those who have need of them. Most striking of all, Augustine declares that not distributing our excess in such a way is actually robbery, for "you are keeping what belongs to someone else."[118]

Following Augustine's two texts is a reference to Gregory the Great's *Homilies on the Gospels* 20.12.[119] In this particular passage Gregory likens the spiritual reward shared by a prophet and his financial supporters to the virtues of the poor shared by a poor person and those who meet the

---

117. PL 37.1922; the critical editions are Augustine, *Enarrationes in Psalmos 101-150, Pars 5: Enarrationes in Psalmos 141-150*, ed. Franco Gori and Iuliana Spaccia, CSEL 95, part 5 (Vienna: Österreichische Akademie der Wissenschaften, 2005) 211-12; id., *Sancti Aurelii Augustini Enarrationes in Psalmos CI-CL*, ed. D. Eligius Dekkers and J. Fraipont, CCSL 40 (Turnhout: Brepols, 1956) 2148. ET: Maria Boulding, *Augustine. Expositions of the Psalms (Enarrationes in Psalmos) 121-150*, WSA 20 (New York: New City Press, 2004) 453-454.
118. Augustine, *Exposition of the Psalms* 147.12 (ed. Gori and Spaccia, CSEL 95.5, 211-12; transl. Boulding, *Expositions of the Psalms*, 454): Res alienae possidentur.
119. PL 76.1165; the critical editions are Gregory the Great, *Homiliae in Evangelia*, ed. Raymond Étaix, CCSL 141 (Turnhout: Brepols, 1999) 163-164; id., *Homiliae in Evangelia*, ed. and transl. Michael Fiedrowicz, Fontes Christiani 28.1 (Freiburg: Herder, 1997) 359-360. ET: David Hurst, *Gregory the Great. Forty Gospel Homilies*, 43-44. Due to a different numbering scheme for the homilies in this English translation, it places sixth the twentieth homily found in the PL and the critical editions.

needs of the poor. Interestingly, the CST document does not cite the wider context, to include 20.10-11, since it is in this wider context that the larger theological point is established. This larger context is Gregory's exegesis of Luke 3:9, Jesus' teaching that every tree which does not bear good fruit will be cut down. One way of bearing good fruit, according to the biblical passage, is to share your second tunic with the person who has no tunic. Gregory draws from this several implications for persons with superfluous resources. First and foremost, sharing one's excess with a poor person is a demonstration of the dictum that one must love his or her neighbor as much as he or she loves himself or herself. Second, works of mercy are "fruits worthy of repentance"[120] and so generosity ought to be cultivated. Finally, and this returns us now to 20.12, the virtues of self-restraint and helping the poor are direct teachings of Jesus, who taught that any who receive a prophet share in the prophet's reward (cf. Matt 10:41). Gregory draws a comparison between the small number of prophets and the larger number of their supporters and the small number of wealthy individuals and the larger number of poorer persons they ought to support. This comparison suggests Gregory believed God had allowed the wealthy to acquire what they have for the very purpose of redistributing it to those in need. In so doing, the wealthy individuals exercise love of neighbor, generosity, and self restraint, all of which are fruits for repentance. This teaching of Gregory is an important component to the theology of social justice that undergirds the CST document.

The last patristic source in this footnote is a reference to Gregory's *Rules for Pastors* III.21.[121] Gregory admonishes two groups of people, those who are not greedy but do not give of their excess to the poor, and those who share with the poor but do so without discretion and so are always in a position of having to demand the return of what they previously distributed. Both groups of people end up hurting the poor. The contribution to the CST document is substantial, for Gregory identifies the need for a healthy balance between charity and discretion, between making sure one's own needs are met and meeting the needs of the poor with any excess. Moreover, Gregory articulates what is a refrain in several

120. Gregory, *Homilies on the Gospels* 20.11 (ed. Étaix, CCSL 141, 163-164; transl. Hurst, *Gregory the Great. Forty Gospel Homilies*, 43): fructum dignum paenitentiae.

121. PL 77.87; the critical edition is Gregory the Great, *Règle pastorale*, ed. Floribert Rommel, transl. Charles Morel, SC 382 (Paris: Éditions du Cerf, 1992) 394-400. ET: Henry Davis, *Gregory the Great: Pastoral Care*, ACW 11 (Westminster, MD: The Newman Press, 1950), 158-162.

CST documents, that the goods of the earth belong to all. No one person ought control what God has given for the enjoyment and use of all persons. In furtherance of this point, Gregory quotes Psalm 112:9, "He has distributed freely, he has given to the poor; his righteousness (δικαιοσύνη αὐτοῦ; צִדְקָתוֹ) endures for ever; his horn is exalted in honor" (RSV). Gregory understands the Psalmist's choice of δικαιοσύνη or צִדְקָתוֹ as an intention to exclude language of "mercy." Thus, it is a matter of justice or righteousness, not mercy, when those with superfluous wealth give it to the poor. Perhaps this is Gregory's greatest contribution to the CST document, for justice language places this issue within a framework that often invokes God's wrath when it is violated, whereas mercy language suggests the activity is optional.

Altogether, these six patristic source references at *GS* 69 contribute to the CST document's larger point by elaborating upon several important practical implications and theological underpinnings. *GS* commands simply that everyone contribute to alleviating the suffering of the poor. It is Basil who tells us that "the wealthy" includes any person who possesses more than he or she needs for survival. It is Lactantius who dispels any notion that food and other goods taken from the earth are to be held privately, for God had created the earth for the common good; in fact, it is the spirit of generosity that must return in order that justice may reign supreme once again on the earth. Augustine provides us a Christological angle through which to view that generosity, for in whatever manner we share our surplus goods with others we demonstrate our faithfulness to Christ. Not to share these goods is, in fact, robbery of the poor, for surplus goods belong to them already. Gregory the Great furthers this point by affirming that God had intentionally assigned surplus goods to wealthy people *for the very purpose* of facilitating the virtues of self-restraint and generosity within them when they give such goods away to others. As well, Gregory challenges the notion that caring for the needs of the poor is an act of mercy; on the contrary, it is an act of righteousness or justice, and this places human responsibility to care for the poor in a framework that has soteriological and eschatological consequences.

In sum, *Gaudium et spes* refers to patristic sources eighteen times. Only one is cited as a quotation within the body of the document, and most of the rest are known only by footnote markers in the text. On the one hand, the number of patristic sources in *GS* surpasses by far the number found in previous documents; on the other hand, the role these patristic sources play is rather understated. Relegating most of them to a footnote has the advantage that the main text can simply rely on the foundation these patristic texts have laid. This is especially important with respect to seemingly complicated theological arguments that *GS* does not want to take the time to re-explain. Even so, their role as articulators of the theology that undergirds CST surely equals their role as historical witnesses to the continuity of the Church's teaching. When placed alongside citations of biblical texts, Aquinas, Bonaventure, and previous CST documents, just to name a few authorities, the patristic sources affirm that what is being taught in *GS* is, in the final analysis, nothing new. The Church continues to teach what it has always believed, even if the modern world has demanded a new articulation of those teachings.

Populorum progressio (1967)

This encyclical of Paul VI challenged existing notions of "development" by tying it to the factors that comprise daily human life. It is these factors which are as important, or more so, than the economic ones. *PP* incorporates two patristic source citations in furtherance of its aims. Both are found in *PP* 23.

The first is a quotation from Ambrose's *On Naboth* 12.53.[122] I quote the original language of both texts and provide the CST document's English translation below.

On Naboth 12.53[123]	*PP* 23[124]	*PP* 23[125]
Non de tuo largiris pauperi sed de suo reddis. Quod enim commune est in omnium usum datum solus usurpas. Omnium est terra, non divitum.	Non de tuo largiris pauperi sed de suo reddis. Quod enim commune est in omnium usum datum, tu solus usurpas. Omnium est terra, non divitum.	You are not making a gift of your possessions to the poor person. You are handing over to him what is his. For what has been given in common

122. PL 14:747; the critical edition is Ambrose, *De Iacob, de Ioseph, de Patriarchis, de fuga saeculi, de interpretatione Iob et David, de apologia David, apologia David altera, de Helia et ieiunio, de Nabuthae, de Tobia*, ed. Carolus Schenkl, CSEL 32 (Vienna: F. Tempsky, 1897) 498. ET: Boniface Ramsey, *Ambrose*, The Early Church Fathers (London and New York, NY: Routledge, 1997) 135; Martin R. P. McGuire, *S. Ambrosii De Nabuthae: A Commentary, with an Introduction and Translation*, Patristic Studies 15 (Washington D.C.: Catholic University of America Press, 1927) 83.

123. PL 14:747.

124. AAS 67, 268-69.

125. CST:DocHer, 245.

for the use of all, you have
arrogated to yourself. The
world is given to all, and not
only to the rich.

The CST document is quoting Ambrose's text from the PL edition,
and this it does verbatim.[126] It is left to compare the contextual frameworks of both Ambrose's text and *PP*. Ambrose's *On Naboth* is a sermon
he delivered sometime in the late 380s.[127] It is an exposition on the story
of King Ahab's covetous desire for the nearby vineyard of the poor man,
Naboth (1 Kings 21). When Naboth refused to sell the vineyard to the
king, on account of the fact that it had been in his family's possession for
some time, Ahab's wife Jezebel stepped in to arrange for the murder of
Naboth. Ambrose's exposition of the story allows him to condemn the
vagaries, plunderings, jealousies, and covetousness of rich people.
Ambrose chastises the rich for looking out only for their own interests,
never content with their current wealth, and as quick to eat the bread off
another person's plate as they are to decorate themselves with yet another
jewel. The point of *On Naboth* 12.53, then, is emphasized throughout the
work. There is even a parallel passage in *On Naboth* 1.2.[128]

In the context of the CST document, this quotation from Ambrose
was intended to supplement the biblical claim that a person's love of
God correlates with a person's concern for the needs of a fellow human.
Ambrose's text is made to supplement this claim by arguing that a person cannot base his or her refusal to meet the needs of another on the
grounds that meeting such a need restricts his or her use of privately-
held property.[129] *PP* finds in Ambrose's statement a claim that private

---

126. Between the PL and the CSEL edition are two differences. One is the editorial
decision related to punctuation. The CSEL edition places a semicolon after *reddis*,
whereas the PL ends the first sentence here with a period. One is advised not to read too
much into this, however, for it may well be the case that the CSEL editor sought to
minimize sentence divisions and chose instead to use semicolons more frequently than
periods. The second difference is PL's inclusion and CSEL's exclusion of the word *tu*
that, according to the CSEL apparatus, is found in only a limited field of manuscripts.
This too is a minor issue, for it functions as the subject of the verb *usurpas*, and since
the verb itself is in the second person, the addition of *tu* to the sentence is unnecessary.

127. Ramsey, *Ambrose*, 117.

128. McGuire, *S. Ambrosii: De Nabuthae*, 182, indicates his awareness of the parallel.
His commentary on §1.2, pp. 106-107, lists parallel passages in four other works by
Ambrose, and it suggests a Ciceronian connection.

129. Ambrose's own understanding of private property, quite apart from the claims of
the CST document, is the subject of a monograph by Vincent Vasey, *The Social Ideas in
the Works of St. Ambrose: A Study on De Nabuthe*, Studia Ephemeridis Augustinianum

property is no longer private when another person needs that property for survival. "The right to private property must never be exercised to the detriment of the 'common good.'"[130]

The CST document lifts the quotation from Ambrose out of a context of condemning the excesses and malcontent of the rich and places it into a new context where the concern is about one's love for God. The expression of that love is the love one has for a neighbour, and this latter love ought be expressed in the tangible ways one handles private property. Yet, Ambrose himself does not make these same connections in his own text; rather, he states the problem of riches bluntly, without recourse to a larger theological framework of love for God and neighbour. One may argue the CST document has enriched the theological setting for Ambrose's own words; equally, one may lament the loss of the rebukes of the rich in the process.

Later in *PP* 23, and functioning as something of a summary of the argument to which Ambrose's text contributed, one encounters the second patristic source citation. It is a general reference to the Church Fathers and is set within *PP* 23's quotation of a 1964 papal letter to an annual gathering of French social activists. The relevant text at *PP* 23 reads, "In a word, 'according to the traditional doctrine as found in the Fathers of the Church and the great theologians, the right to property must never be exercised to the detriment of the common good.'"[131] No citation or quotation of a particular Church Father is included in the papal letter, leaving the reader there to imagine what is to be found in

---

(Rome: Institutum Patristicum "Augustinianum," 1982), esp. pp. 105-142. Vasey recognizes that a reading of one text or another of Ambrose could lead a reader to conclude that Ambrose either rejected or accepted the notion of private property. From a reading of all Ambrose's extant works, Vasey concludes that Ambrose accepted that private property is a consequence of discontent that came with the fall of Adam, that people have the right to inherit and hold property, but that ownership was dictated both by use and need. When property is needed by another person for his or her survival, it ceases to be the private property of someone else. Noteworthy as well is that Ambrose himself shared an inherited land trust between his two siblings.

130. *PP* 23 (AAS 67, 269; transl. in CST:DocHer, 245): numquam proprietatis iure utendum est cum boni communis detrimento.

131. *PP* 23 (AAS 67, 269; transl. in CST:DocHer, 245): Ne multa, *secundum traditam doctrinam Ecclesiae Patrum praeclarorumque Theologorum, numquam proprietatis iure utendum est cum boni communis detrimento.*

For the French text, cf. John Paul II, "L'homme et la révolution urbaine: Citadins et ruraux devant l'urbanisation," *La documentation Catholique* 62 (1-15 August, 1965) 1365. It reads, "… selon la doctrine traditionnelle chez les Pères de l'Église et les grands théologiens. Il y a là sans nul doute un douloureux conflit à surmonter entre droits privés acquis et exigences communautaires primordiales."

the patristic writings. Excerpting the quote from the earlier letter was simply a way to ornament the argument of *PP* 23 already established with the quotation of Ambrose. The quotation from this papal letter adds nothing new to the argument; rather, it appears to have been included precisely because of its general reference to the Church Fathers. Thus, it is a rhetorical ornament whose summarizing purpose is made clear by the words introducing the quote, "In a word, …"

Overall, the two patristic source citations in *PP* comprise only 1.1% of the total word count for the encyclical. Yet, for the first time in this study of CST documents we have encountered a patristic source being used to buttress the claim that private property is no longer private when it is needed by another person for survival. This is a helpful, practical extension of the argument at *PP* 23, and is an important argument made by other CST documents as it was also made by other patristic writers. Indeed, the second patristic citation suggests other such sources do exist. However, a general reference to the Church Father such as it is, the second citation is little more than an ornamental addition to the first. There was room in *PP* for greater use of patristic sources than the two identified here.

Evangelii nuntiandi (1975)

Promulgated in 1975, *EN* addressed various aspects of the evangelizing work of the Church.[132] It exhorted the faithful and the clergy always to live an authentic life of faith so as not to detract from the Church's message. It recognized that authentic human development would only come with a wider knowledge of God in the world and with humanity's acceptance of God as the source and ultimate end of their humanity. Equally important, the Church's promotion of justice, peace, and human rights, in the view of *EN*, are inseparable from its evangelistic mission. In furtherance of these ends, *EN* relied on no less than fifteen patristic sources, including six quotations, six footnote-only references, and three general references in the main text. We examine each patristic source in turn.

The first patristic source citation is a footnote reference to Augustine's *Sermon XLVI* 1-2 at *EN* 15.[133] The title for this sermon is "On the

132. The encyclical defines "evangelism" at *EN* 17-18.
133. PL 38.270-71; the critical edition is Augustine, *Sermones de Vetere Testamento, id est sermones I-L secundum ordinem Vulgatum insertis etiam novem sermonibus post*

Shepherds," and it is one of a two-part sermon series, the other being *Sermon XLVII*, titled, "On the Sheep."[134] Both were preached in the context of the Donatist controversy, the former chastising the bishops and priests for giving cause to the Donatists' complaints, and the latter chastising the laity for their own lapses of faith and Christian charity. In the first two sections of *Sermon XLVI*, Augustine began his exposition of the text for that day, Ezekiel 34. Ezekiel is told by God to preach against the shepherds, for they neglect the sheep and feed only themselves. Augustine extended this complaint to the shepherds of churches, the priests who, in his day, cared only for their own needs and sought the priesthood only for the social honors it bestowed. Augustine reminded his lay audience that bishops and priests must guard not only their own manner of life and speech, but also that of their flock. Thus, they have a greater responsibility before God, and so it is shameful when they put their own interests ahead of caring for their flock. These criticisms of Augustine are joined with the Pauline claim that "what we preach is not ourselves, but Jesus Christ as Lord" (2 Cor 4:5; RSV) in a footnote at the end of this statement in *EN* 15, "The Church herself sends out evangelizers ... To preach not their own selves or their personal ideas, ..."[135] The statement itself comes at the end of a section in the CST document in which it is claimed that the Church has been sent by Christ into the world to proclaim the Gospel, and this mission also includes ongoing preaching of the Gospel within its own community. What is more, the evangelizers whom the Church sends out both to the non-Christian peoples of the world and to its own communities are obligated to preach the message of Jesus. They neither may seek personal gain nor should interject their own ideas about that message. The citation of Augustine at this point is interesting, for Augustine is not concerned with the content of the shepherds' message, but the conduct of their lives. If the CST document wanted to remain focused on the content of the evangelizers' preaching, then it could have cited §31-32 later in this same sermon by Augustine. It is possible the drafters of the CST document had not read further in Augustine's sermon and so were not aware of these

---

Maurinos repertis, ed. Cyril Lambot, CCSL 41 (Turnhout: Brepols, 1961) 529-530. ET: Edmund Hill, *Augustine: Sermones II (20-50) on the Old Testament*, WSA, Part 3.2 (Brooklyn, NY: New City Press, 1990) 263-264.

134. On a date of 414 for both sermons, and for a discussion of the likelihood that they were separated in time by perhaps no more than three months, see Hill, *Augustine: Sermones II (20-50)*, 292 n. 1 and 323-324 nn. 1 and 7.

135. *EN* 15 (AAS 68, 15; transl. in CST:DocHer, 308): Ecclesia ... ipsa vicissim evangelizatores mittit ... scilicet non ad se ipsos, non ad sua cogitata ... praedicandum.

later, content-oriented exhortations. Yet it seems appropriate in this context to strengthen the responsibility of the Church's evangelizers by including not only their speech but also their actions. This is what Augustine contributes to the argument, though one wishes this had been more explicit in the main text.

The next patristic citation is at *EN* 16; in fact, three patristic sources are grouped together in one footnote as corroborating evidence for the words of Luke 10:6 which are found in the main text, "Anyone who rejects you rejects me." The wider context of *EN* 16 challenges the notion that someone can love or listen to Christ but not love or listen to the Church, and it laments that so many live this misguided way. In support of these concerns, *EN* turns first to Cyprian's *On the Unity of the Church* 14.[136] At the outset, it should be noted there is some confusion in the footnote as to exactly what text the CST document is referring. The footnote cites Cyprian's *On the Unity of the Church* 14 and then directs the reader to PL 4.527. The problem is that §14 begins on PL 4.528; the end of §12 and the beginning of §13 are on column 527. The problem could easily be overcome if the contexts of §12 and 14 were different, but the fact is that both could contribute to the argument made in the CST document itself. Thus, it is best to acknowledge what both §12 and 14 contribute to *EN* 16, not knowing for certain to which passage the document's drafters were referring. In the former, Cyprian points out that Jesus condemned discord among his followers when he said, "For where two or three are gathered in my name, there am I in the midst of them" (Matt 18:20; RSV). Jesus supports the two or three who pray in harmony rather than the multitude who pray as dissenters. In the latter, Cyprian declares that the dissenters who die as martyrs, ostensibly for being Christians, are not purged of their guilt of schism. True martyrs are united with the Church. Thus, the CST document's concern with Christians separated from the Catholic Church is shared by Cyprian, although Cyprian is clearly more punitive, suggesting that the dissenters' prayers are not heard by Christ (§12) and that their acts of martyrdom go unrewarded (§14).

The second patristic citation in this footnote at *EN* 16 is of Augustine's *Expositions of the Psalms* 88, Sermon 2.[137] While the footnote here

---

136. PL 4.527-28; the critical edition is Cyprian of Carthage, *Ad Quirinum, Ad Fortunatum, De lapsis, De ecclesiae catholicae unitate*, ed. Maurice Bévenot, CCSL 3, part 1 (Turnhout: Brepols, 1972) 257-260. ET: Maurice Bévenot, *Cyprian. De Lapsis and De Ecclesiae Catholicae Unitate*, Oxford Early Christian Texts (Oxford: Clarendon Press, 1971) 75-80.

137. PL 37.1140; the critical editions are Augustine, *Enarrationes in Psalmos 51-100, Pars 5: Enarrationes in Psalmos 141-150*, ed. Franco Gori and Iuliana Spaccia, CSEL 95,

cites Sermon 2, much of the sermon has nothing to do with Christian unity; rather, one must look to Sermon 2.14, where it is argued that unity with the Church is essential for the Christian. Indeed, *EN* likely included this passage from Augustine because Sermon 2.14 is quoted at length at the end of Leo XIII's encyclical, *Satis cognitum*, which also concerned the unity of the Church.[138] At Sermon 2.14 Augustine argues that it is not appropriate for a person to live in a manner pleasing to God the Father while at the same time offending the Church as his or her mother. Alternatively, it is not appropriate to offend the Father by one's lifestyle or beliefs and regularly attend and support the Church. The true Christian embraces both God as his or her father and the Church as his or her mother. Having employed this argument from Augustine, *EN* expands its critique to include those who attend Mass but do not honor God with their lifestyle throughout the week. As well, the citation of Augustine expands *EN*'s soteriology, for Augustine's comments about the Church as a mother are preceded by a brief exposition of Jesus's words in Matthew 23:37-38, "How often would I have gathered your children together as a hen gathers her brood under her wings, ..." (RSV). Augustine concluded from this, "Christians must never rely on themselves; anyone who wants to grow strong needs to be fostered by a mother's warmth."[139] Thus, coming to the Church as one's mother is nothing less than coming to Christ himself. With such an understanding, a person's search for Christ inevitably leads him or her to the Church. The two are equal in Augustine's mind, and they are equal in *EN*, and yet the development of this claim has been left by the CST document to Augustine and relegated to a footnote.

The third patristic source citation for this footnote is that of John Chrysostom's *Homily on the Capture of Eutropius* 6.[140] This text bears

part 5 (Vienna: Österreichische Akademie der Wissenschaften, 2005) 211-212; id., *Enarrationes in Psalmos LI-C*, ed. Eligius Dekkers and Johannes Fraipont, CCSL 39 (Turnhout: Brepols, 1956) 1243-1244. ET: Maria Boulding, *Augustine: Expositions of the Psalms (Enarrationes in Psalmos) 73-98*, WSA 18 (New York, NY: New City, 2004) 301-02.

138. Leo XIII, *Satis cognitum* 16 (29 June, 1896; cf. ASS 28, 739). This encyclical also cites the Chrysostom text that follows and several passages in Cyprian's *On the Unity of the Catholic Church*, although not §12-14.

139. Augustine, *Expositions on the Psalms* 88.2.14 (ed. Dekkers and Fraipont, *Enarrationes in Psalmos LI-C*, CCSL 39, 1243-1244; transl. Boulding, *Expositions of the Psalms 73-98*, 301-302): Non enim de se debet sperare christianus: si uult esse firmus, uapore materno nutriatur.

140. PG 52.402; no critical edition of the text exists. ET: W. R. W. Stephens, "Two Homilies on Eutropius," in *John Chrysostom: On the Priesthood; Ascetic Treatises; Select Homilies and Letters; Homilies on the Statues*, NPNF I.9 (Edinburgh: T. & T. Clark, 1889) 255-256.

weight of authority as a traditional source because of the author to which it is ascribed, but it is surprising to find this homily identified with John Chrysostom in the CST document for in 1975 it was generally acknowledged to be a spurious work.[141] Alan Cameron tried to resurrect interest in the homily by arguing its subject was not Eutropius, but was instead a Count John who had denounced Chrysostom at the Synod of the Oak. Cameron, however, relegates discussion over the homily's authenticity to a footnote at the beginning of the article, and proceeds with his article as though the homily was genuinely Chrysostomian.[142] His judgment still holds some sway, but a very recent article has once again cast some doubt on Chrysostom being its author.[143] Whether it will, in fact, be accepted within the authentic, Chrysostomian canon is yet to be decided; the fact remains that it was considered a spurious work in the CST document's own day. It was probably included here because it too is found in Leo XIII's encyclical, *Satis cognitum*. All told, these facts suggest a casual treatment of patristic sources by the drafters of *EN*, a point which cannot be understated. Nevertheless, it is a text emerging from the patristic world, and we are still interested in how the argument of the text was deemed to support the point in question at *EN* 16.

Therefore, turning to an examination of the text, one finds in the context of this homily a pastoral exhortation not to envy the life of the rich, and not to covet the goods of others. Such attitudes contributed to the downfall of the homily's subject. Instead, the homily urges its hearers to lay hold of Christ and to judge the things of the world correctly. Connected to that, one reads,

> Do not remain apart from the Church: for nothing is stronger than the Church. The Church is your hope; your salvation, your refuge. It

---

The reader should be careful to distinguish this homily from one with a similar title that is well within the accepted Chrysostom corpus, *On Eutropius*, whose Greek text is PG 52.391-396 and whose English translation is available both in the NPNF volume and in Wendy Mayer and Pauline Allen, *John Chrysostom*, The Early Church Fathers Series (New York, NY: Routledge Press, 2000) 132-139. It is instructive to review this well-accepted homily for context on the life of Eutropius, if indeed he is the subject of this second homily.

141. Cf. Geerard, ed., *Ab Athanasio ad Chrysostomum*, CPG 2, 548, no. 4528.

142. Alan Cameron, "A Misidentified Homily of Chrysostom," *Nottingham Mediaeval Studies* 32 (1988) 34-48. For the treatment of Count John, see 39; for its discussion of the authenticity debate, see 35 n. 9.

143. S. Voicu, "La volontà e il caso: La tipologia dei primi spuri di Crisostomo," in *Giovani Crisostomo: Oriente e Occidente tra IV e V secolo*, Studia Ephemeridis Augustinianum 93 (Rome: Institutum Patristicum "Augustinianum," 2005) 101-118.

is higher than the heavens and wider than the earth. It never grows old, but is always full of vitality. For these reasons, pointing to its strength and stability, Holy Scripture calls it a mountain.[144]

It may seem odd that the homily's author shifted so quickly from a critique of riches to a praise of the Church, but the homily's overall context is Chrysostom's spurning its subject from seeking asylum in the Church. Eutropius, or whoever it might have been, had long been a critic of the Church but was now begging for its assistance, and Chrysostom refused to oblige. Thus the critique of riches and the exhortation to cleave to the Church go hand-in-hand. If you love one, you cannot love the other; Eutropius had made his choice already, making the insincerity of his asylum-seeking all the more patent.

Within the context of the CST document, though, this entire framework is absent. All that remains of this distinction between two loves is the exhortation to love the Church. Rhetorically, then, the homily is included in the CST document merely as an appeal to authority. Insofar as such appeals go, there is often more to the argument in the original version. The attentive reader to this CST document would do well to apprise himself or herself of that larger context.

The next two patristic citations also appear together in a footnote at *EN* 21. In this context, the CST document has moved on to consider how evangelization takes place. It begins with the "wordless witness" of a Christian in a community, a witness marked by sharing, solidarity, living by values that exceed those of the community, and maintaining a hope in things that are unseen. These are the first "essential elements" of evangelization, and it is in support of them as such that the CST document turns to Tertullian's *Apology* 39 and to Minucius Felix's *Octavius* 9 and 31.[145] The former had also been quoted in *RN* 24, and so the reader is directed back to that earlier discussion where Tertullian's rationale for

---

144. (Pseudo-)Chrysostom, *Hom. on the Capture of Eutropius* 6 (PG 52.402; transl. Stephens, "Two Homilies on Eutropius," 256, with some modifications by this author): Μὴ ἀπέξου Ἐκκλησίας, οὐδὲν γὰρ Ἐκκλησίας ἰσχυρότερον. Ἡ ἐλπίς σου ἡ Ἐκκλησία, ἡ σωτηρία σου ἡ Ἐκκλησία, ἡ καταφυγή σου ἡ Ἐκκλησία. Τοῦ οὐρανοῦ ὑψηλοτέρα ἐστί, τῆς γῆς πλατυτέρα ἐστίν. Οὐδέποτε γηρᾷ, ἀεὶ δὲ ἀκμάζει. Διὰ τοῦτο τὸ στερρὸν αὐτῆς καὶ ἀσάλευτον δηλοῦσα ἡ Γραφὴ ὄρος αὐτὴν καλεῖ.

145. PL 3.260-263 and 335-338; the critical edition is Minucius Felix, *Octavius*, ed. Michael Pellegrino, CSLP (Turin: G. B. Paravia, 1972) 11-13, 47-48. ET: Rudolph Arbesmann, *Minucius Felix. Octavius*, FOTC 10 (Washington D.C.: Catholic University of America Press, 1950) 335-338 and 387-389; G. W. Clarke, *The Octavius of Marcus Minucius Felix*, ACW 39 (New York, NY: Newman Press, 1974) 82-85 and 109-111.

monetary offerings by Christians is explained.[146] In this new context, Tertullian's explanation of Christian tithes is important because it is evidence of some practical ways this "wordless witness" was expressed. Christians used their money to express in a tangible way their solidarity with the poor. The latter text, Minucius Felix's *Octavius* 9 and 31, a near contemporary to Tertullian's own text,[147] is a dialogue between the Christian Octavius and the pagan Caecilius. In §9 Caecilius argued that Christians are deplorable for their incestuous relationships (presumed to exist based upon their "holy kisses" and referring to one another as brother or sister) and for infanticide (believing that an infant is sacrificed for the "body" and "blood" elements of the eucharistic meal). In §31 Octavius refutes the charges as mere lies spread about the empire by demons; on the contrary, he argued Christians within and without the walls of their meeting places lead praiseworthy lives and are models of good character. It is rather the Romans, he argued, who indulge in promiscuous relationships and celebrate such relationships among the gods in their poetry and in the performances at the theaters. Thus, Octavius joins Tertullian in affirming what *EN* 21 has claimed, that the manner in which Christians live differentiates them from the larger culture. However, the contexts are quite different. Tertullian and Octavius explained Christianity so as to reduce its perceived threat to the empire, and if pagans like Caecilius become Christians as a result, then all the better. *EN*, by contrast, addresses a context in which Christians already possess the right to exist, and so its appeal to Christian charity and solidarity has as its goal the evangelization of the world's communities. In a final analysis, the uniting of these two contexts creates a new argument altogether, that Christians ought to live in a particular way regardless of the circumstances in which they find themselves.

At *EN* 53 four more patristic sources are incorporated into this document, the first three of which are identified only in a footnote, and the fourth is named in the main text itself. The first three are cited for their use or support of the phrase, "seeds of the Word" (*seminibus Verbi*) which *EN* argues are what the non-Christian religions of the world are

146. See above, 20.

147. The parallels between Tertullian's *Apology* and Minucius Felix's *Octavius* are striking, such that most scholars have concluded that one is dependent on the other, or that both are dependent on a third source. A helpful summary of this debate since the early nineteenth century is available in Michael E. Hardwick, *Josephus as an Historical Source in Patristic Literature through Eusebius*, Brown Judaic Studies 128 (Atlanta, GA: Scholars Press, 1989) 21-22. Examination of the interdependency is also in Clarke, *The Octavius of Marcus Minucius Felix*, 9-10 (supports priority of Tertullian).

vis-à-vis Christianity. These three patristic sources are Justin Martyr's *First Apology* 46,[148] Justin's *Second Apology* 7, 10, and 13,[149] and Clement of Alexandria's *Stromata* I.19, 91, and 94.[150] The relationship between Justin Martyr's two apologies are the subject of some disagreement in scholarship.[151] The second is a far shorter version of what may be found in the first. The first is a general defense of Christians against the baseless accusations of their enemies in the public sphere; the second has in view the particular persecution of a Christian teacher. With respect to the particular passages cited at *EN* 53, however, the arguments are very much the same in both books. *First Apology* 46 argues that, since Christians believe Jesus was the Logos of God and the first-born of God, any who contemplated or believed in the Logos prior to the Incarnation were, in fact, proto-Christians. Thus, the Greek philosophers who taught a Logos doctrine were teaching, in seed form and incompletely, Christianity. The full and proper expression of the teaching of those earlier philosophers came to pass only when the Logos made himself known as Jesus. *Second Apology* 8, 10, and 13 expanded the comments from the first book to include also the Stoic teachings. As well, §10 acknowledged that there were contradictions among the earlier philosophers as to what the Logos was, but that was due to their incomplete knowledge since Jesus had not yet come. All told, Justin believed Christianity was as much a part of the Greco-Roman heritage as any of the pagan religions and, on moral and theological grounds, even better. Clement's *Stromata* argued similarly, and went a step further by citing several biblical texts that also embraced this perspective on non-Christ-

148. PG 6:397-400; the critical editions are Justin Martyr, *Apologies: Introduction, texte critique, traduction, commentaire et index*, ed. André Wartelle, Études Augustiniennes, Série antiquité 117 (Paris: Études Augustiniennes, 1987) 160; id., *Apologie pour les Chrétiens*, ed. Charles Munier, Paradosis: Études de littérature et de théologie anciennes (Fribourg, Switzerland: Éditions Universitaires, 1995) 94; id., *Apologiae pro Christianis*, ed. Miroslav Marcovich, PTS 38 (Berlin: Walter de Gruyter, 1994) 97. ET: Leslie William Barnard, *Justin Martyr: The First and Second Apologies*, ACW 56 (Mahwah, NJ: Paulist Press, 1997) 55.

149. PG 6:456-468; the critical edition is Justin Martyr, *Apologies*, Études Augustiniennes, 206, 210-16; id., *Apologiae pro Christianis*, PTS 38, 149, 151-152, and 157. ET: Barnard, *Justin Martyr. The First and Second Apologies*, 79-84.

150. PG 8.805-13; the critical editions are Clement of Alexandria, *Les Stromates: Stromata I*, ed. Marcel Caster, SC 30 (Paris: Éditions du Cerf, 1951) 117-120; id., *Stromata: Buch I-VI*, ed. Otto Stahlin and Ludwig Früchtel, GCS 52 (Berlin: Akademie Verlag, 1985) 58-61. ET: John Ferguson, *Clement of Alexandria. Stromateis: Books One to Three*, FOTC 85 (Washington D.C.: Catholic University of America Press, 1991) 92-95.

151. Cf. introductory comments by Barnard, *Justin Martyr. The First and Second Apologies*, 10-12.

ian philosophies. Clement recalled Paul's speech to the Athenians in Acts 17. As well, he argued 1 Corinthians 13:12, "For now we see in a mirror dimly," (RSV) took account of how all persons in history have looked for the divine element within them despite imperfections of that knowledge. In sum, the apologies of Justin Martyr and of Clement reclaim religious ground lost to the Greco-Roman state religions. What is more, they argued the best of Greco-Roman culture and philosophy actually anticipated the truths revealed when the Logos himself, Jesus Christ, appeared on earth. What Justin and Clement do not do, however, in contrast to the CST document, is call for a renewed vigor in studying those esteemed philosophies and religious systems. Christianity was the truth, and it was this religion that deserved the attention of the Greco-Roman world. It is not clear that these patristic authors would support a call to mine the non-Christian religions of our present world for their own "seeds of the Word."

Related to the above three patristic sources is the fourth at *EN* 53, Eusebius of Caesarea's *Preparation for the Gospel* I.1.[152] The CST document claims that the "seeds of the Word" that may be found in the world's non-Christian religions constitute a "preparation for the Gospel," and so it was natural to turn to this patristic document bearing that phrase as its title. Eusebius's treatise began by saying that both converts to Christianity and pagans need a demonstration of the proof of the Christian faith so as to deflect criticism about the religion. Eusebius divided his demonstrations into two parts, the first of which is our present treatise and which repudiates the teachings and claims of the Greco-Roman philosophies and religious cults, and the second of which is called *Demonstration of the Gospel* and which repudiates Judaism in favor of Christianity. *EN* 53 cites the first chapter of the first part, in which this two-part structure is explained. Although the phrase "preparation for the Gospel" is found here, it is likely the CST document has in mind the contents of this entire treatise, which are an explanation of how the myriad teachings and the history of the Greco-Roman peoples have anticipated or prepared the way for the life and teachings of Jesus that are manifest now in the Christian religion.

152. PG 21:26-28; the critical editions are Eusebius of Caesarea, *Die Praeparatio Evangelica: Einleitung, die Bücher I bis X*, ed. Édouard des Places, GCS 43.2 (Berlin: Akademie Verlag, 1982) 5-8; id., *La préparation évangélique, Livre I*, ed. Jean Sirinelli, SC 206 (Paris: Éditions du Cerf, 1974) 96-104. ET: Edwin H. Gifford, *Eusebii Pamphili. Evangelicae praeparationis Libri XV. Ad codices manuscriptos denuo collatos recensuit Anglice nunc primum reddidit notis et indicibus instruxit*, Vol. 3.1 (Oxford: Typographeo Academico, 1903) 1-5.

The next patristic source citation is at *EN* 59 and is a quotation from Augustine's *Expositions on the Psalms* 44.23.[153] The relevant Latin text from the critical edition of Augustine's text cited by *EN*, and the Latin and English texts of the quote in the CST document follow.

Ex. on Psalms 44.23[154]	EN 59[155]	EN 59[156]
Praedicaverunt verbum veritatis et genuerunt ecclesias…	Praedicaverunt verbum veritatis et genuerunt ecclesias.	They preached the word of truth and brought forth Churches.

The only textual issue of note is that the CST document drops the last four words of Augustine's text, *non sibi, sed illi* ("not for themselves, but for him"). These words refer to the Apostles who founded churches in Christ's name and not their own. At this point in his exposition of Psalm 44:8 (45:8), Augustine likened the ivory palaces to the human soul and the king's daughters to the converts won to Christianity by the preaching of the Gospel by particular souls. Augustine explained the Apostles are the "brothers" of Christ, for Christ referred to them as such (Mt 28:10; Jn 20:17), who, in following the Jewish levirate custom (Dt 25:5), married themselves to Christ's teaching after his departure from the world and birthed children (i.e. converts) not for themselves, but for Christ.

The CST document, however, has inserted this quotation into a different context, and this new context makes sense only when the last four words from Augustine's text are absent. It should be acknowledged, however, that *EN* includes the Augustine text only because it is relying here on the preface to the Vatican II document, *Ad gentes*, which also used this Augustine quote.[157] That said, the context of *EN* 59 argues the Church is a sign and instrument of Christ's kingdom here on earth, a reality strengthened daily by the ever-expanding presence of the Church on earth through its missionary activity. The concern of *EN* 59 is to substantiate the evangelistic mission of the Church by an appeal to the

---

153. PL 36:508-509; the critical editions are Augustine, *Enarrationes in Psalmos 1-50, Pars 2: Enarrationes in Psalmos 34-50*, ed. Franco Gori and Iuliana Spaccia, CSEL 103, part 5 (Vienna: Österreichischen Akademie der Wissenschaften, 2005) 211-212; id., *Enarrationes in Psalmos I-L*, ed. D. Eligius Dekkers and Johannes Fraipont, CCSL 38 (Turnhout: Brepols, 1956) 510-511. ET: Maria Boulding, *Augustine. Expositions of the Psalms (Enarrationes in Psalmos) 33-50*, WSA 16 (New York: New City Press, 2000) 300-302.

154. Augustine, *Enarrationes in Psalmos I-L*, CCSL 38, 510.

155. AAS 68, 50.

156. CST:DocHer, 327.

157. AAS 58 (1966), 947.

practice of the Apostles, a point not lost on Augustine either. It takes "Churches" in the Augustine quote to refer to "the Church." Augustine, rather, connected the missionary activity of the Apostles with the expansion of Christ's children here on earth, i.e. individual churches. The difference may be trivial, as one sees missionary activity resulting in an expansion of the Church's presence (*EN*), and the other sees it resulting in an expansion of individual churches (Augustine). The dilemma is easily solved, of course, if *EN* believes the Church is equal to the myriad of individual churches, but this ecclesiology is nowhere stated at *EN* 59. The Augustine text makes some of these connections for the reader by calling individual churches "Christ's children," but they are connections lost on the reader of the CST document due to the loss of the final four words in Augustine's sentence. To have left them in would have demanded *EN*, or at least *Ad gentes*, to explain what Augustine meant (particularly his recall of the Hebrew Bible's levirate marriage provision) and, in so doing, provide a fuller ecclesiology. Later in the CST document some attempt at this fuller explanation is provided through an evaluation of the relationship between the universal church and individual churches (cf. *EN* 62). Yet, a full citation of the Augustine text would have invited that discussion here.

Two sections later in the CST document, at *EN* 61, one finds two further patristic source citations. The context recalls the earliest Christians who believed the Church both was and ought to be universal, bounded neither by time nor by geography. The two patristic source citations appear in the same sentence, which reads, "They [i.e., the first Christians] were fully conscious of belonging to a large community which neither space nor time can limit: 'From the just Abel right to the last of the elect', 'indeed to the ends of the earth', 'to the end of time'."[158] Of the three quotations that complete the sentence, the first is from Gregory the Great's *Homily on the Gospel* 19.1,[159] and the second is from Acts 1:8, but a corollary passage may be found in *Didache* 9.1.[160]

---

158. *EN* 61 (AAS 68, 51; transl. in CST:DocHer, 328): A justo Abel ad ultimum electum; usque ad ultimum terrae; usque ad consummationem saeculi.

159. PL 76.1154; the critical editions are Gregory the Great, *Homiliae in Evangelia*, CCSL 141, 143; id., *Homiliae in Evangelia*, Fontes Christiani 28.1, 320. ET: David Hurst, *Gregory the Great: Forty Gospel Homilies*, 78. Due to a different numbering scheme of the homilies in this English translation, it labels as Homily 11 what is the nineteenth homily found in the PL and the critical editions.

160. The most recent edition is that of Bart Ehrman, ed., *The Apostolic Fathers, Volume I: I Clement, II Clement, Ignatius, Polycarp, Didache*, LCL, 2 vols (Cambridge, MA: Harvard University Press, 2003) I.430. Ehrman's base text relies substantially on

With respect to Gregory's homily, it is an exposition of Jesus' parable about the vineyard workers in Matthew 20. The master of the vineyard is likened to God, and the vineyard itself is the universal church, whose branches are the elect of God from all times of history. The workers who arrived at different hours of the day are those who have come to faith in God at different points in history, and yet all the workers will receive the same reward of heaven at the end, much as all the workers in the vineyard received the same pay. Indeed, therefore, Gregory's homily reflects this consciousness of a large community of faith that *EN* 61 claims exists. *Didache* 9.1 also reflects this same mindset when it compares the bread served in the eucharist, which had been made from many scattered grains, to the Christian people that will one day be gathered from many places, to the ends of the earth. It is not clear from what source the drafters of *EN* were aware of the passage in Gregory's homily, but the *Didache* passage had been quoted one decade earlier in Paul VI's encyclical, *Mysterium fidei* (cf. §41, n. 44).

Next, at *EN* 67, a footnote directs the reader to passages in four of Pope Leo I's *Sermons*.[161] The footnote appears at the end of the sentence, "It is precisely for this reason [i.e., Peter was entrusted by Christ with the pre-eminent teaching office] that Saint Leo the Great describes him as he who has merited the primacy of the apostolate."[162] Two of the four sermons to which the CST document refers are sermons given by Leo in commemoration of the anniversary of his election to the bishopric in Rome (*Sermons* 3 and 4). Naturally, Leo reflects in these on the founding of his see and recalls the words of Jesus to Peter that it is upon "this rock" that the Church would be built. Leo confirms that to whatever

the edition of Karl Bihlmeyer, *Die apostolischen Väter*, Sammlung Ausgewählter Kirchen- und Dogmengeschichtlicher Quellenschriften (Tübingen: Mohr Siebeck, 1924, repr. 1956) 6, which itself is a revision of Franz-Xavier Von Funk's two-volume edition of 1913. ET: Cf. also Ehrman, LCL, I.431.

161. Specifically, *Sermons* 3.3; 4; 82.3; 83.2 (following the CCSL numbering scheme) or *Sermons* 69.3; 70.1-3; 94.3; and 95.2 (following the SC numbering scheme). There is some confusion in the sermon numbering, occasioned by the fact that *EN* 67 cites the SC edition. This study joins the English translation in FOTC in following the CCSL scheme. The critical editions are Leo I, *Tractatus septem et nonaginta*, ed. Antoine Chavasse, CCSL 138 and 138A (Turnhout: Brepols, 1973) 12, 16-21, 511-512, 520-521; id., *Sermons, Tome IV*, ed. René Dolle, SC 200 (Paris: Éditions du Cerf, 1973) 50-52, 58-66, 258-260, 268. ET: Jane P. Freeland and Agnes J. Conway, *St. Leo the Great: Sermons*, FOTC 93 (Washington D.C.: Catholic University of America Press, 1996) 22-23, 25-29, 354, 357-358.

162. *EN* 67 (AAS 68, 56; transl. in CST:DocHer, 330-31): Quamobrem, Sanctus Leo Magnus eum meritum esse dicit apostolatus principatum.

extent he and the Christians in Rome attest to the Gospel, they participate in and continue the ministry of Peter. The other two sermons cited
in the CST document were occasioned by the annual feast of Sts. Peter
and Paul (*Sermons* 82 and 83). In these, too, we find reference to the primacy of Peter among the apostles. Leo reminded his hearers that Peter
commanded a worldwide audience; having been sent by God to Rome,
he preached to the many expatriates from the world's people groups
who had made the city their home (including, as well, the leaders and
soldiers of many invading armies). Here again, Leo called upon his congregants to participate in the ministry of Peter by judging the peoples
and things of this world correctly and in sharing the Gospel with others. All told, the recollection of Peter in these sermons has a humbling
effect on Leo. He is aware of the responsibility given to him to carry on
the preaching of Christ that Peter himself had begun in Rome. Having
been handed the same keys to the kingdom as given to Peter, Leo must
judge fairly the things of the world and those who seek out the
Christian religion. The CST document, somewhat contrastively, does
not reflect on the humbling responsibility given to the bishopric in
Rome; instead, it explains the distinctions in evangelistic roles between
that office and the other bishops, the priests, the religious, and the laity.
The bishop in Rome, according to *EN* 67, preaches the Gospel and
authorizes others to do the same on its behalf. It is the job of the bishop
in Rome, and only that of the bishop in Rome, both to preach and to
oversee the preaching of others. Rhetorically, Leo's sermons are little
more than appeals to an historical authority for a point in the encyclical
that Leo had not himself elaborated.

The final patristic source citation in this CST document is at *EN* 71.
Having turned its attention to the evangelistic potential of individual
families, *EN* recalls the phrase "domestic church" recovered in Catholic
teaching less than a decade earlier by the Vatican II documents, *Lumen
gentium* and *Apostolicam actuositatem*.[163] Here, though, passages from
two sermons of John Chrysostom, *Sermons on Genesis* 6.2 and 7.1,[164] are
included in the footnote as a patristic witness to the same teaching. The
sermons, delivered a day apart from each other, begin by examining

163. For a study of the history of the phrase, including especially its "recovery" and
usage in Catholic teaching, cf. Florence Caffrey Bourg, *Where Two or Three Are Gathered: Christian Families as Domestic Churches* (Notre Dame, IN: University of Notre
Dame Press, 2003).

164. PG 54:607-608; the critical edition is John Chrysostom, *Sermons sur la Genèse*,
ed. Laurence Brottier, SC 433 (Paris: Éditions du Cerf, 1998) 296, 302.

whether or not Adam possessed "knowledge of good and evil" prior to eating fruit from the tree by the same name. Having concluded in his sixth homily that Adam did, Chrysostom goes on to say in the seventh homily that eating from the tree proved to Adam that obedience is good and disobedience is evil. What is more, the tree of salvation (i.e., the cross) is a far better tree for having introduced knowledge of greater goods and for conquering the evil powers (i.e., the devil and demons). Both at the end of the sixth sermon and at the beginning of the seventh sermon, set in between the two parts of his exposition about the tree of knowledge of good and evil, Chrysostom exhorts the heads of households in his audience to make these teachings a part of the family's lives and beliefs. "Make your house a church, for you are liable to give an account for the salvation both of your children and of your servants."[165] This exhortation is not particular to the teachings surrounding it; indeed, Chrysostom has used it in a variety of other contexts.[166] It is, instead, a rhetorical device intended to break down any barriers a congregant might presuppose between his or her "spiritual life" and his or her "private life."[167] Chrysostom wants his teaching to permeate the way in which his congregants live and think, particularly with respect to the responsibility men had to manage the affairs of their children and households. While not placing any particular focus on the heads of households, *EN* 71 shares Chrysostom's concern for families to believe the Gospel and to share the Gospel with other people. Parents are obligated to share the Gospel with their children; children are obligated, in return, to evangelize their parents by faithfully living out the Gospel; parents and children alike are called to evangelize other families.

All told, the fifteen patristic source citations in *EN* support and extend its arguments and assumptions. At times, the patristic voices are little more than prooftexts for what had already been argued in the body

---

165. John Chrysostom, *Sermons on Genesis* 6.2 (ed. L. Brottier, *Sermons sur la Genèse*, SC 433, 296; translation is my own): Ἐκκλησίαν ποίησόν σου τὴν οἰκίαν, καὶ γὰρ ὑπεύθυνος εἶ καὶ τῆς τῶν παιδίων καὶ τῆς τῶν οἰκετῶν σωτηρίας.

166. Vigen Guroian, "Family and Christian Virtue: Reflections on the Ecclesial Vision of John Chrysostom," in *Ethics after Christendom: Toward an Ecclesial Christian Ethic* (Grand Rapids, MI: Eerdmans, 1994) 133-154, examines Chrysostom's use of this phrase in other homilies.

167. Laurence Brottier, "De l'église hors de l'église au ciel anticipé sur quelques paradoxes Chrysostomiens," *Revue d'histoire et de philosophie religieuses* 76 (1996) 277-292 considers a variety of phrases in Chrysostom's writings, including this one, where Chrysostom teaches his people to let the spiritual life invade and transform the private life.

of the CST document. Its three citations of Augustine, though, added real depth to the arguments. Augustine's *Sermon XLVI* challenged the Church's evangelizers to take stock of their actions as well as their preaching. His *Expositions on the Psalms* 88.2 added a Christological dimension to the ecclesiology operative at *EN* 16. Then finally, his *Expositions on the Psalms* 44 contributed yet another ecclesiological element when it compared the Church's daughter churches throughout the world to the Hebrew levirate marriage custom. Still, one hesitates to suggest the contributions of these three texts from Augustine overshadow the proof text and ornamental function played by the remaining patristic citations in *EN*.

Puebla Documents (CELAM III, 1979)

The CELAM meetings challenged the Catholic Church's vision of "church" in the Latin American world. They took seriously the calls of Vatican II to correct the ills of the Church, to read the signs of the times, and to rethink how best to evangelize those in its sphere of influence. The documents of this third CELAM meeting generally renewed the commitment of the Latin American churches to the ideals put forth in the previous meeting at Medellin twelve years prior. This included calls for "liberation" of the Latin American peoples and for the furtherance of the base communities movement so widespread across that region. As indicated at the beginning, the documents of Medellin contained no patristic source citations, but we find two in the Puebla documents. Both are general references to the patristic period, the first oblique, the second straightforward.

The first citation is actually not a citation, properly speaking, but is a general reference to the teachings of the Church that could not help but include the theologians of the patristic period. It comes in Part II, chapter 1, §1.1. The text of the Puebla document reads,

> It is our duty to proclaim clearly the mystery of the Incarnation, leaving no room for doubt or equivocation. This mystery includes both the divinity of Jesus Christ, *as it is professed by the faith of the Church*, and the reality and force of his human and historical dimension.[168] (italics added for emphasis)

---

168. Conference of Latin American Bishops, *Puebla and Beyond: Documentation and Commentary*, transl. John Drury, ed. John Eagleson and Philip Scharper (Maryknoll, NY: Orbis Books, 1980) 145.

The fact is that the debate over the divinity of Jesus Christ took place in the patristic period. Whether one considers the question from a Trinitarian perspective (i.e., was Jesus another form of God, and thus the third- and fourth-century debate over the teachings of Sabellus), or whether one considers the question from a Christological perspective (i.e., what does it mean for Christians to say Jesus was a divine being, and thus the fourth century debates over the ὁμοούσιος language used at the Council of Nicaea, or how is Jesus' divine nature consonant with his human nature, and thus the fifth century debate leading to Chalcedon), the fact remains that Jesus' divinity was hotly contested during the patristic period. As far as the Church's adherents in the ages since that time have been concerned, it is largely a matter of settled doctrine. Thus, Puebla's reference to "the faith of the Church" inevitably leads the attentive reader to the patristic world.

The second patristic reference may be found in Part II, chapter 2, §4.2. The context is the history of Catholic social teaching. The relevant passage here reads, "These teachings have their source in Sacred Scripture, in the teaching of the Fathers and major theologians of the Church, and in the magisterium (particularly that of the most recent popes)."[169] This Puebla document acknowledges a role for the patristic world in the formulation of CST; however, it does not cite patristic authors or texts when it has the occasion to do so. For example, Part III, chapter 1, §1.2, draws on biblical texts and comments from Pope John Paul II in evaluating how Jesus reached out to the poor in support of Puebla's own interest in proclaiming a preferential option for the poor. The evidence from sacred scripture and the magisterium is not supplemented with teachings from the Fathers or any other major theologian of the Church, and yet it would not have been difficult to identify patristic commentaries on the relevant Gospel texts.

To conclude, the two, patristic source references in Puebla are hardly consequential. Only the first of these two draws substantively on patristic theology, and even then the historical context for the theological claim is by no means explicit.

---

169. Conference of Latin American Bishops, *Puebla and Beyond*, 189.

Familiaris consortio (1981)

Following more than a year after the synod of bishops gathered in Rome to discuss issues related to contemporary family life, *FC* defended marriage and family from what it saw were negative, cultural encroachments. It is written in *FC* 1,

> Knowing that marriage and the family constitute one of the most precious of human values, the church wishes to speak and offer her help to those who are already aware of the value of marriage and the family and seek to live it faithfully, to those who are uncertain and anxious and searching for the truth, and to those who are unjustly impeded from living freely their family lives. Supporting the first, illuminating the second and assisting the others, the church offers her services to every person who wonders about the destiny of marriage and the family.[170]

FC returned to the patristic phrase used at *EN* 71 and in two of the Vatican II documents, "domestic church," in articulating its vision of family life.[171] In four parts, this CST document evaluated the cultural forces at work both supporting and undermining the family, it explained the realization of true humanity within the context of a family, it addressed several aspects of family life (including birth control, education of children, and roles for women), and it concluded with exhortations for pastors to renew their care for and attention to the needs of families. In furtherance of its aims, *FC* cited four patristic sources, to an examination of which this discussion now turns.

The first patristic source citation is at *FC* 6; it is a loose quotation of Augustine's *City of God* 14.28.[172] In this context, the CST document situated the cultural forces affecting families in terms of the opposing forces of light and darkness. On the side of light are the efforts to

---

170. *FC* 1 (AAS 74.1, 81-82; transl. at www.vatican.va): Ecclesia sibi conscia matrimonium et familiam unum e bonis pretiosissimis generis hominum esse, nuntium suum cupit afferre et auxilium polliceri iis qui, vim bonumque matrimonii et familiae iam cognoscentes, inde fideliter vivere student, qui haerentes et anxii veritatem exquirunt et qui iniuste praepediuntur ne libere in vita sua ad effectum adducant propositum suam circa familiam. Illos confirmando, hos illuminando, ceteros iuvando Ecclesia paratam se praebet unicuique ministrare, qui de sorte matrimonii et familiae sit sollicitus.

171. See above, 72.

172. PL 41.429-430; the critical editions are Augustine, *De civitate Dei, libri XI-XXII*, ed. Bernardus Dombart and Alphonsus Kalb, CCSL 48 (Turnhout: Brepols, 1955) 451; id., *De civitate Dei libri XXII, Vol. II: Libri XIV-XXII*, ed. Emanuel Hoffmann, CSEL 40.2 (Vienna: F. Tempsky, 1899) 56-57. ET: R. W. Dyson, *Augustine. The City of God Against the Pagans*, 632.

strengthen interfamily relationships, to rediscover the family's ecclesial mission, and a new awareness of the dignity of women, among others. On the side of darkness are abuses of authority in families, the increasing divorce rates, and increasing recourse to artificial contraception, among others. Consequently, *FC* 6 argued that history is not one positive progression after another, but is instead an "event of freedom, and even a struggle between freedoms."[173] What follows is a paraphrase of Augustine, whose text is used to put a theological spin on the problem of opposing, cultural forces. Below are the relevant Latin texts from Augustine's *City of God* and *FC* 6, alongside its English translation.

City of God 14.28[174]	*FC* 6[175]	*FC* 6[176]
Fecerunt itaque ciuitates duas amores duo, terrenam scilicet amor sui usque ad contemptum Dei, caelestem vero amor Dei usque ad contemptum sui.	amorem videlicet Dei, qui usque ad contemptum sui pervenit, et amorem sui ipsius, qui ad contemptum Dei progreditur.	the love of God to the point of disregarding self, and the love of self to the point of disregarding God.

Augustine has characterized the two cities, the heavenly and earthly, in terms of their affections. The heavenly city is created by a love for God and a rejection of the self; the earthly city is created by a love for self and a rejection of God. *FC* did not introduce its paraphrase with a reference to the two cities, but by saying this is a well-known expression of Augustine's. Textually, its paraphrase has reversed Augustine's own order, and *FC* likely did so to match its earlier claim that the cultural forces may be characterized in terms of light and darkness. Since light was first in that earlier expression, so too must the positive affections Augustine finds in the heavenly city be recalled first. Additionally, removed as it is from its reference point of the two cities, *FC* must supply its paraphrase of Augustine with the necessary verbs, *pervenit* and *progreditur*, to take the place of *fecerunt* in Augustine's text.

On the one hand, this paraphrase of Augustine may seem to be little more than rhetorical ornament for *FC* already characterized the cultural problem in terms of light and darkness. However, Augustine's text

173. *FC* 6 (AAS 74.1, 88; transl. at www.vatican.va): sed eventum libertatis, quin immo luctationem inter libertates.

174. CCSL 48, 451.

175. AAS 74.1, 88.

176. Text available at www.vatican.va.

clarifies what is meant by light and darkness. The cultural forces that uplift families really find their source in those loves for which the heavenly city is known, and, thus, it may be argued by *FC* that only in loving God can true marital and familial joy be found (cf., e.g., *FC* 9-10). The forces that discourage families find their source in the loves of the earthly city. The love of oneself will inevitably lead to marital and familial unhappiness. In the final analysis, Augustine's text provides theological clarity to the CST document; however, not having expanded on Augustine's themes of the two cities, *FC* set aside a convenient word picture for the cultural forces facing families to supplement its own light/darkness distinction.

The second patristic source citation is at *FC* 13, at which place is a quotation of Tertullian's *To His Wife* II.8.6-8.[177] Below are the relevant texts for Tertullian and the CST document.

To His Wife II.8.6-8[178]	*FC* 13[179]	*FC* 13[180]
Unde <vero> sufficiamus ad enarrandum felicitatem eius matrimonii, quod ecclesia conciliat et confirmat oblatio et obsignat benedictio, angeli renuntiant, pater rato habet? ... Quale iugum fidelium duorum unius spei, unius uoti, unius disciplinae, eiusdem seruitutis! Ambo fratres, ambo conserui; nulla spiritus carnisue discretio, atquin vere duo in carne una. Ubi caro una, unus et spiritus.	Unde sufficiamus ad enarrandum felicitatem eius matrimonii, quod Ecclesia conciliat, et confirmat oblatio, et obsignat benedictio, angeli renuntiant, Pater rato habet? ... Quale iugum fidelium duorum unius spei, unius disciplinae, eiusdem servitutis! Ambo fratres, ambo conservi, nulla spiritus carnisve discretio. At quin vere duo in carne una; ubi caro una, unus et spiritus.	How can I ever express the happiness of the marriage that is joined together by the church, strengthened by an offering, sealed by a blessing, announced by angels and ratified by the Father? ... How wonderful the bond between two believers, with a single hope, a single desire, a single observance, a single service! They are both brethren and both fellow servants; there is no separation between them in spirit or flesh. In fact they are truly two in one flesh, and where the flesh is one, one is the spirit.

177. PL 1.1300-02; the critical editions are Tertullian, *Opera, Pars I: Opera Catholica, Adversus Marcionem*, CCSL 1, 392-394; id., *À son épouse*, ed. Charles Munier, SC 273 (Paris: Éditions du Cerf, 1980) 144-150. ET: William P. Le Saint, *Tertullian. Treatises on Marriage and Remarriage: To His Wife, An Exhortation to Chastity, Monogamy*, ACW 13 (Westminster, MD: Newman Press, 1951) 33-36.

178. Tertullian, *Opera, Pars I*, CCSL 1, 393.

179. AAS 74.1, 94.

180. Text available at www.vatican.va.

There are a few textual differences between the Latin of the CCSL edition and the *FC*, which is quoting the latter. One is the minor, orthographic preference for "v" rather than "u" in *FC*. A second is another, minor, orthographic preference for captializing *ecclesia* and *pater* in FC, both of which are found in the lower-case at CCSL. Yet a third minor difference is the punctuation choices of the two texts. *FC* initiated new sentences with the clauses the CCSL edition strung together into a longer chain. Fourth, and more significant, the *FC* missed the phrase *unius uoti* in the CCSL text without providing an ellipsis, which it dutifully provided after *Pater ratio habet?*. One suspects the scribal error of homoeoarchy here, for it would be easy to miss the second of the three *unius* expressions. What is most interesting, however, is that the English translation did not miss the phrase, but included it with the translation, "a single desire." The English translation must have been prepared from an earlier draft of *FC* that included *unius uoti*. Thus, the scribal error arose during preparation of the final edition of the encyclical rather than with its earlier drafts.

With respect to the two contexts, *FC* placed this quotation of Tertullian within an argument that conjugal love is a living symbol of what Christ accomplished on the cross. Christ's sacrifice for people was selfless and complete; so too ought to be spousal love. According to *FC*, conjugal love finds its true identity only in the life of Christ, and so conjugal love is able to be experienced in its true sense only by those who are baptized and "live the charity of Christ."[181] The quotation of Tertullian is then made to supplement this teaching insofar as it offers a concrete picture of what this beautiful, conjugal love looks like. Like *FC*, Tertullian writes of this beautiful marriage as one that exists between two Christian people. In the sections that precede this quotation in Tertullian's treatise, Tertullian specifically denounced the types of marriages Christians would find themselves in had they been married to a non-Christian, as well as denouncing the marriage of both a pagan man and woman. Thus, the CST document is fair to Tertullian's own context by ensuring that its own, ideal picture of conjugal love is set within the marital bond of two Christian persons. Tertullian has added practical, pastoral depth to what is otherwise a theoretical discussion about Christian love vis-à-vis the life of Christ.

Next is a quotation of John Chrysostom's *On Virginity* 10[182] at *FC* 16. Below is the Greek text from Chrysostom's treatise, the Latin translation

181. *FC* 13 (AAS 74.1, 94): participant ipsam Christi caritatem.
182. PG 48.540; the critical edition is John Chrysostom, *La virginité*, ed. Herbert Musurillo, SC 125 (Paris: Éditions du Cerf, 1966) 122-124. ET: Sally Rieger Shore, *John*

of it in the PG edition to which *FC* refers, the Latin and English texts
of the encyclical, and an English translation of Chrysostom's treatise
based on the Greek text.

On Virginity 10[183]	*FC* 16[184]	*FC* 16[185]
... qui matrimonium damnat, is virginitatis etiam gloriam carpit; qui laudat, is virginitatem admirabiliorem augustioremque reddit. Nam quod deterioris comparatione bonum videtur, id haud sane admodum bonum est; quod autem omnium sententia bonis melius, id excellens bonum est: ...	Qui matrimonium damnat, is virginitatis etiam gloriam carpit; qui laudat, is virginitatem admirabiliorem augustioremque reddit. Nam quod deterioris comparatione bonum videtur, id haud sane admodum bonum est; quod autem omnium sententia bonis melius, id excellens bonum est.	Whoever denigrates marriage also diminishes the glory of virginity. Whoever praises it makes virginity more admirable and resplendent. What appears good only in comparison with evil would not be particularly good. It is something better than what is admitted to be good that is the most excellent good.

'Ο μὲν γὰρ τὸν γάμον
κακίζων καὶ τὴν τῆς
παρθενίας ὑποτέμνεται
δόξαν, ὁ δὲ τοῦτον ἐπαινῶν
μᾶλλον ἐκείνης ἐπαίρει τὸ
θαῦμα καὶ λαμπρότερον
ποιεῖ. Τὸ μὲν γὰρ τῇ πρὸς
τὸ χεῖρον παραθέσει φαινό-
μενον καλὸν οὐκ ἂν εἴη
σφόδρα καλόν, τὸ δὲ τῶν
ὁμολογουμένων ἀγαθῶν
ἄμεινον, τοῦτό ἐστι τὸ μεθ'
ὑπερβολῆς καλόν ...

On Virginity 10[186]
The detractor of marriage also reduces the glory of virginity, whereas one who praises marriage increases admiration for it and makes it more significant. For what appears good in comparison with something inferior would not be very good; but that which is better than what is acknowledged as good is exceedingly good, ...

The encyclical clearly relied on the Latin translation of Chrysostom's
text in the PG edition, for the two texts are exactly the same; the
encyclical dropped only the first word of the sentence, *etenim*, and the
last phrase, *cujusmodi nos virginitatem esse docemus* ("which is what we
show virginity to be"). In this case, the encyclical's reliance on the Latin
translation and not the Greek original did not involve any alteration of

Chrysostom: On Virginity, Against Remarriage, Studies in Women and Religion 9 (New York: Mellen Press, 1983) 13-14.
    183. The Latin and Greek texts in this column are from PG 48.540. The Greek text of the PG edition is the same as that found in the SC critical edition.
    184. AAS 74.1, 98.
    185. Text available at www.vatican.va.
    186. This translation of the Greek text is in Shore, *John Chrysostom: On Virginity, Against Remarriage*, 13.

Chrysostom's point. He had argued for virginity in the face of parents upset with their daughters choice for the virgin life over marriage and the bearing of children. Both virginity and marriage are to be esteemed, and insofar as marriage is good, virginity is better still. Indeed, Chrysostom had made this point clear in one section earlier, in *On Virginity* 9, when he wrote, "[W]hen I recommend virginity, I do not bring discredit to marriage or denounce one for not obeying."[187] For its part, the encyclical explained that virginity is a further proof of the good of marriage, and that a virgin's commitment to fidelity parallels the marital couple's own commitment to the same. Rhetorically, Chrysostom's text is neither a proof of the argument's validity nor an extension of its points; rather, it re-states and ornaments what has already been expressed.

The final patristic source citation is a quotation of Ambrose's *Hexameron* V.7.19[188] at *FC* 25. Ambrose has followed substantially the series of homilies on the creation narrative written by Basil, whose works he so admired.[189] In this homily, Ambrose exposits the meaning of the creation of the fish in the sea that occurred on the fifth day (cf. Gen 1:20-23). He describes at length the parts of their bodies, their abilities in the sea, and makes constant comparison to what his audience already understands about the body parts and habits of land creatures. Ambrose even goes so far as to compare the big fish that prey on little fish to rich men who pursue the weak and unjustly acquire the goods of others. Just as predatory fish will one day meet their end on a fish hook, so too does Ambrose warn the rich that justice will one day overcome them. Having drawn this analogy, Ambrose is now free in the latter part of this homily to make additional parallels between the sea of fish and humans. Ambrose reminds his audience that the Gospels taught Peter would be a fisher of men. As well, and this brings us to the relevant text for our

---

187. Chrysostom, *On Virginity* 9 (ed. Musurillo, *La virginité*, SC 125, 118; transl. Shore, *John Chrysostom: On Virginity, Against Remarriage*, 12): ὁ δὲ κωλύων παραιρεῖται καὶ αὐτὴν τὴν ἐξουσίαν αὐτοῦ. Πρὸς τούτοις ἐγὼ μὲν παραινῶν οὐ κακίζω τὸ πρᾶγμα, οὐδὲ τοῦ μὴ πεισθέντος κατηγορῶ.

188. PL 14.214; the critical edition is Ambrose, *Opera, Pars prima qua continentur libri: Exameron, De paradiso, De Cain et Abel, De Noe, De Abraham, De Isaac, De bono mortis*, ed. Carol Schenkl, CSEL 32, part 1 (Vienna: F. Tempsky, 1897) 154-55. ET: John J. Savage, *Ambrose: Hexameron, Paradise, and Cain and Abel*, FOTC 42 (New York: Fathers of the Church Inc., 1961) 174-175.

189. Cf. introductory remarks by John Savage, *Ambrose. Hexameron, Paradise, and Cain and Abel*, vi-vii. For Basil's text, see Basil of Caesarea, *Homilien zum Hexaemeron*, ed. Emmanuel Amand de Mendieta, GCS 2 (Berlin: Akademie Verlag, 1997).

study here, Ambrose says it is often the case that husbands must go on sea journeys, and that wives remain behind to manage the household. This is a perfect occasion for pastoral exhortation, and Ambrose uses it. He exhorts the wives to remain faithful to their husbands while they are away, and he exhorts the husbands to be kind to their wives once they return as a matter of gratitude for what the wife has had to endure in his absence. It is this latter exhortation that is recalled in the CST document, and the Latin text for Ambrose and the Latin and English texts for FC follow.

Hexameron V.7.19[190]	*FC* 25[191]	*FC* 25[192]
Non es dominus, sed maritus, non ancillam sortitus es, sed uxorem … Redde studio uicem, redde amori gratiam.	'Non es dominus', ita scribit Sanctus Ambrosius, 'sed maritus: non ancillam sortitus es, sed uxorem … Redde studio vicem, redde amori gratiam'.	'You are not her master', writes St. Ambrose, 'but', her husband; she was not given to you to be your slave, but your wife … Reciprocate her attentiveness to you and be grateful to her for her love'.

There are no differences between the Latin texts of the CST document and the critical edition of Ambrose's text upon which the CST document relied. The same may be said of the two literary contexts as well. The CST document has couched Ambrose's text within the framework of equal dignity among the husband and wife, stemming, as it does, from the woman's creation out of the same substance as man. The balance in Ambrose's exhortations, some to wives and some to husbands, too, is replicated in this CST document. However, the exhortations to wives come later in the encyclical and are not as concerned with fidelity as they are to being committed to proper management of the home. The CST document has relied here on Ambrose to state its case for how husbands may practically express conjugal love. Only would that the quotation had been longer, and so capture Ambrose's further pastoral directives to husbands on how to love their wives.

In sum, the drafters of FC gave due attention to the patristic arguments they employed. Three of the four extend the arguments of FC in theological or practical ways. Chrysostom's text is ornamental here in FC, but his treatise as a whole offered a practical and theological defense of

190. CSEL 32.1, 154.
191. AAS 74.1, 110.
192. Text available at www.vatican.va.

virginity. None of the patristic sources are set within a literary, historical, or theological context, but that is a regular theme for most of the CST documents and so is not a surprise here.

The Challenge of Peace (USCCB, 1983)

In response to *GS*' call for Catholics around the world to "read the signs of the times" in their own communities, and out of concern for the seemingly unstoppable nuclear arms race around the globe, the USCCB issued this pastoral letter to Catholics and to their fellow citizens in the United States. The document is unequivocal in its affirmation that peace ought to be the goal of every Christian person, and indeed also of every nation on the planet. Beyond this affirmation, though, it tries to balance a number of competing interests, regularly digressing to an acknowledgment that fair-minded people may well disagree on how peace is achieved and to what extent Christians may participate in military actions. In the end, the document calls for greater efforts at peaceful resolution to international conflicts and a reduction in nuclear stockpiles. With respect to just war theory, the document reminds its readers that promoting just war is akin to promoting peace insofar as "just wars" are only those for which military action is the least preferable option of last resort in settling international conflict. The patristic literature on Christians and military service was about as diverse as the positions this CST document presumes exist still in the Church today.[193] However, only a small window

---

193. Literature affirming a univocal pacifism in the Early Church begins, as far as the twentieth century is concerned, with C. John Cadoux, *The Early Christian Attitude Toward War* (London: Headley Brothers, 1919), continuing with Roland Bainton's chapter on early Christian pacificism in his book, *Christian Attitudes Towards War and Peace* (New York, NY: Abingdon, 1960) 66ff; Jean-Michel Hornus, *Evangile et labarum: étude sur l'attitude du christianisme primitif devant les problèmes de l'État, de la guerre et de la violence*, Nouvelle série théologique 9 (Geneva: Labor et Fides, 1960); John Howard Yoder, *The Original Revolution: Essays on Christian Pacifism*, Christian Peace Shelf Series 3 (Scottsdale, PA: Herald Press, 1971).

Balancing these readings of patristic sources are Adolf von Harnack, *Militia Christi: die christliche Religion und der Soldatenstand in den ersten drei Jahrhunderten* (Tübingen: Mohr Siebeck, 1905), available in English as *Militia Christi: The Christian Religion and the Military in the First Three Centuries*, transl. David McInnis Gracie (Philadelphia, PA: Fortress Press, 1981); John Helgeland, "Christians and the Roman Army A.D. 173-337," *Church History* 43 (1974) 149-163; id., *Christians and the Roman Army from Marcus Aurelius to Constantine* (Berlin: Walter de Gruyter, 1979); id., "Time and Space: Christian and Roman," in *Religion (Vorkonstantinisches Christentum: Verhältnis zu römischem Staat und heidnischer Religion [Forts.])*, Aufstieg und Niedergang der römischen Welt, series 2, vol. 23, part 2, ed. Wolfgang Haase (Berlin: Walter de Gruyter, 1980) 724-834; Louis J.

into that diversity is evidenced here, for the document cites only five patristic sources, and four of those are brought together in one section in support of a stand for non-violence. That having been said, we examine first the citation of Augustine's *City of God* IV.15[194] at *ChP* 81.

The Catholic Church's support of the rights of states to defend themselves can be traced back, according to this CST document, to Augustine. Augustine's contribution to a theory of just war is based on his having emphasized the latter half of the "already, not yet" status of the kingdom of God on earth. *PT* had already cited *City of God* IV.4, agreeing with Augustine that sin and states' disordered ambitions are real and they adversely affect the lives of innocent human beings. Now here in this CST document, *City of God* IV.15, the standard passage for a just war theory in Augustine, is cited in a footnote arguing that just wars are only those taken up to protect the lives of innocent people, that it is a matter of Christian charity to restrain a person or a state harming others unjustly. Augustine's own text makes these claims in the context of an appraisal of how the Roman Empire itself had gained its ascendancy. It was not through greed on its own part, but was a consequence of defeating wicked and injurious neighbors. In an ideal world, according to Augustine, "if men were always peaceful and just, human affairs would be happier and all kingdoms would be small, rejoicing in concord with their neighbors. There would be as many kingdoms among the nations of the world as there are now houses of the citizens of a city."[195] Augustine shares with Aquinas the historical spotlight with respect to the support of the Catholic Church for a just war. That said, *ChP* acknowledges the predominant position among American Catholics is pacifism. In support of that position, the document looks to four patristic sources, two from the second, and one from each of the third and fourth centuries.

Swift, *The Early Fathers on War and Military Service*, Message of the Fathers of the Church, 19 (Wilmington, DE: Michael Glazier Press, 1983); John Helgeland, Robert J. Daly, and J. Patout Burns, *Christians and the Military: The Early Experience* (Philadelphia, PA: Fortress Press, 1985); James T. Johnson, *The Quest for Peace: Three Moral Traditions in Western Cultural History* (Princeton, NJ: Princeton University Press, 1987) esp. 4-66; J. Daryl Charles, "Pacifists, Patriots or Both? Second Thoughts on Early Christian Attitudes toward Soldiering and War," unpublished paper, Annual Meeting of the Evangelical Theological Society (Philadelphia, PA, 2005).

194. PL 41:124-25; the critical editions are Augustine, *De civitate Dei, Pars I*, CSEL 40.1, 182-183; id., *De civitate Dei, Libri I-X*, CCSL 47, 111. ET: Dyson, *Augustine: The City of God Against the Pagans*, 161.

195. Augustine, *City of God* IV.15 (eds. Dombart and Kalb, *De civitate Dei, Libri I-X*, CCSL 47, 111; transl. Dyson, *Augustine: The City of God Against the Pagans*, 161): sic felicioribus rebus humanis omnia regna parua essent concordi uicinitate laetantia et ita essent in mundo regna plurima gentium, ut sunt in urbe domus plurimae ciuium.

Refreshingly, three of the four patristic voices in support of non-violence in this CST document are introduced by name and set within their historical context. The first two of these citations are a quotation from Justin Martyr's *Dialogue with Trypho* 110[196] together with an additional footnote reference to his *First Apology* 14 and 39.[197] The CST document says Justin lived during the middle of the second century and introduces its quotation from his *Dialogue* with an explanation that Justin draws on the writings of the Hebrew prophet Isaiah. The quotation, in English, from the CST document and the Latin text from the most recent critical edition are below.

Dialogue 110[198]

Καὶ οἱ πολέμου καὶ ἀλληλοφονίας
καὶ πάσης κακίας μεμεστωμένοι ἀπὸ πάσης
τῆς γῆς τὰ πολεμικὰ ὄργανα ἕκαστος, τὰς
μαχαίρας εἰς ἄποτρα καὶ τὰς ζιβύνας εἰς
γεωργικὰ <ὄργανα>, μετεβάλομεν, καὶ
γεωργοῦμεν εὐσέβειαν, δικαιοσύνην,
φιλανθρωπίαν, πίστιν, ἐλπίδα τὴν παρ᾽
αὐτοῦ τοῦ πατρὸς διὰ του σταυρωθέντος
<δοθεῖσαν ἡμῖν ἔχοντεη>.

ChP 112[199]

And we who delighted in war, in the slaughter of one another, and in every other kind of iniquity have in every part of the world converted our weapons into implements of peace – our swords into ploughshares, our spears into farmers' tools – and we cultivate piety, justice, brotherly charity, faith and hope, which we derive from the Father through the crucified Savior...

The quotation is set within the context of Justin explaining that the Messianic prophecies of the Hebrew Bible promise two advents. The first advent had, of course, already taken place; the world now awaits the Messiah's second advent. In this interim period, Christians live in various ways, including those described in this quotation. Since the CST document does not situate the response of non-violence within a framework of an interim period between two advents for the Messiah, this quotation from Justin adds a new dimension, an eschatological one, to the discussion. At the second advent, according to Justin, the Christians will be removed from the earth. They who have been oppressed by the world will be restored at this second advent. It is not necessary, then, for Christians to defend themselves from oppression; rather, Christians wait for Christ's return and for God to restore justice.

196. PG 6.729-32; the critical edition is Justin Martyr, *Dialogus cum Tryphone*, PTS 47, 258-59; ET: Thomas B. Falls, *Writings of Saint Justin Martyr*, FOTC 6, 318
197. PG 6.348-49, 388; the critical editions are Justin Martyr, *Apologies*, Études Augustiniennes, 114 and 148-50; id., *Apologie pour les Chrétiens*, Paradosis 39, 54 and 84; id., *Apologiae pro Christianis*, PTS 38, 52-53 and 87. ET: Barnard, *Justin Martyr. The First and Second Apologies*, ACW 56, 31-32 and 49-50.
198. PG 6.729.
199. CST:DocHer, 517.

Following the quotation of Justin Martyr is one from Cyprian of Carthage's *Letter 60, To Cornelius*. Incidentally, *ChP*'s footnote to Cyprian's text is rather inadequate, for it simply directs the reader to "Cyprian, 'Collected Letters', Letter to Cornelius,"[200] as if only one such letter exists. The fact is Cyprian wrote many letters to Cornelius;[201] only with great difficulty could an average reader of this CST document unearth the original, patristic material. Still, the main body of the CST document dates Cyprian to the third century and introduces the quotation with a claim that it agrees with the preceding quotation from Justin's *Dialogue*. The Latin text of Cyprian's letter from the recent critical edition and the English translation available in the CST document itself are presented below.

Letter 60.2[202]	*ChP* 113[203]
… nec repugnare contra inpugnantes, cum occidere innocentibus nec nocentes liceat, sed prompte et animas et sanguinem tradere, ut cum tanta in saeculo malitia et saeuitia grassetur, a malis et saeuis uelocius recedatur.	They do not even fight against those who are attacking since it is not granted to the innocent to kill even the aggressor, but promptly to deliver up their souls and blood that, since so much malice and cruelty are rampant in the world, they may more quickly withdraw from the malicious and the cruel.

The larger context of the quotation is Cyprian's praise of Cornelius, bishop of Rome, who had withstood the verbal and, perhaps also, physical assaults of those persecuting Christians in the city. Cyprian points to Satan as being the one ultimately responsible for the persecutions, and that this adversary of God will be driven back time and again by the faith and vigor of Christians. Christians will not fight their adversaries, according to Cyprian, and this brings us to the quotation above, because by death Christians can escape more quickly the wickedness of the present world. Cyprian is merely acknowledging how Christians respond when confronted with those persecuting them *on account of* their being Christian. He is not, as the CST document would have the reader

---

200. CST:DocHer, 566 n. 47.

201. In addition to *Letter 60*, cf., among those extant, *Letters* 44, 45, 47, 48, 51, 52, 57, and 59.

202. The critical edition is Cyprian of Carthage, *Epistularium*, ed. G. F. Diercks, CCSL 3B.3 (Turnhout: Brepols, 1996) 376. ET: G. W. Clarke, *The Letters of St. Cyprian of Carthage: Volume III, Letters 55-66*, ACW 46 (New York, NY: Newman Press, 1986) 90.

203. CST:DocHer, 517. The English text for the quotation was taken directly from Rose B. Donna, *Cyprian. Letters (1-81)*, FOTC 51 (Washington D.C.: Catholic University of America Press, 1964) 194.

believe, promoting non-violence in response to all aggressors. Cyprian may or may not have been a pacifist, but that is certainly not the point of this letter to Cornelius.

Finally, *ChP* 114 quotes Sulpicius Severus' *Life of St. Martin* 4.3.[204] In this passage, St. Martin renounces his earlier military service and counters that soldiers of Christ are not allowed to fight. As a matter of history, the CST document argues the idolatry prevalent in the Roman army offended the sensibilities of Christians. Equally disturbing was the military's training to fight and kill other people; it was for these reasons many Christians refused military service. In St. Martin's case, being a convert to Christianity while still a soldier, such things led to his exodus from the military. Below is the Latin text from the critical edition and the English translation of the passage found in the CST document.

Life of St. Martin 4.3[205]	*ChP* 114[206]
hactenus, inquit ad Caesarem, militaui tibi; patere ut nunc militem Deo ... Christi ego miles sum: pugnare mihi non licet.	Hitherto I [i.e., Martin] have served you as a soldier. Allow me now to become a soldier of God ... I am a soldier of Christ. It is not lawful for me to fight.

More so than the previous two quotations, this one from *Life of St. Martin* conforms to the argument of the CST document. The day prior to a battle, Martin and other soldiers were offered a bonus by the emperor as an encouragement to fight bravely. Martin had earlier resolved to request a discharge and so used this occasion of receiving a bonus from the emperor to formally do so. The ellipsis in the quotation was Martin's offer to the emperor, *donatiuum tuum pugnaturus accipiat* ("let the one who will fight receive your gift"). The emperor was impressed neither by Martin's request nor by his deferral to being a soldier for Christ, and so Martin offered himself as an unarmed soldier. The next day, however, the opposing army surrendered before the battle even began and, as hagiographer, Severus attributed the surrender to

204. PL 20.162; the critical edition is Sulpicius Severus, *Vie de Saint Martin, Tome I*, ed. Jacques Fontaine, SC 133 (Paris: Éditions du Cerf, 1967) 260. ET: F. R. Hoar, "The Life of Saint Martin of Tours," in *Soldiers of Christ: Saints and Saints' Lives from Late Antiquity and the Early Middle Ages*, ed. Thomas Head and Thomas F. X. Noble (University Park, PA: Pennsylvania State University Press, 1995) 1-29; Bernard Peebles, *Sulpicius Severus. Writings*, FOTC 7 (Washington D.C.: Catholic University of America Press, 1949) 108-109.

205. Sulpicius Severus, *Vie de Saint Martin*, SC 133, 260.

206. CST:DocHer, 517. It is clear that the English translators of the CST document relied, with minor modifications, on Alexander Roberts, "Life of St. Martin," in *The Works of Sulpicius Severus*, NPNF II.11 (Edinburgh: T & T Clark, 1894) 6.

Martin's stand as a Christian. Neither Severus nor Martin (through Severus) explained what led to Martin's desire for a discharge; that Martin had contemplated it for some period prior to this battle suggests it was not just the physical act of fighting that he believed was discordant with Christianity. Something about even the day-to-day tasks of soldiering troubled Martin, and it is quite possible the CST document is correct that Christians such as Martin disapproved of the training to fight as much as of the fighting itself.

On average, the five patristic source citations in *ChP* are allotted more space in the text (nearly 110 words per citation) than any other CST document in this study. The first of the five citations pays a nod to Augustine's reflection that wars are sometimes necessary (indeed, they are a matter of Christian charity) in order to protect innocent people from injurious neighbors. The remaining four, however, substantiated the feelings of most Catholics today that war and military service are not appropriate for the Christian. *ChP*, more than most of the earlier CST documents, has grounded most of its citations in their historical and literary context. Still, it was shown that only the first and last of the five citations actually corresponded to the particular argument of the document as a whole. The others extended or modified the arguments of *ChP* in theological ways that are certainly helpful, but would otherwise escape the reader of *ChP* who does not also turn to the patristic sources themselves.

Economic Justice for All (USCCB, 1986)

Whereas the USCCB's pastoral letter of 1984 challenged the U.S.'s commitment to peace and to a reduction of nuclear stockpiles, this second letter took aim at the U.S.'s commitment to act justly towards workers, the poor, families, farmers, and others. To that end, the letter makes two references to patristic sources, the first of which is a quotation of Cyprian of Carthage's *On Works and Almsgiving* 25[207] at *EJA* II.34. It is the last phrase at the end of the argument that proceeds,

---

207. PL 4.620; the critical edition is Cyprian of Carthage, *La bienfaisance et les aumônes*, ed. Michel Poirier, SC 440 (Paris: Éditions du Cerf, 1999) 150-154. ET: Roy J. Deferrari, *Cyprian: Treatises*, FOTC 36 (Washington D.C.: Catholic University of America Press, 1958) 251-252.

To stand before God as the creator is to respect God's creation, both the world of nature and of human history. *From the patristic period to the present, the Church has affirmed that misuse of the world's resources or appropriation of them by a minority of the world's population betrays the gift of creation since "whatever belongs to God belongs to all"*[208] (italics in the pastoral letter)

In the context of Cyprian's treatise, the quotation is set within an exhortation to put aside the things of this world (i.e., the earthly garment, cf. *On Works and Almsgiving* 24) and instead to put on a heavenly garment, which takes little account of the things of this world. Cyprian reminds his readers that the earliest Christians shared their goods as if owned in common (Acts 2). God allows rain, sunshine, wind, and sleep to fall upon the righteous and unrighteous, argues Cyprian, and so a proper imitation of God is for Christians liberally to share their own goods with any – Christian or non-Christian – who has need. Cyprian, of course, writes in a context where wealth is largely tied to land and its usability. It is not difficult to argue that the land actually belongs to God, for it was he who made it as the earth's creator. It is rather more complicated to use this text, as the CST document intends, in order to challenge people to consider modern "goods" (e.g., money earned in the financial sectors) as coming from the hand of God. Of course, *EJA* is aware of the difficulty, and it eventually becomes clear that what is really at stake in the argument is not one's need to consider "whatever belongs to God belongs to all," but to appreciate the larger theological point Cyprian has made. That is, people must exchange their earthly clothes for heavenly ones, one manifestation of it being a reduction in the esteem one holds for private possession of goods. Cyprian adds an important theological dimension to *EJA*, one which is not so clear from the partial citation incorporated here, but which is evident from the larger context of the passage in Cyprian's treatise.

The second patristic source citation is a general reference to the "Church Fathers" at *EJA* II.57. It is set within the words,

In the first centuries, when Christians were a minority in a hostile society, they cared for one another through generous almsgiving. In the patristic era, the church fathers repeatedly stressed that the goods of the earth were created by God for the benefit of every person without exception, and that all have special duties toward those in need.[209]

208. ET: CST:DocHer, 586. The Latin text for the quotation of Cyprian (ed. Poirier, *La bienfaisance et les aumônes*, SC 440, 152): Quodcumque enim Dei est in nostra usurpatione commune est.

209. CST:DocHer, 592.

This is two references, really. The first, to the earliest Christians who were a persecuted minority, makes one think of the apologies by Justin Martyr, Tertullian, and Minucius Felix. Tertullian, in particular, pointed to the generosity of Christians in *Apology* 39, a text employed at *RN* 24 and elsewhere.[210] The second reference is to the patristic era and to the Church Fathers, suggesting something of a distinction from the previous era. Likely, *EJA* has in mind here the writings of the fourth century onward. Within the larger context, this reference to the Church Fathers at *EJA* II.57 is employed as an historical authority intended to support the argument that Christians have, throughout their history, both within Catholic and Protestant circles, carried on the mission of advancing the kingdom of God initiated by Christ.

EJA identifies in its numerous remaining pages the injustices plaguing American society. The details of these injustices did not, apparently, lend themselves to any further recourse to patristic source materials. The patristic source citations at *EJA* II.34 and 57, then, contribute to the larger document by helping lay a groundwork for justice. They join the biblical witnesses in saying that God intended for humans to live differently, to live with a concern for the common good.

Sollicitudo rei socialis (1987)

Twenty years after *Populorum progressio*, it was deemed appropriate to reaffirm to the world the Church's commitment to social justice. This CST document moves past general critcisms of both Marxism and liberalism, choosing instead to articulate a different vision of human development. This new vision emphasizes the essential dignity of each human person, believing them to be more than a laborer for goods or services in the world's economies. Solidarity is once again the watchword. *SRS* incorporates six patristic source citations into its text, yet all are concentrated in two footnotes in one section of the document, §31.

SRS 31 correlates the work of Christ in history with the dignity of human persons. Whenever a person performs a work that contributes to the furtherance of God's kingdom here on earth, it participates in the same work as Christ who came to bring that kingdom and now works through the Church to complete it. Importantly, this teleology makes possible an abstraction of human work from the day-to-day tasks to a

210. See above, 20 and 65.

notion of "development." Humans are to be about development, and the Church is obliged to proclaim what is authentic human development (orientation towards God; likeness to Christ). To the extent that the Church's own witness is hampered by superfluous displays of wealth, it is necessary for such wealth to be dispensed for relief of the poor. In support of these ideas are the two footnotes referencing patristic sources.

The first of the two footnotes cites Basil of Caesarea's *Longer Rules* Q. 37.1-2,[211] Theodoret of Cyrus' *Concerning Providence* Oration 7[212] and Augustine's *City of God* 19.17.[213] The footnote appears at the end of the sentence,

> ... one can find in the teaching of the Fathers an *optimistic vision* of history and work, that is to say of the *perennial value* of authentic human achievements, inasmuch as they are redeemed by Christ and destined for the promised kingdom.[214] (italics in the Latin text and official English version)

Despite their name, Basil's *Rules* were not written for monastics, but for the "mature." This is not an unimportant consideration with respect to the CST document, for Basil's proclamation of the value of work applies to all Christians. Specifically, Basil argues that human labor accomplishes two things. It brings into subjection the otherwise undisciplined human body, and it generates goods which may be shared with the weak and the poor. With respect to this latter point, Basil wants Christians to work hard *in order that* the needs of weaker or poorer Christians may be met. For the able-bodied labor is a means of caring for the poor. Basil framed labor in terms of its ability to balance the socio-ethical system, and in so doing further the kingdom of God on earth. Surprisingly for a socio-ethical document, this framework is supplanted in *SRS* with a concern instead to express labor in terms of international development and in terms of how the Church evaluates its own

---

211. PG 31:1009-1012; no critical edition of the Greek manuscripts exists. ET: M. Monica Wagner, *Basil: Ascetical Works*, FOTC 9 (Washington D.C.: Catholic University of America Press, 1950) 306-307.

212. PG 83:665-686; no critical edition exists. ET: Thomas Halton, *Theodoret of Cyrus. On Divine Providence*, ACW 49 (New York, NY: Newman Press, 1988) 88-100.

213. Augustine, *De civitate Dei, Pars II*, CSEL 40, 402-405; id., *De civitate Dei, Libri XI-XXII*, CCSL 48, 683-685. ET: Dyson, *Augustine. The City of God against the Pagans*, 945-947.

214. *SRS* 31 (AAS 80.1, 555; transl. in CST:DocHer, 416): Aliis verbis in doctrina Patrum tam historia quam hominis labor *in optimam partem accipi* potest, id est *perenne bonum* quod rerum ab homine perfectarum est proprium, quippe quae sint a Christo redemptae promissoque Regno destinatae.

financial priorities. Admittedly, the CST document addressed a wider and more diverse audience than did Basil, and its praise of all genuine human achievements may accomplish on a wider scale what Basil's view of the labor of particular individuals accomplished on a smaller scale. That said, the loss of that particularity cannot help but dilute Basil's pastoral exhortation for every person to labor for the benefit of the weaker and poorer among us.

Following the citation of Basil is that of Theodoret of Cyrus' *Concerning Providence* Oration 7. This oration defends two seemingly contradictory points at the same time, that all humans are to be treated equally for God created humans with equal natures, and that it is a matter of providential care that God directed the separation of peoples into masters and slaves, rulers and ruled. The creation of Eve from the nature of Adam, according to Theodoret, assures us that God never intended for any one person to rule over any other person or persons (cf. 7.8). Such equality of persons remained until the post-diluvian period, after which God "divided mankind into rulers and the ruled, so that fear of rulers might lessen the volume of crime."[215] The separation of humans into rulers and ruled is proof, then, of God's providential care in administering the affairs of the earth promoting justice and reducing sin. To Theodoret, this is the fundamental theological basis for promoting the value of the work of slaves and subjects who are quick to complain against their masters. Although slaves perform the greater share of physical labor in producing goods, they do not bear the further responsibility (indeed, the burden, according to Theodoret) held by the master of having to sell those goods and provide for the welfare of a large household. Thus, in addition to God's providential decision to separate humans into classes of rulers and ruled, God's providence is seen further still in his balance of labor and responsibility. The labor of a slave, then, has a value equal to the responsibilities born by a master. In the context of the CST document, Theodoret's text seems misplaced. Theodoret defends God's providence, not the value of human labor or human achievements, he neither connects labor with a furtherance of the kingdom of God nor argues that the value of a slave's labor is redeemed by the coming of Christ. By the same token, the CST document cited all

---

215. Theodoret of Cyrus, *On Divine Providence* 7.10 (PG 83:672; transl. Halton, *Theodoret of Cyrus. On Divine Providence*, ACW, vol. 49, 91): ...εἰς ἄρχοντας καὶ ἀρχομένους διεῖλε τῶν ἀνθρώπων τὸ γένος, ἵνα τῶν ἀρχόντων τὸ δέος σμικρύνῃ τῶν ἁμαρτημάτων τὸ πλῆθος.

of Theodoret's oration and not just a part. Perhaps a broad theology of providence was to be understood as undergirding the CST document's own theology of the kingdom of God. If that is the case, then this citation of Theodoret is better placed elsewhere, perhaps in the preceding section of the document where the "will of God" is connected with the idea of human development.

The last of the three patristic sources cited in this footnote at *SRS* 31 is Augustine's *City of God* 19.17. This text too seems oddly placed, for Augustine is concerned here with the establishment of peace in the earthly city and the use of such peace by the heavenly city. The earthly city establishes peace by laws and religious customs; the heavenly city uses that peace to direct humans that long for a lasting and perfect peace toward God. Citizens of the heavenly city are merely pilgrims in the peace of the earthly city and are even considered corrupters of that peace by the authorities for they harbor different religious beliefs. Such citizens live by faith in the peace of the heavenly city, yet, with every good act directed towards God or one's neighbor, contribute to furthering its reality in the earthly city. As with Theodoret, Augustine is not defending the value of human labor or development for the present world. Rather, Augustine believed human labor had eschatological implications. Yet here too, perhaps this is the point the CST document wants the reader to understand. Human labor and achievements are to be celebrated, but not so much for what they accomplish now as for how they direct the laborer to his or her Creator.

The second of the two footnotes, following closely after the previous footnote, cites John Chrysostom's *Homilies on St. Matthew* 50.3-4,[216] Ambrose's *On the Work of the Ministry* II.28.136-40[217] and Possidius's *Life of St. Augustine* 24.[218] The footnote appears at the end of the CST document's claim that the early Church Fathers both taught and lived out the need to relieve the suffering of the poor. Indeed today, such relief

216. PG 58:508-510; no critical edition presently exists. ET: George Prevost, "The Homilies of St. John Chrysostom, Archbishop of Constantinople, on the Gospel of St. Matthew," in *Saint Chrysostom: Homilies on the Gospel of Saint Matthew*, NPNF I.10 (Edinburgh: T&T Clark, 1888) 312-313.

217. PL 16:139-41; the critical edition is Ambrose, *De officiis*, CCSL 15, ed. Maurice Testard (Turnhout: Brepols, 2000) 146-148. ET: Ivor J. Davidson, *Ambrose. De officiis, Volume I: Introduction, Text, and Translation*, Oxford Early Christian Studies (Oxford: Oxford University Press, 2001) 343-347.

218. PL 32:53-54; the critical edition is Anthony A. R. Bastiaensen, ed., *Vita di Cipriano, Vita di Ambrogio, Vita di Agostino*, Scritti greci e latini: Vite dei santi, vol. 3 (Milan: Fondazione Lorenzo Valla, 1997). ET: John E. Rotelle, *Possidius: The Life of Saint Augustine*, The Augustinian Series 1 (Villanova, PA: Augustinian Press, 1988) 97-99.

may even need to come at the expense of selling the Church's superfluous ornaments and furnishings. Chrysostom argued similarly in his
Homilies on St. Matthew 50.3-4. According to Chrysostom, it is a trav-
esty to decorate the house of God or to participate in the eucharist with
golden chalices if the funds used to pay for such adornment should have
rather been spent on the poor. However, Chrysostom's social ethic runs
much deeper than mere arguments for poor relief, and this deeper men-
tality supports a healthy balance between gifts designated for ornamen-
tation and those for the poor. The entire discussion of 50.3-4 is framed
by Chrysostom's evaluation of the eucharistic meal, explaining that,
since Christ spared not himself to bring peace to our souls, so too ought
we not spare any of our wealth thinking that it brings peace to our
souls. In other words, the mystery of the eucharist is the peace of Christ,
and we should receive the peace of Christ through the eucharist and not
through any pursuit of wealth. This, then, is the platform upon which
Chrysostom can now stand to say that too many Christians are ostenta-
tious in their displays of wealth, particularly when they flaunt their
wealth with gifts of ornament for the church. To the extent that one
keeps wealth in proper perspective, and to the extent one gives generously of his or her wealth for the relief of the poor, it is not a problem,
in Chrysostom's mind, for such a person also to contribute to the
adornment of a church.

> If thou desire to honor the sacrifice [i.e., of the eucharist], offer thy
> soul, for which also it was slain; ... Let not this therefore be our aim,
> to offer golden vessels *only*, but do so from honest earnings likewise
> ... And these things I say, not forbidding such offerings to be pro-
> vided; but requiring you, *together with them*, and before them, to give
> alms.[219] (italics mine)

In sum, Chrysostom is eminently pastoral here, encouraging maturity of Christian faith that inevitably manifests itself in financial stew-
ardship, including care for the poor.

Following the citation of Chrysostom is that of Ambrose's *On the Work
of the Ministry* II.28.136-40. Taking a cue from Cicero's *De officiis*,
Ambrose prepares this three-volume work on the proper life and duties of
clergy for those under his charge in the diocese of Milan. In the section

---

219. Chrysostom, *Hom. on Matthew* 50.4 (PG 58.508-509; transl. Prevost, "Homilies
on Saint Matthew," NPNF I.10, 313): Εἰ γὰρ βούλει τιμῆσαι τὴν θυσίαν, τὴν ψυχὴν
προσένεγκε, δι' ἣν καὶ ἐτύθη, ... Μὴ τοίνυν τοῦτο σκοπῶμεν, ὅπως χρυσᾶ σκεύη προσ-
φέρωμεν μόνον, ἀλλ' ὅπως καὶ ἐκ δικαίων πόνων .... Καὶ ταῦτα λέγω, οὐ κωλύων ἀναθή-
ματα κατασκευάζεσθαι τοιαῦτα, ἀξιῶν δὲ μετὰ τούτων, καὶ πρὸ τούτων, τὴν ἐλεημοσύνην
ποιεῖν.

pertinent to this discussion, Ambrose recalls a time when he melted down some sacred vessels in order to raise money for relief of the poor. "It was far more advantageous to preserve souls for the Lord than to preserve gold,"[220] Ambrose wrote. Indeed, the true treasures of the Church are the poor, as Ambrose recalls a certain martyr Lawrence as having previously taught. Like Chrysostom, Ambrose connects the church's own efforts to deprive itself of material goods for the benefit of the poor with the work of Christ who, in his own suffering, relieved the suffering of human souls. Also like Chrysostom, Ambrose sees this portrayed most clearly in the eucharistic meal, but, in contrast to Chrysostom, says that the chalices with the greatest ornament in that meal are the men and women whose blood has been redeemed by Christ's own blood on the cross. In other words, the redemption of the poor and the slaves for the cause of Christ is the best ornament for churches; there is no need for decorous chalices at the eucharistic meal when you have their own lives before you.

A final patristic contribution to the argument of the CST document is that of Possidius' comments about Augustine's own dispassionate behavior vis-à-vis church finances in his *Life of Augustine* 24. According to Possidius, Augustine reluctantly engaged in financial matters for the diocese, concerned only that the needs of the poor were met first and that buildings were constructed modestly. When it came to receiving gifts of land or other entitlements from wealthy congregants, Augustine first made sure that the needs of the wealthy patron's own family were met. As well, Augustine did not hesitate to sell church ornaments when the needs of the poor were great and money was not otherwise available. Possidius strung together these anecdotes and mentalities of Augustine without further theological reflection, but the point is not lost on the reader. Christians and their churches are obliged to hold the wealth of this world lightly, for the poor have a greater claim on these resources.

In summary, two points at *SRS* 31 have sought support from the patristic world. The first is that human labor has eternal value insofar as it contributes to overall human development and directs the laborer to God. Of the three patistic citations on this point, Basil most nearly

---

220. Ambrose, *On the Work of the Ministry* II.28.137 (ed. Maurice Testard, *De officiis*, CCSL 15, 146; transl. Davidson, *De officiis*, 345): ut animas Domino quam aurum seruaremus.

approximated the CST document, but Basil praised labor for its ability to balance social inequities, and this was not the point of *SRS*. Theodoret and Augustine moved the focus away from labor for its own sake (i.e., labor itself being an expression of the kingdom of God) and towards a particular understanding of labor's contribution to the kingdom of God. Labor is a by-product of God's providential care for the world in Theodoret, and labor for God or one's neighbor is the path to the heavenly city in Augustine. In the final analysis, the patristic texts on this point about labor have added new reasons for praising it, rather than supporting the CST document's particular teaching.

Similarly for the second point at *SRS* 31 that relied on a set of patristic citations, the early Christian sources seem to both challenge and extend the point made in the CST document. In furtherance of the previous point, which argued labor is an earthly expression of the kingdom of God, this second point called upon the Church not to be a hindrance to the furtherance of the kingdom of God by withholding its wealth from the poor, those unable to earn a living wage despite their hard labor. The patristic texts were clearly concerned about the Church's wealth (both in terms of its sacred vessels made of gold and silver and in terms of its landholdings) in the face of the dire poverty of so many. However, the patristic texts were agreed that the seeming contradiction between the Church's wealth and its ministry to the poor was not easily solved by simply selling off the Church's wealth, which might easily be concluded from a surface reading of the CST document. On the contrary, the patristic authors recognized that the Church's wealth came from wealthy congregants, that it is the motive of these congregants which is of greatest concern, and that once alms had been given by these congregants it was not inappropriate for them also to make gifts to the Church either for its sustenance or for its adornment. Simply put, for all the patristic citations at *SRS* 31, the patristic texts say much more than does the main text. It is incumbent upon the CST reader to apprise himself or herself of this fuller context.

Centesimus Annus (1991)

A century of years having passed since *Rerum novarum*, it was appropriate that John Paul II issue a social encyclical both in honor of Leo XIII's earlier letter and in furtherance of his own social agenda.

This CST document is divided roughly into two parts, the first one being a review of Leo XII's encyclical and its effects, and the second being an appraisal of new challenges facing the Church in her calls for social justice in the world. In *CA*'s introduction, the argument is made that the Church's appreciation for *RN* is one example of how the "tradition" is alive and well. The foundation of that tradition is argued to have been "laid by our fathers in the faith, and particularly upon what 'the Apostles passed down to the church' in the name of Jesus Christ."[221] The inset quotation, 'the Apostles passed down to the church' was taken from Irenaeus of Lyon's *Against Heresies* I.10.1[222] and III.4.1.[223] It is a paraphrase of what Irenaeus wrote," … it is not necessary to seek the truth among others which it is easy to obtain from the Church, since the apostles … lodged in her hands most copiously all things pertaining to the truth,"[224] and "The Church, indeed, though disseminated throughout the world, even to the ends of the earth, received from the apostles and their disciples the faith in one God the Father Almightly, …"[225] This is the only patristic source citation within the document, although a perfect opportunity to include another one was overlooked at *CA* 57. As is clear, it has little connection to the socio-ethical argument of either *RN* or of *CA*. It is, rather, a rhetorical ornament corroborating *CA*'s claim to lie within the Church's social teaching tradition.

221. *CA* 3 (AAS 83.2, 795; transl. in CST:DocHer, 440): aedificat a nostris in fide patribus actum et praecipue super fundamentum quod Apostoli Ecclesiae tradiderunt Iesu Christi nomine.

222. PG 7.549; the critical editions are Irenaeus of Lyon, *Contre les hérésies, Livre I*, ed. Adelin Rousseau and Louis Doutreleau, SC 264 (Paris: Éditions du Cerf, 1979) 154; id., *Epideixis Adversus Haereses*, ed. Norbert Brox, Fontes Christiani 8.1 (Freiburg: Herder, 1993) 198-200. ET: Dominic J. Unger and John J. Dillon, *Irenaeus of Lyons: Against the Heresies, Book 1*, ACW 55 (Mahwah, NJ: Paulist Press, 1992) 48-49.

223. PG 7.855; the critical editions are Irenaeus of Lyon, *Contre les hérésies, Livre III*, SC 211, 44; id., *Adversus Haereses*, Fontes Christiani 8.3, 38. ET: Alexander Roberts and James Donaldson, "Against Heresies," in *The Apostolic Fathers with Justin Martyr and Irenaeus*. ANF 1, 416.

224. Irenaeus, *Against Heresies* III.4.1 (ed. Brox, *Adversus Haereses*, Fontes Christiani 8.3, 38; transl. Roberts and Donaldson, "Against Heresies," 416): non oportet adhuc quaerere apud alios veritatem quam facile est ab ecclesia sumere, cum apostoli … in eam contulerint omni quae sint veritatis.

225. Irenaeus, *Against Heresies* I.10.1 (ed. Brox, *Epideixis Adversus Haereses*, Fontes Christiani 8.1, 198; transl. Unger and Dillon, *Irenaeus of Lyons. Against the Heresies, Book 1*, 48-49): Ἡ μὲν γὰρ ἐκκλησία, καίπερ καθ' ὅλης τῆς οἰκουμένης ἕως περάτων τῆς γῆς διεσπαρμένη, παρά τε τῶν ἀποστόλων καὶ τῶν ἐκείνων μαθητῶν παραλαβοῦσα τὴν εἰς ἕνα Θεὸν πατέρα παντοκράτορα...

Santo Domingo Documents (CELAM IV, 1992)

The criticisms heard following CELAM III at Puebla that it was but a small step forward from the bold claims of CELAM II at Medellin, reverberated in the aftermath of Santo Domingo. Apart from a special focus on the concern of the Latin American churches to confront the growing threat of evangelical and fundamentalist-oriented sects, *SDomingo* largely repeated and re-emphasized the mission already put forth at Medellin for the Latin American churches. With respect to patristic source citations in *SDomingo*, here too there is a comparison with Puebla, for the two patristic citations in *SDomingo* seem relatively inconsequential to the larger context of which they are a part.

The first of the two citations is a footnote-only citation of the anonymous *Epistle to Diognetus* 8 at *SDomingo* I.1.9.[226] It should be pointed out that footnotes in *SDomingo* are actually parenthetical notes embedded within the main body of the text, yet this parenthetical citation functions much as a footnote would insofar as it points the reader to *Epistle to Diognetus* for more information. The passage from *SDomingo* at which this citation is found says, "The renewed evanglization that we are now undertaking must be an invitation to the conversion of personal and collective conscience alike (cf. *OA* 18) so that we Christians may be the soul, as it were, in all realms of society (cf. *Letter to Diognetus* 8)."[227] The *Epistle to Diognetus* 8 is understood to contribute to the recognition that Christians are the soul of society. The larger context of this claim in *SDomingo* is a recitation of the New Testament teaching about the mercy of God towards sinners in sending the Son and in the Son's reconciliation of sinners back to God. The individual and collective sins of Latin America – wars, terrorism, drugs – are able to be overcome when the people of Latin America return to the grace offered by God. The return of the people to God must be, as the above quote makes clear, the evangelistic work of the Latin American churches. That having been said, a reading of *Epistle to Diognetus* 8 does not seem to contribute to

226. The critical editions are *A Diognète: Introduction, édition critique, traduction et commentaire*, ed. Henri I. Marrou, SC 33 (Paris: Éditions du Cerf, 1951) 70-72; Bart Ehrman, ed., *The Apostolic Fathers, Volume II: Epistle of Barnabas, Papias and Quadratus, Epistle to Diognetus, The Shepherd of Hermas*, LCL (Cambridge, MA: Harvard University Press, 2003) II.146-148. ET: Cf. also Ehrman, LCL, II.147-149.

227. Conference of Latin American Bishops, *Santo Domingo and Beyond: Documents and Commentaries from the Historic Meeting of the Latin American Bishops' Conference*, ed. Alfred T. Hennelly (Maryknoll, NY: Orbis Books, 1993) 75.

this overall picture. In fact, I suspect there is an error in the reference; rather than citing §8, the citation should be to §6. In the former, the epistle defends the view that we may understand the kindness of God when we acknowledge that this kindness was revealed to the world through the Son. Nothing in §8 suggests the presence of Christians in the world. The latter, however, mentions this presence explicitly. Consider *Epistle to Diognetus* 6.1,6-8,

> To put the matter simply, what the soul is in the body, this is what
> Christians are in the world ... The soul loves the flesh that hates it,
> along with its limbs; Christians love those who hate them. The soul
> is imprisoned in the body, but it sustains the body; Christians are
> detained in the prison of the world, but they sustain the world. The
> soul, which is immortal, dwells in a mortal tent; Christians tem-
> porarily dwell in perishable surroundings but await that which is
> imperishable in the heavens.[228]

The *Epistle to Diognetus* dates to the mid-second century, and the first ten of its twelve sections are an apology for Christianity. The sixth section concludes the first main part of the apology which is a critique both of the Greek's pagan gods and of the Jews. The sixth section, in particular, defends Christians against charges that, despite their disrespect for the pagan gods and for the Jewish religion, they are not strangers to Greek society. Christians live in many regions, they dress, eat, and carry about their work and commerce like everyone else, and, indeed, are as much a part of the world as anyone else. This diffusion of Christians and of Christianity is responsible for its ever-expanding appeal to the Greeks and Romans. Thus, *SDomingo's* (now corrected) citation of *Epistle to Diognetus* 6 offers an expanded, pastoral elaboration to its otherwise abstract wish that Christians would be the "soul" of the Latin American world calling that world's inhabitants to repentance. The appeal to this patristic source teaches that Christians in Latin America need to continue identifying themselves with the common people in order that the Christian appeal for conversion comes from the mouth of those who have already earned the respect of the larger community. Perhaps the message of *SDomingo* as a whole captures this

---

228. *Epistle to Diognetus* 8.6-8 (ed. Ehrman, LCL II.142): Ἁπλῶς δ' ἐστὶν ἐν σώματι ψυχή, τοῦτ' εἰσὶν ἐν κόσμῳ Χριστιανοί ... .ἡ ψυχὴ τὴν μισοῦσαν ἀγαπᾷ σάρκα καὶ τὰ μέλη, καὶ Χριστιανοὶ τοὺς μισοῦντας ἀγαπῶσιν. ἐγκέκλεισται μὲν ἡ ψυχὴ τῷ σώματι, συνέχει δὲ αὐτὴ τὸ σῶμα, καὶ Χριστιανοὶ κατέχονται μὲν ὡς ἐν φρουρᾷ τῷ κόσμῳ, αὐτοὶ δὲ συνέχουσι τὸν κόσμον. ἀθάνατος ἡ ψυχὴ ἐν θνητῷ σκηνώματι κατοικεῖ, καὶ Χριστιανοὶ παροικοῦσιν ἐν φθαρτοῖς, τὴν ἐν οὐρανοῖς ἀφθαρσίαν προσδεχόμενοι.

spirit, for having buried this patristic reference in a parenthetical note blunts its otherwise helpful teaching at this particular place in the document.

The second patristic source citation is a general reference to the Nicene-Constantinopolitan Creed at *SDomingo* II.1.4.3. In this passage, *SDomingo* encourages the Latin American churches to join in ecumenism as a pastoral activity. Eight suggestions are given for how this may accomplished, the second of which says, "Deepen relationships of convergence and dialogue with those Churches who pray the creed of Nicea-Constantinople, who share the same sacraments and who revere Holy Mary, Mother of God, even if they do not acknowledge the primacy of the Roman pontiff."[229] This general reference to the creed proffered at the Council of Constantinople (381) suggests that the faith of the Church as it is expressed in this document is one of three criteria by which to judge potential partners in ecumenical dialogue. The creed from the Council of Constantinople was a revision of the earlier, Nicene Creed issued at the Council of Nicaea (325). The revised creed both affirmed the *homoousion* language of the earlier creed, and it expanded the earlier creed's teaching about the person and work of the Holy Spirit. Interestingly, the Nicene-Constantinopolitan Creed was later revised again to include a reference to the Spirit's procession as being both from the Father and the Son. Although this addition to the Creed dates to at least the sixth century, it was not made official until 1014.[230] It should be assumed that this interpolated creed with the addition of *filioque* is actually the one to which *SDomingo* refers, and not the creed

229. Conference of Latin American Bishops, *Santo Domingo and Beyond*, 110.

230. The Council of Toledo (589) was the first to include *filioque* in its creed, although it appears as though they thought the original creed was worded that way. (The second canon of the council anathematized any who departed from the Nicene-Constantinopolitan creed "according to the form of the Eastern Churches." Since their text of this creed included *filioque* it seems clear they were unaware *filioque* was not original). The Spanish bishop Fulgentius of Ruspe (d. c. 533) had even taught procession of the Spirit from the Son as having apostolic origin. (De filio quoque procedere Spiritum Sanctum, prophetica atque apostolica nobis doctrina commendat. ["Of the son also proceeds the Holy Spirit, as also prophesied by our apostles who commended the doctrine."] PL 65, 696). Belief in the Spirit's double procession as a creedal statement, at least in Spain and other western regions, may go back into the fifh or earlier centuries.

The Council of Gentilly (767) marked the beginning of imperial sanction of an interpolated creed, but Rome continued to denounce modification of the Nicene-Constantinopolitan creed until 1014. That year, at the coronation of King Henry II of Germany, Pope Benedict VIII allowed an interpolated creed to be read. Rome used the *filioque* in its creeds thereafter.

of the Council of Constantinople (381). Regardless, the rhetorical contribution of this general reference is that it provides practical, pastoral guidance to Latin American ministers wondering what is the theological dividing line between themselves and non-Christian religious movements. The Nicene-Constantinopolitan creed affirms particular doctrines of the Trinity, of Christ, and of the Spirit. If this is the standard of theological orthodoxy, then it helps the local minister and national churches alike to keep particular expressions of worship from being hindrances to genuine dialogue.

SDomingo's two patristic source citations function as practical, pastoral elaborations of what is taught in the document at the places in which the citations are found. Yet, these two citations hardly stand out amidst the larger document. That the first citation is likely mistaken in its attribution to §8 rather than §6 perhaps bears some testimony to its seeming inconsequentiality. What is more, *SDomingo* neither explains its choice of these particular citations nor elaborates on their pastoral implications. Considering the fact that *Puebla* had only two citations of patristic sources and *Medellin* none, *SDomingo* is another document in the line of those emerging from CELAM that shows little recourse to patristic sources for its consideration of present, pastoral challenges.

Compendium of Catholic Social Thought (2004)

As the introductory remarks in the volume indicate, The Pontifical Council for Justice and Peace responded to a request from Pope John Paul II that a compendium of the Church's social teachings be prepared.[231] Completed and published in 2004, the compendium is divided into three parts. The first part is a theology for social action by the Church, including both the inherent dignity of human persons, the social mission of the Church given to it by God, and a survey of its guiding principles (e.g., common good, subsidiarity, solidarity). The second part is a survey of the the Church's social doctrine on a variety of topics, including family life, economic rights, political systems, international

231. The compendium was published originally both in English and in Italian. Both are official texts for the compendium, as no Latin *ur*-text was preferred, if one ever had existed. Likely, the English text was prepared by the American Msgr. Frank Dewane, a member of the Justice and Peace council. The Italian text was the basis for the German edition published in 2005.

law, third-world development, peace movements, and environmental concerns. The third part is a series of exhortations to the Church, to its pastors, and to its laity for continued commitment to justice in the world. Following the body of the compendium is a substantial index of sources and of topics treated.

The compendium is largely a series of quotations from papal documents going back to Leo XIII (e.g., encyclicals, homilies), from the *Catechism of the Catholic Church*, and from the documents of Vatican II strung together by a series of interpretive reflections by the compendium's compilers. Relying as it does on some of the documents included in this study, it is not surprising that, with respect to its use of patristic sources, this compendium draws on some of the same texts. However, most are new texts that were not identified earlier in this study. Thus, this compendium is as much its own document in the CST tradition as it is an attempt to summarize that tradition. That having been said, the nineteen patristic sources incorporated into this document will be examined in turn.

The first patristic source citation is found in a footnote at *ComCST* 53. Set within a quotation of John Paul II's earlier encyclical *Redemptor hominis* (1979) is a general reference to the "Fathers of the Church."[232] Rhetorically, this appeal to an authority in *ComCST* is an appeal to the earlier encyclical, but the weight of that earlier encyclical's treatment of this subject rests on an appeal to the authority of the Fathers. The argument in both texts is that Christians are to be open to the ideas of non-Christians and to dialogue with them in the common quest for truth, for God is believed to have sown the seeds of truth throughout the human landscape. *Redemptor hominis* incorporates a general reference to the Church Fathers here in support of its claim that, indeed, seeds of truth do exist in other religious and philosophical traditions.[233] Doubtless, *Redemptor hominis* is referring to the Church Fathers Justin Martyr, Clement of Alexandria and Eusebius of Caesarea, whose texts associated with this idea were cited in *EN* 53 discussed earlier.[234] As noted above, these patristic authors believed the Christian expression of truth was the fruition of any earlier "seeds" and supercedes them, yet such a disclaimer is not present in either *Redemptor hominis* or *ComCST* 53. Indeed, *Redemptor hominis* uses the imagery of a mountain upon which people

---

232. *ComCST* 53, 29 n. 65.
233. John Paul II, *Redemptor hominis*, AAS 71 (1979) 276.
234. See above, 66-68.

of all religious backgrounds are ascending in their pursuit of truth. Certainly *ComCST* is not suggesting Christians leave their faith tradition in the pursuit of truth, but the authority of the Fathers seems rather misconstrued in furtherance of the view that other religious traditions have an equally valid claim to the rightness of their way of pursuing truth.

Another general reference to the "Fathers of the Church" is found at *ComCST* 87. The sentence in which it is found reads,

> [The Church's doctrinal heritage concerning society] has its roots in Sacred Scripture, especially the Gospels and the apostolic writings, and takes on shape and body beginning from the Fathers of the Church and the great Doctors of the Middle Ages, constituting a doctrine in which, even without explicit and direct Magisterial pronouncements, the Church gradually came to recognize her competence.[235]

The Fathers of the Church are a part of the historical heritage of the Church's understanding of society and of how society may be just. Rhetorically, this general reference is intended as a practical elaboration on what that doctrinal heritage entails. However, just what those practical elements are is left to the imagination of the reader, for no explanation is given as to what may be found in the writings of either the Fathers or the scholastics. This study has identified some of those texts from other CST documents.

The next patristic citation is found at *ComCST* 114 and is a quotation of Augustine's *Confessions* I.1.[236] "You have made us for yourself, O Lord, and our hearts are restless until they rest in you."[237] This is the same patristic source recalled in *MM* 214 and *GS* 21,[238] although the compendium does not reference these earlier CST documents here. Rhetorically, the quotation from Augustine is a crowning ornament to the end of the argument made by the CST document. Specifically, *ComCST* 114 began with the metaphysical claim that human persons can know themselves. It goes on to suggest that such knowing reveals a set of faculties within human persons (i.e., reason, discernment, free will) that owe their existence to the Creator. It concludes the section with the Augustine quote, which furthers its argument by explaining that awareness of these faculties ought to draw human persons into a relationship with the

---

235. *ComCST* 87, 49.
236. PL 32.661; the critical editions are Augustine, *Confessionum libri XIII*, CCSL 27, 1; id., *Confessionum libri tredecim*, CSEL 33, 1. ET: Chadwick, *Aurelius Augustinus: Confessions*, 3.
237. *ComCST* 114, 65.
238. See above, 26 and 41-42, respectively.

God who created them. The CST document is rather positive here on the ability of a human person to apprise himself or herself of God simply as a result of being conscious of his or her constitution. The CST document does not make clear by what mechanism a person "listens to the deep aspirations of his heart" or how "the heart indicates the spiritual faculties which most properly belong to man."[239] Augustine, for his part, believed it was necessary for God to move the heart of human persons in order that they might come to know their creator.[240]

A footnote reference to Gregory of Nyssa, *Life of Moses* II.2-3,[241] may be found at *ComCST* 135. The larger context of the CST document concerns humanity's free will, which is acknowledged as one of the highest signs of the *imago Dei*. The CST document further argues that human persons accept personal responsibility for the choices they make in creating and expanding their personal and social worlds. To the extent a person exercises freedom, says the CST document, his or her growth as a person may be measured. The citation of Gregory's text is incorporated into the summary sentence for this section, "In this way man generates himself, he is *father* of his own being, he constructs the social order" (italics in the original).[242] Gregory is said to support the claim that every human person is a "father of his own being."

With respect to Gregory's text, *Life of Moses* II.2-3, one discovers an entire set of biblical-exegetical baggage associated with this claim. To unpack the baggage, it must be clear that Gregory's text is divided into two parts. The first part is a summary of the events in Moses' life, according to the latter four books of the Pentateuch. The second part, in which is found this citation in *ComCST*, revisits these details in Moses's life, but this time with an interest in how these details may be connected to the lives of those in Gregory's own audience. The exegetical method at work here is often called allegory, or sometimes spiritual interpretation.[243] Gregory believed the events in Moses' life were

239. *ComCST* 114, 65.

240. In Augustine, *Confessions* I.1, the quotation included in this CST document is preceded by the explanation, "You, O Lord, move us to delight in praising you." (Tu excitas, ut laudare te delectet).

241. PG 44.327-328; the critical edition is Gregory of Nyssa, *De vita Moysis*, ed. Herbertus Musurillo, Gregorii Nysenni Opera 7, part 1 (Leiden: Brill, 1964) 33-34. ET: A. J. Malherbe and Everett Ferguson, *Gregory of Nyssa: The Life of Moses*, CWS (New York, NY: Paulist Press, 1978) 55-56.

242. *ComCST* 135, 75.

243. The exegetical methods of the Church Fathers have been the focus of much study. A new, standard reference for this field is Charles Kannengiesser, *Handbook of Patristic Exegesis: The Bible in Ancient Christianity*, 2 volumes, The Bible in Ancient

recorded neither for curiosity's sake nor for the benefit of the Israelites alone. On the contrary, God intended the story to be of benefit to persons in every age, but especially those living with the hindsight of the incarnation of the Son. That having been said, Gregory opened his second part of the treatise with an explanation as to how the story of Moses' birth may be applied in the lives of people in his audience. "Someone will rightly raise the objection that it does not lie within our power to imitate in our own birth that famous birth."[244] Gregory wondered what kind of birth we may experience, and his answer was that birth is really about change. He argued each person may initiate those changes he or she wishes to take place.

> Being born, in the sense of constantly experiencing change, does not come about as the result of external initiative, as is the case with the birth of the body, which takes place by chance. Such a birth [i.e. constant change] occurs by choice. We are in some manner our own parents giving birth to ourselves by our own free choice in accordance with whatever we wish to be.[245]

Just as Moses was a male born at a time when Hebrew males were being slaughtered by the pharoah (cf. Exodus 1:16), Gregory urged his hearers to give birth to "male" and not "female" choices. This is another feature of Gregory's biblical exegesis, for he connects the contrast between male and female Hebrew children in Exodus 1 with the Fall narrative in Genesis 3, at which place it is described how the female first succumbed to the temptations of the devil. "Sober and provident rational thoughts ... are the parents of the male child,"

Christianity (Leiden: Brill, 2004) esp. I.206-258 and, for a particular discussion of *Life of Moses*, see II.753-754. Among others, also important is Frances M. Young, *Biblical Exegesis and the Formation of Christian Culture* (Cambridge: Cambridge University Press, 1997). Young underscores the difficulty readers of early Christian exegesis will have in teasing out distinctions between typology and allegory in their attempts to define spiritual exegesis. Finally, the legacy of patristic exegesis into the medieval period with its four senses of Scripture is traced in Henri de Lubac, *Medieval Exegesis*, 2 volumes, transl. Mark Sebanc and E. M. Macieroweski (Grand Rapids, MI: Eerdmans, 1998-2000).

244. Gregory of Nyssa, *Life of Moses* II.1 (ed. Musurillo, *De vita Moysis*, Gregorii Nysenni Opera 7, part 1, 33; transl. Malherbe and Ferguson, *The Life of Moses*, CWS, 55): οὐ γὰρ δὴ καὶ τοῦτο τῶν ἐφ᾽ ἡμῖν εἶναι πάντως ἐρεῖ τις ὥστε μιμήσασθαί τινα τῇ καθ᾽ ἑαυτὸν γενέσει τὸν εὐδόκιμον τόκον.

245. Gregory of Nyssa, *Life of Moses* II.3 (ed. Musurillo, *De vita Moysis*, Gregorii Nysseni Opera 7, part 1, 34; transl. Malherbe and Ferguson, *The Life of Moses*, CWS, 55): τὸ δὲ οὕτως γεννᾶσθαι οὐκ ἐξ ἀλλοτρίας ἐστὶν ὁρμῆς καθ᾽ ὁμοιότητα τῶν σωματικῶς τὸ συμβὰν ἀπογεννώντων, ἀλλ᾽ ἐκ προαιρέσεως ὁ τοιοῦτος γίνεται τόκος. καὶ ἐσμὲν ἑαυτῶν τρόπον τινὰ πατέρες, ἑαυτοὺς οἵους ἂν ἐθέλωμεν τίκτοντες καὶ ἀπὸ τῆς ἰδίας προαιρέσεως εἰς ὅπερ ἂν ἐθέλωμεν εἶδος.

argued Gregory.[246] To draw the argument together now, the types of choices to which Gregory referred are those that lead to ever higher states of virtue. It is in regard to virtue, then, that a person may be and rightfully ought to consider himself or herself to be a "father of his own being." This is the point of the CST document, although it has side-stepped the exegetical and theological baggage important in Gregory's defense of the point. Instead, *ComCST* 135 substituted that baggage for another one: freedom. Only in the context of freedom, it seems to be arguing, can a person then make the choices for virtue to which Nyssa is referring. Still, rhetorically, by including Gregory in a footnote on this point, *ComCST* has indicated its intention for the reader to turn there for the theological elaboration.

In a footnote reference at *ComCST* 142, the CST document returns again to Augustine's *Confessions*, this time to *Confessions* II.4.9[247]. The footnote comes at the end of the sentence, "The natural law, which is the law of God, cannot be annulled by human sinfulness."[248] Earlier, at *ComCST* 140, the natural law was said to be the "light of intellect" infused within humans by God. Natural law unites together humans across the globe in so far as they share common principles (cf. *ComCST* 141). Thus, human sinfulness neither obviates nor obfuscates it. Augustine, in his text, affirms this to be true in light of his own past activities of thievery. The footnote reference at *ComCST* 142 quotes the opening sentence of *Confessions* II.4.9, "Theft receives certain punishment by your law (Exod 20:15), Lord, and by the law written in the hearts of men (Rom 2:14) which not even iniquity itself destroys."[249] Augustine has referred here both to a divine law revealed in the biblical text (what the CST document has called the "revealed law"; cf. *ComCST* 141) and to a natural law present within human hearts. That the latter is unmoved by sin is made clear by Augustine in comments that follow in *Confessions* II.4.9, "For what thief can with equanimity endure

---

246. Gregory of Nyssa, *Life of Moses* II.7 (ed. Musurillo, *De vita Moysis*, Gregorii Nysseni Opera 7, part 1, 35; transl. Malherbe and Ferguson, *The Life of Moses*, CWS, 56): οἱ δὲ σώφρονές τε καὶ προνοητικοὶ λογισμοί, οἱ τῆς ἀνδρείας γονῆς πατέρες …

247. PL 32.678; the critical editions are Augustine, *Confessionum libri XIII*, CCSL 27, 21-22; id., *Confessionum libri tredecim*, CSEL 33, 35-36. ET: Chadwick, *Aurelius Augustine. Confessions*, 28.

248. *ComCST* 142, 78.

249. Augustine, *Confessions* II.4.9 (PL 32.678; transl. Chadwick, *Confessions*, 28): Furtum certe punit lex tua, Domine, et lex scripta in cordibus hominum, quam ne ipsa quidem delet iniquitas. In its footnote reference, the CST document only provides the Latin text from the PL edition.

being robbed by another thief?"[250] To Augustine, his sins, his violations of the natural law, made clear his love for evil itself. That thievery is not permitted by the natural law made stealing all the more enjoyable to him. This served as further evidence to him of the depravity of human persons. In short, the natural law existed to shame and to convict Augustine, but this context of shame and conviction is absent in the discussion of the natural law in *ComCST*. Rather, *ComCST* uplifts natural law as a fundamental building block to healthy, human society. To the extent human communities acknowledge its existence, they free themselves to pursue peace with one another. The footnote of Augustine at *ComCST* 142 functions as an appeal to an historical authority, and, with respect to human sinfulness, Augustine validates the point being made. However, the reader of the CST document should be aware that Augustine did not in this passage reflect on the contribution of natural law to the common good; rather, it was a cause of conviction for his own sin.

The next patristic citation is a quotation from Gregory the Great's *Rules for Pastors* III.21[251] at *ComCST* 184, a text to which it will return again in a footnote at §329. This patristic source was also used at *GS* 69, but neither *ComCST* 184 nor 329 include a reference to *GS*. As well, *ComCST* 184 and 329 are quotations from different parts of the text and not a general reference as found in *GS*. With respect to the quotation of Gregory at *ComCST* 184, the Latin text of Gregory's passage is paired with the Latin text and English translation provided in this CST document in the columns below.

Rules for Pastors III.21[252]	*ComCST* 184[253]	*ComCST* 184
Nam cum qualibet necessaria indigentibus ministramus, sua illis reddimus, non nostra largimur; iustitiae potius debitum soluimus, quam misericordiae opera implemus.	Nam cum qualibet necessaria indigentibus ministramus, sua illis reddimus, non nostra largimur; iustitiae potius debitum soluimus, quam misericordiae opera implemus.	When we attend to the needs of those in want, we give them what is theirs, not ours. More than performing works of mercy, we are paying a debt of justice.

In the earlier discussion of Gregory's text in *GS* 69 it was noted that Gregory identified the need for a healthy balance between charity and

---

250. Augustine, *Confessions* II.4.9 (ed. Verheijen, *Confessionum libri XIII*, CCSL 27.1, 21-22; transl. Chadwick, *Confessions*, 28-29): quis enim fur aequo animo furem patitur?

251. PL 77.87; the critical edition is Gregory the Great, *Règle pastorale*, SC 382, 394-400. ET: Henry Davis, *Gregory the Great. Pastoral Care*, ACW 11, 158-162.

252. PL 77.87.

253. This and the following column are at *ComCST* 184, 104 n. 392.

discretion, between making sure one's own needs are met and meeting the needs of the poor with any excess. Gregory affirmed that the goods of the earth belong to all; no one person ought to control what God had given for the enjoyment and use of all persons. Within that context this quotation argues that our giving to those with needs is a matter of justice and not charity. It is those with excess goods who are in debt, as it were, to the poor. The CST document uses this quotation in further-ance of its goal to explain poverty relief in terms of justice rather than charity. Poverty is a visible expression of injustice in the world, and it is incumbent upon the wealthy to restore justice. The transfer of wealth from the rich to the poor is not optional, it is not a matter of charity.

At *ComCST* 265 and 266 are six patristic source citations, of which five are footnote-only references and one is a reference made in the main text. They all contribute to the one claim made at the beginning of *ComCST* 265, "The Fathers of the Church do not consider work as an 'opus servile' ... but always as an 'opus humanum'."[254] The six patristic citations but-tress supporting arguments for this main point. The first such supporting argument says, "Idleness is harmful to man's being, whereas activity is good for body and soul."[255] To this is attached a footnote reference to John Chrysostom's *Homilies on Acts* 35.3[256] The homily is an examination of Acts 16:13-24. Paul and Silas cast out a demon that enabled a slave girl to earn money for her master by working as a fortune-teller. With the demon gone, the slave's owners were upset at the loss of this revenue stream and promptly dragged Paul and Silas before the local magistrate. Chrysostom lamented the treatment accorded Paul and Silas at the hands of the Roman officials; yet, he juxtaposed their willingness to suffer for Christ with the luxurious living of Christians in his own audience. In the final paragraphs of the homily, that to which the CST document refers, Chrysostom redressed the problem by promoting a life of hard work. A commitment to labor is one way of taming the body's passions, its love for idleness and, by extension, its enjoyment of riches. "Nothing is more miserable than leisure, and nothing is more miserable than idleness," Chrysostom argued.[257] Chrysostom fulfills his duty as an argument from

---

254. *ComCST* 265, 154.

255. *ComCST* 265, 154 and cf. n. 577.

256. PG 60.256-58; no critical edition of this homily exists. ET: H. Browne and G. B. Stevens, "Homilies on the Acts of the Apostles," in *John Chrysostom, Homilies on the Acts of the Apostles and the Epistle to the Romans*, NPNF I.11 (Edinburgh: T. & T. Clark, 1889) 221.

257. John Chrysostom, *Homilies on Acts* 35.3 (PG 60.257; translation is my own): Οὐδὲν σχολῆς μοχθηρότερον, οὐδὲν ἀργίας.

authority in support of the point made here at *ComCST*. However, if *ComCST* had made reference to the entirety of Chrysostom's homily, the reader of the CST document would have been impressed by a broader, theological point. One's commitment to labor is an acknowledgment that Christ did not promise his followers an easy life, Paul and Silas being but two examples.

Immediately following the Chrysostom citation is a footnote of two further patristic sources. They are in support of another corresponding argument, which reads, "Christians are called to work not only to provide themselves with bread, but also ... to give food, drink, clothing, welcome, care and companionship [to their poorer neighbors]."[258] The two patristic sources identified in the associated footnote are Basil of Caesarea's *Longer Rules* Q. 42[259] and Athanasius's *Life of Antony* 3.[260] In the former, Basil argues labor has two ends: both to meet the needs of the poor and, in so doing, to further purification. Basil dismissed the objection that the apostle Paul exhorted people to work in order that they might not be a burden to others (cf. 2 Thess 3:11-12); on the contrary, Basil explained Paul taught such things to those who had grown indolent and idle, not to laborers. In the latter text, Athanasius's *Life of Antony*, one finds something rather different than in Basil's text. Whereas Basil spoke of a laborer's contribution to the poor, Athanasius nowhere speaks of Antony *working* to support the poor. Rather, Antony renounced worldly affairs and sold his goods in order to give the proceeds to the poor. The greater share of his goods that Antony gave to the poor, presumably the less he relied on worldly resources. Yet the sale of one's goods for the benefit of the poor is a one-time event; the CST document, on the other hand, is referring to an ongoing life of work that has as one of its objectives care for the poor. Thus, the reference to Antony seems misplaced. However, I suspect the inclusion of Antony's story is important here not for its exaltation of work, but for its exhortation to give little thought to worldly goods. Such an understanding gives theological depth to what is otherwise a straightforward pastoral exhortation to work for the benefit of others. That is to say, giving away one's goods to the poor fosters a correct view of the human person, a

258. *ComCST* 265, 154 and cf. n. 578.

259. PG 31.1023-27; no critical edition of the text exists. ET: Wagner, *Basil: Ascetical Works*, 317-318.

260. PG 26.846; the critical edition is Athanasius of Alexandria, *Vie d'Antoine*, SC 400, 134-138. ET: Gregg, *Athanasius of Alexandria. The Life of Antony and the Letter to Marcellinus*, 31-32.

being that is himself or herself dependent on another. A worker might be tempted to think that he or she provides for his or her own needs, but the reality is that, just as the poor person relies on the worker for sustenance, so too does the worker rely on God for his or her sustenance. It is God who is the ultimate provider of every physical and spiritual need. The footnote reference to Antony makes this theological point clear; however, the point will be entirely lost on the reader of the CST document who does not take the time to examine carefully this footnote citation.

Following the footnote reference to Basil and Athanasius is a general reference to Ambrose, who supports another corroborating argument to the claim that work is human and not servile. According to the CST document, Ambrose argued in his *Consolation on the Death of Valentinus* 62[261] that "every worker … is the hand of Christ that continues to create and do good."[262] In Ambrose's own text one reads, "for every good laborer is the hand of Christ."[263] He makes this statement at the end of a claim that Valentinian had served the empire justly and his decrees reflected a constancy of spirit. As well, Valentinian was always careful to correct the actions of others, and for this Ambrose writes what he does about laborers. Ambrose praised Valentinian for being an emperor that helped his subjects be good laborers. That Valentinian did so can be attributed to good kingship, and not necessarily to an interest on Valentinian's part to help his subjects see their work as ultimately for the glory of Christ. True, Ambrose praises Valentinian for his interest in religious affairs and even for his interest in receiving Christian baptism (cf. *On Valentinian* 51), but the context here suggests this is a pastoral comment by Ambrose himself. Thus, although the citation of Ambrose does not extend the argument of the CST document, *ComCST* has appealed to Ambrose's authority in faithfully repeating what he believed.

261. PL 16.1438; the critical editions are Ambrose of Milan, *Opera Pars VII*, CCSL 73, 358. ET: Roy J. Deferarri, "Consolation on the Death of Emperor Valentinian," in *Funeral Orations by Saint Gregory Nazianzen and Saint Ambrose*, FOTC 22 (Washington, D.C.: Catholic University of America Press, 1968) 291.
Cf. also Thomas A. Kelly, *Sancti Ambrosii. Liber de consolatione Valentiniani: A Text with a Translation, Introduction and Commentary*, Patristic Studies 58 (Washington, D.C.: Catholic University of America, 1940) 223 with associated commentary on 295-296.
262. *ComCST* 265, 155 and cf. n. 579.
263. Ambrose, *Consolation on the Death of Emperor Valentinian* 62 (ed. Faller, *De obitu Valentiniani*, CSEL 73, 358; transl. Deferrari, *Funeral Orations*, FOTC 22, 291): omnis enim bonus operarius manus Christi est.

The last two patristic citations associated with this discussion of human labor at *ComCST* 265 and 266 are footnote references, one to Irenaeus of Lyon's *Against Heresies* V.32.2[264] and the other to Theodoret of Cyrus' *Concerning Providence* Ors. 5-7.[265] The citation of Irenaeus comes at the end of this sentence in the CST document, "By his work and industriousness, man – who has a share in the divine art and wisdom – makes creation, the cosmos already ordered by the Father, more beautiful."[266] However, a reading of Irenaeus's *Against Heresies* V.32.2 reveals nothing related to human labor or even to the improvement of the created realm. On the contrary, in this section Irenaeus makes it clear the promises made by God to Abraham with regard to a promised land and numerous heirs will be fulfilled in the context of the Church, and that even in the Eschaton (or, the "resurrection of the just"; resurrectione justorum).[267] Only if one reads further in the text, in V.33-35, is it possible to see a connection between the fulfillment of these promises in the Church and the point of the CST document. Irenaeus makes the point that the Church's labor in the Eschaton will consist of building a new Jerusalem, a city in which nature will yield bountiful food, the animals would not kill one another, and where all of creation would be in perfect subjection to humans.[268] At least two points should be made with respect to the CST document's use of this Irenaeus passage. First, its citation of Irenaeus is inadequate to buttress any concern about the role of human labor. Second, it has confused its own context with that of Irenaeus'. The CST document appeals to humans to use their labors for the improvement of creation *as we now know it*. Irenaeus, again reading a broader context than *ComCST* cites, elaborates on what will come of human labors in the creation *as we will know it* in the Eschaton. It remains then to ask why the CST document cites the passage it does

264. PG 7.1210-1211; the critical editions are Irenaeus of Lyon, *Contre les hérésies*, SC 153, 398-404; id., *Adversus haereses*, Fontes Christiani 8.5, 238-240. ET: Roberts and Donaldson, "Against Heresies," in *The Apostolic Fathers with Justin Martyr and Irenaeus*, ANF 1, 561. The English text of *ComCST* incorrectly points the reader to the PL rather than to the PG in this footnote reference to Irenaeus. The Italian text of *ComCST* does not do so.

265. PG 83:625-686; no critical edition exists. ET: Halton, *Theodoret of Cyrus: On Divine Providence*, ACW 49, 59-100.

266. *ComCST* 266, 155.

267. Irenaeus, *A.H.* V.32.2.

268. Cf. esp. Irenaeus, *A.H.* V.33.3-4; 34.4; 35.1. Cf. Hans Boersma, "Irenaeus, Derrida, and Hospitality: On the Eschatological Overcoming of Violence," *Modern Theology* 19 (2003) 163-180, here 172. I have checked also *A.H.* II.32 and IV.32 to ensure there was not an error in the CST document with respect to which book was being cited.

within this context. Of course, it is possible the reference is simply to the wrong text in *Against Heresies*. Short of that, it may be the drafters of *ComCST* wanted to capture an eschatological sense to human labor. That is to say, although human labor contributes to improving the creation in the here and now, this present creation is not the Christian's ultimate home. A Christian person's labor in the present is really an anticipation of the created order yet to come. To the extent labor in the present experience is frustrated by sin or other factors, it is all the better a tutor of what God has prepared for Abraham's heirs.

The citation of Theodoret in the sentence immediately following the citation of Irenaeus is less troublesome. The footnote appears at the end of the CST document's phrase, "He [i.e. man] summons the social and community energies that increase the common good."[269] The CST document cites three of Theodoret's orations in the series, *On Divine Providence*, a selection broad enough to find support for the point being made. The fifth oration explains the tutorial value of the animal kingdom for humans to appreciate the value of being subservient to God.[270] The sixth oration examines the contribution of wealth and of poverty both to an individual's growth in virtue, and to the common good of a society as a whole.[271] The seventh oration, which was cited also in *SRS* 31, argues both that all humans are to be treated equally, and that it is a matter of providential care that God directed the separation of peoples into masters and slaves, rulers and ruled.[272] Altogether, Theodoret's orations contribute to *ComCST* 265 and 266 by extolling human persons' free will, their ability to act in accordance with reason to control the domain about them, and their desire to order life in accordance with an awareness that God is the source of every good thing. To the extent the CST document is correct, that humans use their abilities to increase the common good, then Theodoret has provided a helpful theological

269. *ComCST* 266, 155.

270. Theodoret explained that the reasoning capacity in humans gives them superiority over the animals. He gives a host of examples of how humans have either tamed or otherwise controlled the movements of animals and fish. To the extent humans marvel at or appreciates the contribution of animals to their lives, they may thereby acknowledge the value of being subservient to their own master, God. Also, the danger to humans posed by some members of the animal kingdom ought to check the pride of humans in thinking of themselves as the sovereigns of the universe. This, too, is a way for humans to enter into an appreciation for God.

271. Wealth and the pursuit of wealth are extremely dangerous, in Theodoret's eyes, for they do not encourage reason to reign in the passions. Wealthy people accept little restraints on their materialistic whims. Poverty, on the other hand, is a sure path to purification (cf. *Or.* 6.11).

anthropology to undergird both the source of those abilities and humans' identification of what is truly "good." Equally, Theodoret has provided practical guidance on how that good is achieved in light of an appreciation for the drawbacks of wealth and the benefits of poverty.

Later in this CST document, at *ComCST* 328, a general reference is made to the "Fathers of the Church." In this section, the argument for a universal destination of goods is rehearsed. Christianity frees humanity from, among other things, possessions in this world. The CST document adds that the Church Fathers believed these truths would best penetrate the culture when the focus is on "conversion and transformation of the consciences of believers [rather than on the] social and political structures of their day. They call on those who work in the economic sphere and who possess goods to consider themselves administrators of the goods that God has entrusted to them."[273] This is a rather confusing point, for, in the first sentence, it says the Church Fathers focused their teaching on "believers" while, in the second sentence, it says they focused on "those who work in the economic sphere ..." Which is true? Did the Church Fathers focus on believers or on the economic power brokers? By the late fourth century, it is true some economic and political power brokers were Christians, but it is not clear that this is the time period to which the CST document is referring. If that is the time period to which it is referring, then one wonders if the drafters of this CST document believed the Church Fathers did not address their teaching on this matter to the large number of Christians outside the economic, social, or political elite. In terms of the larger context of *ComCST* 328, this general reference to the "Fathers of the Church" suggests that appeals to conscience are preferred to advocating structural changes in society or in politics, in keeping with the tenor of most other CST documents.[274] Yet, devoid of a more specific time referent, this general reference to the "Fathers of the Church" functions as little more than an appeal to an historical authority to substantiate the document's presupposed position.

At *ComCST* 329 are five of the remaining patristic source citations, each of which contribute to the CST document's examination of the benefits of wealth in the hands of Christians. The patristic sources extend the argument that opens this section of the document, "Riches

272. Cf. above, 115.
273. *ComCST* 328, 187.
274. This latter point is not lost on commentators of the CST documents, in particular Donal Dorr, *Option for the Poor: A Hundred Years of Vatican Social Teaching* (Dublin: Gill and Macmillan, 1983, rev. 1992) 191-192, 210-211, 222-223, 320-321.

fulfil their function of service to man when they are destined to produce benefits for others and for society."[275] In fact, the first patristic citation is included in a footnote at the end of this opening statement. It recalls Hermas' *Shepherd* III.1.[276] The third of Hermas's books is a series of ten parables, and this first laments the wealthy Christian who has used his wealth to buy land and possessions in a "foreign land" (κατοικεῖτε) rather than in his "own city" (πόλις ὑμῶν) to which he as a Christian is destined. In time, according to the parable, this wealthy Christian will be obliged to choose which laws he will follow – those of the foreign city or those of his own, heavenly city. The greater the wealth, the greater will be the difficulty in choosing to leave the foreign city and return to the heavenly city. The point of the parable is not, surprisingly, that the Christian should despise wealth; instead, the Christian should spend his or her wealth on the afflicted, the widows, and the orphans. They are "fields and houses" in the heavenly city and they are the investments that will pay the greatest dividends. "It is much better to purchase the fields, goods, and houses you find in your own city when you return to it. This kind of extravagance is good and makes one glad."[277] Hermas, therefore, furthers the argument of the CST document here with some practical guidance as to what type of service riches may perform.

Immediately following the footnote reference to *Shepherd* is a quotation from Clement of Alexandria's homily, *"What Rich Man will be Saved?"* 13.[278] The Greek text of the quotation from Clement's homily and the English translation found in the CST document follow.

275. *ComCST* 329, 187.
276. PG 2.954; the critical editions are Hermas, *Le pasteur*, ed. Robert Joly, SC 53 (Paris: Éditions du Cerf, 1958) 218; Ehrman, ed., *The Apostolic Fathers, Volume II*, LCL, II.304-308. ET: Cf. also Ehrman, LCL, II.305-309.
277. Hermas, *Shepherd* III.1 (ed. and transl. Ehrman, *The Apostolic Fathers, Volume II*, LCL, II.308-309): πολὺ βέλτιόν ἐστι τοιούτους ἀγροὺς ἀγοράζειν καὶ κτήματα καὶ οἴκους, οὓς εὑρήσεις ἐν τῇ πόλει σου, ὅταν ἐπιδημήσῃς εἰς αὐτήν. Αὕτη ἡ πολυτέλεια καλὴ καὶ ἱλαρά.
278. PG 9.618; the critical edition is Clement of Alexandria, *Stromata: Buch VII und VIII; Excerpta ex Theodoto; Eclogae propheticae; Quis dives salvetur; Fragmente*, ed. Otto Stählin, Ludwig Früchtel, and Ursula Treu, GCS 17 (Berlin: Akademie Verlag, 1970) 167-68. ET: G. W. Butterworth, *Clement of Alexandria. The Exhortation to the Greeks, The Rich Man's Salvation, and the fragment of an address entitled To the Newly Baptized*, LCL (Cambridge, MA: Harvard University Press, 1919, repr. 1982) 295-97. This Loeb edition has reprinted, with minimal changes, the critical edition cited above (cf. Butterworth's introduction, xvii).

What Rich Man will be Saved? 13[279]	*ComCST* 329[280]
τίς γὰρ ἂν κοινωνία καταλείποιτο	How could we ever do good to our neighbor
παρὰ ἀνθρώποις, εἰ μηδεὶς ἔχοι μηδέν;	if none of us possessed anything?

Clement's homily is certainly a supportive voice within *ComCST* 329's context of acknowledging a positive side to Christians having wealth. In paragraph twelve of his homily, the one preceding that which is cited here, Clement chastises those who dispense with all their wealth out of some new-found concern for the philosophical life. Such people, he argues, end up in a worse situation, having to neglect the very thing they aimed to pursue in order to satisfy their physical needs. This tragic situation is then contrasted in paragraph thirteen with the Christian who both possesses wealth and is concerned only for "higher things" (τὴν γνώμην). The mark of such a Christian is his or her willingness to share his or her wealth with the poor and needy. Thus, Clement is not concerned simply about money, as one might infer simply from reading the CST document's quotation of his homily. Instead, Clement balances the possession of wealth against the passion one has for higher things. If the latter exists, there is no need to worry about the presence of the former. This is an important pastoral teaching that the CST document will continue to unfold through its citation of the remaining patristic citations in this section.

To that end, *ComCST* 329 includes next a general reference to John Chrysostom's *21 Homilies "On the Statues"* 2.6-8.[281] The CST document introduces Chrysostom by saying, "In the perspective of St. John Chrysostom, riches belong to some people so that they can gain merit by sharing them with others."[282] As with the other patristic citations in this document, we are provided no literary or historical context for Chrysostom or his homily cited in the CST document's footnote. The homily series of which this one is a part were likely delivered during Lent in 387, and owe their name "On the Statues" to the events that transpired during Lent of

279. PG 9.618.

280. *ComCST* 329, 187 and cf. n. 686. The footnote in the CST document does not supply here the original language of Clement's text as it does for other quotations of patristic sources.

281. PG 49.41-46; no critical edition exists. ET: W. R. W. Stephens, "The Homilies on the Statues, to the People of Antioch," in *John Chrysostom: On the Priesthood; Ascetic Treatises; Select Homilies and Letters; Homilies on the Statues*, NPNF I.9 (Edinburgh: T. & T. Clark, 1889) 350-353. The paragraphs numbered 17-19, 20-22, and 23-25 in the NPNF translation equate to the sections numbered 6, 7, and 8, respectively, in the PG edition.

282. *ComCST* 329, 187.

that year.[283] Emperor Theodosius had levied a new tax; the Antiochenes responded to the tax by rioting and overturning the statues of Theodosius and members of his family in their city. As Lenten sermons, they were not delivered specifically as a response to the riots, but, of course, Chrysostom could not have avoided mention of the riots or their punitive consequences imposed by the imperial army. Like most of the other sermons, this began with a lament for the suffering of the people of Antioch. Yet, in Chrysostom's mind, all Antiochenes were responsible insofar as they did not heed his own earlier calls to tame the fervor of some youths and intervene to prevent the riots in the first place. In the middle of the homily, though, Chrysostom makes an abrupt turn and ceases further discussion about the situation in Antioch (cf. 2.4). Instead, he gives attention to the original purpose for this Lenten sermon, an examination of 1 Timothy 6:17, "As for the rich in this world, charge them not to be haughty, nor to set their hopes on uncertain riches but on God who richly furnishes us with everything to enjoy" (RSV). Chrysostom explained Paul had not said the rich should not be so, but only that the rich should not be haughty (cf. 2.5). This caveat opens the door, then, for Chrysostom to encourage the rich to see their wealth as tools to expand their own relationship with God. One passage in particular is reminiscent of *ComCST*'s reference to Chrysostom in its own text. Chrysostom writes,

> The rich man is not able to say that he enjoys more of the sunbeams than the poor man; he is not able to say that he breathes more plenteous air: but all these are offered alike to all. And wherefore, one may say, is it the greater and more necessary blessings, and those which maintain our life, that God hath made common; but the smaller and less valuable (I speak of money) are not thus common. Why is this? In order that our life might be disciplined, and that we might have training ground for virtue ... Again, if money was also an universal possession, and were offered in the same manner to all, the occasion for almsgiving, and the opportunity for benevolence, would be taken away.[284]

283. Frans van de Paverd, *St. John Chrysostom, The Homilies on the Statues: An Introduction*, Orientalia Christiana Analecta 239 (Rome: Pontificium Institutum Studiorum Orientalium, 1991) xxi. Mary A. Burns, *Saint John Chrysostom's Homilies on the Statues: A Study of their Rhetorical Qualities and Form*, Patristic Studies 22 (Washington D.C.: Catholic University of America Press, 1930) 1-2, suggests the occasion for the sermons was the rioting, not Lent, but van de Paverd has properly shown the reverse is true.

284. John Chrysostom, *Homilies on the Statues* 2.7 (PG 49.43; transl. W. R. W. Stephens, *Homilies on the Statues*, NPNF I.9, 351): Οὐκ ἔστιν εἰπεῖν ὅτι πλείονος ἀπολαύει τῆς ἀκτῖνος ὁ πλούσιος, ἐλάττονος δὲ ὁ πένης· οὐκ ἔστιν εἰπεῖν, ὅτι δαψιλέστερον ἀέρα ἀναπνέει τοῦ πένητος ὁ πλουτῶν· ἀλλὰ πάντα ἴσα καὶ κοινὰ πρόκειται. Τίνος οὖν ἕνεκεν τὰ

In the final analysis, the rhetorical function of this citation of Chrysostom in the CST document is an appeal to an historical authority. However, the reader of the CST document who takes the time to examine Chrysostom's homily will find within it a wealth of exhortations on how a person may both possess riches and be a Christian.

Still another patristic citation at *ComCST* 329 along these lines is a quotation from Basil of Caesarea's *Homily VII* (*Destruam horrea mea*) 5.[285] It is a homily to which *GS* 69 had also referred, and with a similar point in view, that no one is above the obligation to live justly with respect to other humans.[286] The Greek original of Basil's text and the English translation in the CST document are given below.

Homily VII 5[287]	*ComCST* 329[288]
ὥσπερ ποταμῷ μεγάλῳ πολύκαρπον γῆν δι' ὀχετῶν μυρίων ἐπερχομένῳ, οὕτως αὐτοί, τῷ πλούτῳ διδόντες διὰ ποικίλων ὁδῶν εἰς τὰς τῶν πενήτων οἰκίας κατασχίζεσθαι.	A great torrent rushes, in thousands of channels, through the fertile land: thus, by a thousand different paths, make your riches reach the homes of the poor.

ComCST follows its citation of Gregory's text with this clarification, "Wealth, explains Saint Basil, is like water that issues forth from the fountain: the greater the frequency with which it is drawn, the purer it is, while it becomes foul if the fountain remains unused." In keeping with its citation of the three previous patristic sources, it has once again drawn attention to the need for a right attitude towards wealth. For his part, Basil is not as clear in this text as the other patristic citations about the attitude proper to rich persons. The river imagery in his text is buttressed both by insights into the dangers of wealth and by the value such wealth may bring to the poor when it is in the hands of the right person. In the previous section of the homily, Basil chastised the rich for

μὲν μείζονα καὶ ἀναγκαιότερα καὶ τὴν ζωὴν ἡμῶν συνέχοντα κοινὰ πεποίηκεν ὁ Θεὸς, τὰ δὲ ἐλάττονα καὶ εὐτελέστερα οὐκ ἔστι κοινά, τὰ χρήματα λέγω· τίνος οὖν ἕνεκεν; Ἵνα συγκροτῆται ἡμῶν ἡ ζωή, καὶ ἀρετῆς ἔχωμεν σκάμματα. ... πάλιν εἰ καὶ τὰ χρήματα ἦν κοινὰ, καὶ πᾶσιν ὁμοίως προύκειτο, ἐλεημοσύνης ἀνήρητο πρόφασις, καὶ φιλοφροσύνης ἀφορμή.

285. PG 31.271; the critical edition is Basil, *Homélies sur la richesse*, Collection d'études anciennes, 27-29. ET: Janis (Berzins), "Homily on the Words of St. Luke's Gospel: 'I will pull down my barns and build larger ones' and on Avarice," 14.

286. See above, 52.

287. PG 31.272. The CST document, in citing PG 31.271 betrays its reliance on the Latin translation rather than on the Greek text itself. The Greek text for the quotation is on PG 31.272.

288. *ComCST* 329, 187 and cf. n. 688.

their love of gold and for how they let the acquisition of gold blind their eyes to the existence and plight of poor persons (cf. Hom. VII.4). Just prior to the quotation, Basil had charged the wealthy to consider just what good it does to hoard their wealth, for it is unlikely their beneficiaries will treat it with the same care. Far better in this life, then, to spend it wisely, and that means dispensing it to those working for subsistence wages (Gk: πενής). Following the quotation, Basil chastises the rich person with avarice. The rich person is as unfruitful, spiritually, as are his or her own crops after adverse weather conditions. The quotation above from his text, then, is as much a plea for the wealthy to change as it is a critique of their attitudes towards wealth. The CST document has dropped the plea and framed the quotation within a setting of right attitudes towards wealth. The end result is perhaps very much the same, but one misses the hostile context towards wealth that is clearly present in Basil's homily.

The last patristic citation in this series at *ComCST* 329 is a reference to Gregory the Great's *Rules for Pastors* III.21.[289] This is the third time in this study the text has been used, the second within this CST document. This time, however, the point drawn from Gregory's text is slightly different. Whereas, in the earlier citations, Gregory was employed to corroborate a distinction between justice and mercy with respect to the obligation of the rich to give to the poor, here the point is on the larger question of a rich person's attitude towards wealth. Gregory's text is an historical authority, from which *ComCST* draws the conclusion that the rich person is merely "an administrator of what he possesses."[290] Unique among all the patristic citations in *ComCST*, the reference to Gregory is set within a relative, historical context. The text reads, "Gregory the Great will later say..." Following as it does the quotation of the fourth century father, Basil the Great, the reader of the CST document is made aware that Gregory wrote what he did some time later than Basil. (Yet this chronological reference is not indicative of how the patristic citations are arranged in *ComCST* 329, for Chrysostom and Basil are out of sequence). That having been said, Gregory's text does support the argument of *ComCST* 329. Writing, as Gregory did, within an agrarian-based, economic setting, he argued

---

289. PL 77.87; the critical edition is Gregory the Great, *Règle pastorale*, SC 381, 394-400. ET: Davis, *Gregory the Great: Pastoral Care*, ACW 11, 158-162.
290. *ComCST* 329, 187.

that the fruits and crops of the earth belong to all persons for God had given the earth for the good of all. It is insufficient for a wealthy person to reply that he or she did not go out and despoil others; whenever such a person arrogates to himself or herself all that his or her hands have produced, that is sufficient condemnation.[291] To be an administrator of the earth's goods, then, is to be a distributor of even those things to which one had contributed his or her own labor in the process of production. Perhaps if Gregory was writing in our modern, knowledge-based, economic setting, he would have said even knowledge-based products must be shared, since God had given in common to all men the reasoning capacity of the mind. Within such a framework, no product or service may ever be considered "owned," only "administered," by any one person.

Turning now to the last patristic source citation in this CST document, one encounters a quotation of John Chrysostom's *Homily on Perfect Love* 2[292] at *ComCST* 582. This is largely an unknown homily of Chrysostom's, and it is not clear from what source the drafters of this CST document gleaned it. The quotation from the homily concludes this section of the CST document. Set alongside its Greek text in the PG edition, to which the CST document refers, is the quotation from Chrysostom and its *ComCST* context.

On Perfect Love 2[293]	*ComCST* 582[294]
	[T]he Magisterium highly recommends solidarity because it is capable of guaranteeing the common good and fostering integral human development: love "makes one see in [*sic*] neighbour another self."
Ἡ ἀγάπη δείκνυσί σοι τὸν πλησίον ὡς σεαυτόν.	

291. Gregory recalled the parable of the rich man and Lazarus (Luke 16), wherein it is never said of the rich man that he went out of his way to harm Lazarus. The rich man is condemned to eternal torment simply for ignoring the needs of Lazarus.

292. PG 56.281-82; no critical edition or English translation of the text exists. The CST document has cited both paragraphs one and two in Chrysostom's homily, but the quotation is found at the beginning of paragraph two.

A brief article by Sebastian Haidacher, "Quellen der Chrysostomus-Homilie De perfecta caritate (PG 56, 279-290)," *Zeitschrift für katholische Theologie* 19 (1895) 387-389, explains that the homily is a patchwork of material from a variety of Chrysostom's biblical commentaries, with a small chart demonstrating some of these connections. This is not a denial of Chrysostomian authorship; indeed, it is listed among the authentic works in CPG (cf. n. 4556).

293. PG 56.281.

294. *ComCST* 582, 331.

Chrysostom contributes a definition of love to the argument for solidarity. His homily is largely an exposition on the theme of love from a variety of passages in the books of the New Testament. He wove together, among many others, Jesus's teaching that love will be the defining characteristic of his disciples, the Pauline triad of faith, hope, and love, and the testimony in Acts that the earliest Christians shared everything they had in common. Expanding on the Acts reference, Chrysostom asks whether any society that esteems unity and has drawn itself together through mutual agreement can withstand the assault of an enemy.[295] This is as close as Chrysostom will get to the teaching of the CST document, in which love (manifest in solidarity) is preferred to legal frameworks for the proper governance of society. In the end, the CST document has left to the reader an examination of Chrysostom's text for biblical and theological grounding in the meaning of "love."

As a document summarizing CST, the reader of *ComCST* will be pleasantly surprised to find that it is not simply one quotation of earlier documents after another. It is, instead, an interpretive guide to those earlier documents. Equally so, the reader will be delighted that only four of the nineteen patristic source citations are found in earlier documents. *ComCST* has embraced a wider collection of patristic texts than are found in the earlier documents. That having been said, the patristic sources in *ComCST* function in much the same manner as they do in the other CST documents. Only one of the citations is set within any historical, literary, or theological context. The rest are authoritative voices from the past contributing a theological or practical expansion to the main argument of the text. Oftentimes, even these points reflect a narrow reading of the patristic sources' own contexts. There is also little consistency in how the texts are cited. Some quotations give the Latin text in the footnote, others do not. Some citations are to recent, critical editions, but most are to the older PG or PL editions. However, as with the preceding CST documents of this study, this is an invitation for the reader of *ComCST* to examine carefully its historical sources. *ComCST* has opened a broader window into the patristic world for the student of CST.

---

295. Chrysostom, *Homily on Perfect Love* 2 (PG 56.281).

Deus caritas est (2005)[296]

Signed by Pope Benedict Christmas Day in 2005, but promulgated one month later, this encyclical is comprised of two parts. The first is an exposition on the words for "love" in the biblical and Greco-Roman contexts. The second is a consideration of how Christian love may be made manifest through the lives, teachings, and charitable activities of members of the Church. Among the CST documents included in this study, this is one of the shortest. Sixteen patristic source citations populate its forty-two paragraphs. This, combined with the fact patristic sources far outweigh all other historical sources in the document, gives the impression the document's drafters were deeply impressed by patristic arguments. This study bears out such a conclusion.

The first of the patristic sources may be found at *DCE* 7, a general reference to the "Church Fathers." The sentence in which it is found reads, "In the account of Jacob's ladder, the Fathers of the Church saw this inseparable connection between ascending and descending love, between *eros* which seeks God and *agape* which passes on the gift received, symbolized in various ways."[297] A brief review of *Biblia patristica* revealed a number of patristic authors who incorporated some discussion of Genesis 28 into their writings.[298] One wonders to which of

296. During preparation of this study, the annual AAS to include *Deus caritas est* had not yet appeared. Thus, the Latin text of the encyclical and its English translation are taken from the Vatican's web site. For the Latin, see http://www.vatican.va /holy_father/benedict_xvi/encyclicals/documents/hf_ben-xvi_enc_20051225_deus-cari-tas-est_lt.html. For the English, see http://www.vatican.va/holy_father/benedict_xvi/ encyclicals/documents/hf_ben-xvi_enc_ 20051225_deus-caritas-est_en.html

297. *DCE* 7 (www.vatican.va): Viderunt Patres Ecclesiae variis modis figuratam, in Iacob scalae narratione, hanc coniunctionem inseparabilem inter ascensionem et descensionem, inter *eros* qui Deum conquirit et *agape* qui receptum transmittit donum.

298. For the seven volumes of *Biblia patristica* cf. Université des sciences humaines de Strasbourg. Centre d'analyse et de documentation patristiques, *Biblia patristica: index des citations et allusions bibliques dans la littérature patristique. 1: Des origines à Clément d'Alexandrie et Tertullien* (Paris: CNRS, 1975) 84-85; id., *Biblia patristica: index des citations et allusions bibliques dans la littérature patristique. 2: Le troisième siècle (Origène excepté)* (Paris: CNRS, 1977) 92; id., *Biblia patristica: index des citations et allusions bibliques dans la littérature patristique. 3: Origène* (Paris: CNRS, 1980) 54; id., *Biblia patristica: index des citations et allusions bibliques dans la littérature patristique. 4: Eusèbe de Césarée, Cyrille de Jérusalem, Epiphane de Salamine* (Paris: CNRS, 1987) 45-46; id., *Biblia patristica: index des citations et allusions bibliques dans la littérature patristique. 5: Basile de Césarée, Grégoire de Nazianze, Grégoire de Nysse, Amphiloque d'Iconium* (Paris: CNRS, 1991) 149-150; id., *Biblia patristica: index des citations et allusions bibliques dans la littérature patristique. 6: Hilaire de Poitiers, Ambroise de Milan, Ambrosiaster* (Paris: CNRS, 1995) 43; André Pautler, *Biblia patristica: index des citations et allusions bibliques*

these is *DCE* referring. However, *DCE* comes to its readers aid in identifying at least one such source undergirding its interpretation, for two
sentences later it reads, "A particularly striking interpretation of this
vision is presented by Pope Gregory the Great in his *Pastoral Rule*."[299]
This citation of Gregory, though, is to be considered a separate patristic
reference for purposes of this study since *DCE* clearly suggests a plural-
ity of voices with its generic reference to the "Fathers of the Church."
The claim by the CST document is that it understands *eros* and *agape* in
much the same way as did the Early Church. Giving one example is not
sufficient proof for such a claim; the reader is asked simply to trust this
rhetorical turn to historical authorities.

   That having been said, *DCE* 7's treatment of Gregory the Great's
Rules for Pastors II.5 deserves separate consideration.[300] The CST document connects three points in Gregory's treatise to its own arguments
about *caritas*, the first and third points of which are expressed with quotations from Gregory's text, and the second expressed only in summary
form. A first among all the CST documents of this study, the Latin text
for the quotations are given in the body of the English translation of the
document. Equally interesting, the first of the two quotations is introduced by a paraphrase of the quotation itself, and then the quotation is
given only in Latin in the English edition. For both quotations at *DCE*
7, the Latin text of the quotation from Gregory's *Rules* and the Latin
and English texts of the encyclical are given. An examination of the first
quotation follows.

Rules for Pastors II.5[301]	*DCE* 7[302]	*DCE* 7[303]
	Dicit enim ille: in contem-platione radices agere debet pastor bonus. Hoc dumtaxat modo valebit ipse aliorum intra se suscipere necessitates, ita ut ipsius propriae evadant:	[Gregory] tells us that the good pastor must be rooted in contem-plation. Only in this way will he be able to take upon himself the needs of others and make them his own: *per pietatis viscera in se*

---

dans la littérature patristique. 7: Didyme d'Alexandrie, Antiquité romaine et chrétienne
(Paris: CNRS, 2000) 55.

   299. *DCE* 7 (www.vatican.va): Percellit maxime animum interpretatio quam Pon-
tifex Gregorius Magnus sua in *Regula Pastorali* huius facit visionis.

   300. PL 77.32-34; the critical edition is Gregory the Great, *Règle pastorale, Tome I*,
ed. Floribert Rommel, SC 381 (Paris: Éditions du Cerf, 1992) 196-198. ET: Davis, *Gregory the Great. Pastoral Care*, ACW 11, 56-59.

   301. Gregory the Great, *Règle pastorale*, SC 381, 196.

   302. *DCE* 7 from www.vatican.va.

   303. *DCE* 7 from www.vatican.va.

... per pietatis uiscera in se infirmitatem ceterorum transferat, ...	*"Per pietatis viscera in se infirmitatem caeterorum transferat."*	*infirmitatem caeterorum transferat.*

The CST document has cited the critical edition of the patristic text and not the far older PL edition, a rare occurrence among the CST documents. The only differences between the two texts are orthographic. However, the encyclical extracted the quotation from a larger sentence in Gregory's text. For this reason, it is important to examine the context of Gregory's treatise to determine just how his ideas were transmitted into the encyclical. The quotation comes from the opening sentence in *Rules for Pastors* II.5, which reads,

> Let the ruler be [a *sic*] neighbour in compassion to everyone and exalted above all in thought, so that *by the love of his heart he may transfer to himself the infirmities of others*, and by the loftiness of his contemplation transcend even himself in his aspirations for the invisible things. Otherwise, while he has lofty aspirations, he will be disregarding the infirmities of his neighbours, or in accomodating himself to the weak, will cease to seek that which is above.[304]

From a reading of this whole sentence, it is clear the encyclical tried to summarize its contents with its own introductory remarks to the quotation. The encyclical misses, however, the concern on Gregory's part for the consequences of being too heavily invested either in contemplation or in compassion. In brief, Gregory was concerned that pastors not forsake compassion for contemplation or vice versa; there must be a balance. Another point is that the encyclical argued its quotation from Gregory is a consequence of his reading of Jacob's dream recorded in Genesis 28. The fact is, Jacob's dream is but one of four biblical examples to which Gregory turns in support of his point. The others are Paul (the discussion of whom in Gregory is summarized briefly by the CST document),[305] Moses (from the discussion of whom the next quotation in this

---

304. Gregory the Great, *Rules for Pastors* II.5 (ed. Rommel, *Règle pastorale*, SC 381, 196; transl. Davis, *Pastoral Care*, ACW 11, 56): Sit rector singulis compassione proximus, prae cunctis contemplatione suspensus, ut et *per pietatis uiscera in se infirmitatem ceterorum transferat*, et per speculationis altitudinem semetipsum quoque inuisibilia appetendo transcendat, ne aut alta petens proximorum infirma despiciat, aut infirmis proximorum congruens, appetere alta derelinquat.

305. The CST document summarizes Gregory's use of Paul when it says, "Saint Gregory speaks in this context [i.e., the balance between contemplation and compassion] of Saint Paul, who was borne aloft to the most exalted mysteries of God, and hence, having descended once more, he was able to become all things to all men (cf. 2 Cor 12:2-4; 1 Cor 9:22)." Hoc loco se refert sanctus Gregorius ad sanctum Paulum qui sublime

encyclical was taken) and Jesus. With respect to Gregory's inclusion of Jacob's dream, the angels ascending and descending the ladder are examples of good pastors, who are continually showing devotion to God and compassion to humans in need (in this case Jacob). Importantly, the CST document captured Gregory's argument well by explaining his literary context and by situating the discussion within a theological argument about *caritas* that Gregory certainly shares. Since *DCE* has offerred its vision of *caritas* as a practice for all people, Gregory's own concern with pastors situates his text, rhetorically, as but one illustration of this vision. It is a practical extension of what has already been articulated by *DCE*.

Turning now to the second quotation of Gregory's text at *DCE* 7, the relevant Latin texts and the encyclical's English translation follow.

Rules for Pastors II.5[306]	*DCE* 7[307]	*DCE* 7[308]
		Within [the tent] he is borne aloft through contemplation, while without he is completely engaged in helping those who suffer: *intus*
… intus in contemplationem rapitur, foris infirmantium negotiis urgetur.	intus in contemplationem rapitur, foris infirmantium negotiis urgetur.	*in contemplationem rapitur, foris infirmantium negotiis urgetur.*

Here again the CST document has extracted Gregory's language from a larger sentence, which reads, "Moses frequently goes in and out of the Tabernacle; and while within he is caught up in contemplation, outside he devotes himself to the affairs of the weak." As with the first quotation, *DCE* here introduces this quotation with some literary and biblical context so as to explain that it refers to Moses and his goings in and out of the Tabernacle. Gregory followed this recollection of Moses with an exhortation to secular rulers that they, like Moses, ought to turn to the Lord (which is to say, to the pages of scripture) when having to decide on doubtful matters. Like the earlier quotation, this one too functions rhetorically as a practical extension to *DCE*'s argument of the need for a balance between *eros* and *agape*.

Next, a footnote reference to Pseudo-Dionysius' *Divine Names* IV.12-14[309] is at *DCE* 9. The reference comes at the end of this sentence, "God

---

abripitur summa in Dei arcana sicque descendens omnia omnibus fieri potest (cfr *2 Cor* 12, 2-4; *1 Cor* 9, 22).

306. Gregory the Great, *Règle pastorale*, SC 381, 198.
307. *DCE* 7 from www.vatican.va.
308. *DCE* 7 from www.vatican.va.
309. PG 3.709-13; the critical edition is Pseudo-Dionysius Areopagita, *De divinis nominibus*, PTS 33, ed. Beate Regina Suchla (Berlin: Walter de Gruyter, 1990) 157-160.

loves, and his love may certainly be called *eros*, yet it is also totally *agape*."[310] In the footnote, the reader is told that Dionysius identifies God by both of these terms. *DCE* 9 has moved the discussion about *caritas* away from a definition of the terms involved and into a concrete expression of *caritas* in God. Contrary to the idea of a divine power in Aristotle, which was only an object of love and never a giver of it, according to the CST document, "The one God in whom Israel believes ... loves with a personal love."[311] Dionysius, in *Divine Names*, argued very much along the same lines as the CST document. This section of his treatise, IV.12-14, began with an explanation that the terms *yearning* (ἔρωτος) and *loving* (ἀγάπης) are synonymous. It explained that yearning defines the One, the Good; equally so, such yearning is made manifest in the zeal of God for every part of the creation. In response to that yearning, the creation itself yearns to be united to its creator. Dionysius saw in Paul's language at Galatians 2:20 ("It is no longer I who live, but Christ who lives in me," RSV) an example of how this yearning works. "This divine yearning brings ecstasy so that the lover belongs not to self but to the beloved."[312] The love in God and moving out from God to the creation is met by humans with a zeal to love in return. The zeal is so great, in fact, a person might even think he or she has been taken over by another. Dionysius's text functions rhetorically in the CST document as an appeal to an historical authority in defense of *DCE's* view that God is both *eros* and *agape*. Yet this study has shown that the reader of the CST document will find a rich source of practical expression for this love should that reader engage Dionysius's text directly.

We examine next a short quotation from Augustine's *Confessions* III.6.11 at *DCE* 17.[313] The argument about love in the first part of the encyclical draws to a close here with an appraisal of how maturity of *eros* in a human person fundamentally reorders that person's own will. The person obeys God's will not for some pre-moral reaction to the existence

ET: Colm Luibheid, *Dionysius the Areopagite: The Complete Works*, CWS (New York: Paulist Press, 1987) 81-83.

310. *DCE* 9 (www.vatican.va): Ipse amat, et amor hic eius sine dubio veluti *eros* designari potest, qui tamen est etiam et prorsus *agape*.

311. *DCE* 9 (www.vatican.va): unus Deus, in quo Israel credit, personaliter amat.

312. Ps.-Dionysius, *Divine Names* IV.13 (ed. Suchla, *De divinis nominibus*, PTS 33, 158-59; transl. Luibheid, *Complete Works*, CWS, 82): Ἔστι δὲ καὶ ἐκστατικὸς ὁ θεῖος ἔρως οὐκ ἐῶν ἑαυτῶν εἶναι τοὺς ἐραστάς, ἀλλὰ τῶν ἐρωμένων.

313. PL 32.687-88; the critical editions are Augustine of Hippo, *Confessionum libri XIII*, CCSL 27, 32-33; id., *Confessionum libri tredecim*, CSEL 33, 52-53. ET: Chadwick, *Aurelius Augustine. Confessions*, 42-43.

of biblical commandments, but because that will has become the person's own will. "God's will is no longer for me an alien will, … it is now my own will, based on the realization that God is in fact more deeply present to me than I am to myself."[314] The last words of this passage from *DCE*, "more deeply present to me than I am to myself" (*interior intimo meo*), are taken from Augustine's *Confessions*. Surprisingly, only the Latin text for the encyclical indicates this is a quotation from Augustine. All the vernacular translations of the encyclical avoid placing these words within quotation marks, and so the fact that it is a quotation of Augustine would be entirely lost on the readers of these versions alone. In Augustine's text, these words characterize the end of his search for God. He had examined a variety of philosophical and religious schools of thought, but that search was led by his "mind of the flesh." Had he been led by his reasoning capacity, the *imago Dei* within him, it would have led to him to the truth. The truth, as he discovered it, was that God was *interior intimo meo*. Having understood this, Augustine responded with love for God and lament for all the misdirections his life had taken in previous years (cf. III.7.12 to III.12.21). Without a digression into an examination of all the ways a person might be misdirected by other systems of belief or misunderstand the truth of God's presence, the CST document has appropriated Augustine's text into very much the same context. Augustine is a practical illustration of the CST document's claim that the willingness of a human person to align his or her will to that of God is based on the *realization* (*ex experientia*) that God is in fact *interior intimo meo*.

At *DCE* 19 is another quotation of Augustine, this time from his *On the Trinity* VIII.8.12.[315] The quotation opens the second part of the encyclical, whose theme is the working out of charity in the life of the Church, including the lives of its members. The Latin text of the quotation from Augustine's text and from the encyclical, followed by the English translation of the encyclical follow.

---

314. *DCE* 17 (www.vatican.va): Dei voluntas mihi iam non est extraria voluntas … sed mea eadem est voluntas, eo quod ex experientia Deus re vera «interior intimo meo».

315. PL 42.957-59; the critical edition is Augustine of Hippo, *De Trinitate libri XV, Libri I-XIII*, CCSL 50, eds. W. J. Mountain and F. Glorie (Turnhout: Brepols, 1968) 287. ET: Stephen McKenna, *Augustine. On the Trinity, Books 8-15*, Cambridge Texts in the History of Philosophy (Cambridge: Cambridge University Press, 2002) 19-21.

On the Trinity VIII.8.12[316]	*DCE* 19[317]	*DCE* 19[318]
Immo uero uides trinitatem si caritatem uides.	«Immo vero vides Trinitatem, si caritatem vides», scripsit sanctus Augustinus.	'If you see charity, you see the Trinity', wrote Saint Augustine.

Generally, orthographic differences in the transmission of a quotation from one setting to another are not of great concern; here, however, the decision to capitalize [t/T]rinitatem is rather important. The quotation in *DCE* is followed by a summary of the work of each person of the Trinity. It explains that the Father was moved by love when he redeemed man by sending Jesus into the world. Jesus was moved by love when he washed the disciples feet and gave up his life for humans. The Spirit is now the energy that moves us to love God and our fellow humans. Thus, for the CST document, *caritas* is understood by knowing the work of the Trinity. Augustine, by contrast, explained that *caritas* is understood as a *t*rinity, including the lover, the object of love, and the love itself. To Augustine's mind, the trinity of love helps prove his point that God, who is defined as love, can be a trinity of persons. When human persons love and are loved by others, according to Augustine, they have some cognition of what is that trinity of love. In sum, by capitalizing *T*rinitatem, the CST document glossed over the intervening arguments about the *t*rinity of love in Augustine's text and moved straight to the final point: that the *t*rinity of love is one human glimpse into the *T*rinity that is love. Rhetorically, Augustine provides the theological basis for understanding the Trinity that the CST document does want to take the time to explain. The quotation from Augustine allows *DCE* to move beyond this difficult issue and instead to talk about the economy of the Trinity. This is important for defending the Church's responsibility, as Christ's representative on earth, to express God's love to humanity.

Three patristic citations are found at *DCE* 22 in support of the claim that one of the Church's essential activities – indeed, one for which she has gained worldwide renown – is charity. The CST document introduces the citations in saying, "The Church cannot neglect the service of charity any more than she can neglect the Sacraments and the Word. A few references will suffice to demonstrate this."[319] The first of these "few

316. CCSL 50, 287.
317. *DCE* 19 from www.vatican.va.
318. *DCE* 19 from www.vatican.va.
319. *DCE* 22 (www.vatican.va): Ecclesia neglegere non potest caritatis exercitium sicut Sacramenta et Verbum derelinquere nequit. Exempla quaedam sufficiant ad hoc demonstrandum.

references" is Justin Martyr's *Apology, Book I* 67.[320] The CST document paraphrases Justin's text in this way,

> Justin Martyr († c. 155) in speaking of the Christians' celebration of Sunday, also mentions their charitable activity, linked with the Eucharist as such. Those who are able make offerings in accordance with their means, each as he or she wishes; the Bishop in turn makes use of these to support orphans, widows, the sick and those who for other reasons find themselves in need, such as prisoners and foreigners.[321]

Having offered such a lengthy summary of Justin's text, one wonders why the CST document did not just quote the patristic text directly. The reader of the CST document is given a solid understanding of the literary context. As well, the reader is helped further here by the indication that Justin died in the middle of the second century, adding to that literary context some awareness of the historical setting, a period still very early in Christianity's history and one during which Christianity continues outside the political spectrum. Indeed, Justin's *Apology I* is a defense of Christianity in the face of a Roman society that viewed Christianity as a danger to the welfare of the state. Justin's promotion of the charitable activity of Christian people buttresses, therefore, his claim that Christianity rather contributes to the betterment of the state and to the well-being of the state's citizens. Christian charity is not apart from or in spite of the religion's beliefs, but is part and parcel with its praxis.

Following Justin Martyr is a reference to Tertullian's *Apology* 39.7,[322] a text to which two earlier CST documents had referred.[323] *DCE* summarizes Tertullian's contribution to its argument in saying, "The great Christian writer Tertullian († after 220) relates how the pagans were struck by the Christians' concern for the needy of every sort."[324] As with

320. PG 6.429; the critical editions are Justin Martyr, *Apologies*, Études Augustiniennes, 190-92; id., *Apologie pour les Chrétiens*, Paradosis 39, 122; id., *Apologiae pro Christianis*, PTS 38, 129-30. ET: Barnard, *St. Justin Martyr. The First and Second Apologies*, ACW 56, 71-72.

321. *DCE* 22 (www.vatican.va): Iustinus martyr († c. 155) describit, in contextu dominicalis christianorum celebrationis, etiam eorum navitatem caritatis, coniunctam cum ipsa Eucharistia uti tali. Divites stipes suas pro viribus offerunt, quas quisque iudicat; iis ipse Episcopus pupillos et viduas deinde sustentat eosque qui, morbo aliisque causis afflicti, in necessitate versantur, sicut captivos quoque et peregrinos.

322. PL 1.470; the critical editions are Tertullian, *Opera, Pars I*, CCSL 1, 150-53; id., *Apologeticum*, CSEL 69, 91-95. ET: Daly, *Tertullian. Apologetical Works*, FOTC 10, 98-102.

323. *RN* 24 and *EN* 21; see above, 19-20 and 65-66.

324. *DCE* 22 (www.vatican.va): Tertullianus, praeclarus scriptor christianus († post 220), narravit quomodo admirationem gentilium suscitaret sollicitudo christianorum erga omne genus indigentes.

Justin, the reference to Tertullian also includes an historical reference point. The third century was still a time during which Christianity was outside the religious mainstream of the Roman Empire. Tertullian, for his part, wrote this at *Apology* 39.7, "The practice of such a special love [i.e., the voluntary practice of tithing to the Church] brands us in the eyes of some. 'See,' they say, 'how they love one another'; (for *they* hate one another), 'and how ready they are to die for each other'. (They themselves would be more ready to kill each other)."[325] Tertullian couched his defense of Christianity in terms that foist blame back onto the pagans, a tactic left unacknowledged by the summary of his point in *DCE*. Still, rhetorically, *DCE* incorporates Tertullian's text in much the same way as it did Justin's, as a practical illustration of charity at work in the Church.

Finally at *DCE* 22 is a quotation from the preface to Ignatius of Antioch's *Letter to the Romans*.[326] The respective Greek and Latin texts for Ignatius' letter and the Latin and English texts of the encyclical are presented below.

Ad Romanos[327]	*DCE* 22[328]	*DCE* 22[329]
praesidens in charitate	praesidet in caritate	presiding in charity

Ad Romanos
προκαθημένη τῆς ἀγάπης

The quotation is set within this sentence of the CST document, "And when Ignatius of Antioch († c. 107) described the Church of Rome as 'presiding in charity (*agape*)', we may assume that with this definition he also intended in some sense to express her concrete charitable activity."[330] Noteworthy again is the reference to Ignatius's year of

325. Tertullian, *Apology* 39.7 (eds. Dekkers, Borleffs and Willems, *Opera, Pars I*, CCSL 1, 151; transl. Daly, *Apologetical Works*, FOTC 10, 99): Sed eiusmodi uel maxime dilectionis operatio notam nobis inurit penes quosdam. "Vide, inquiunt, ut inuicem se diligant," ipsi enim inuicem oderunt, "et ut pro alterutro mori sint parati," ipsi enim ad occidendum alterutrum paratiores.

326. PG 5.801; the critical edition is Bart Ehrman, ed., *The Apostolic Fathers, Volume I: I Clement, II Clement, Ignatius, Polycarp, Didache*, LCL, I.268. ET: Cf. also Ehrman, LCL, I.269.

327. The Latin and Greek texts in this column are from the PG 5.802 and 801, respectively, per the citation in the *DCE* footnote.

328. *DCE* 22 from www.vatican.va.

329. *DCE* 22 from www.vatican.va.

330. *DCE* 22 (www.vatican.va): Cum Ignatius Antiochenus († c. 107) Ecclesiam Romanam definit illam esse quae «praesidet in caritate (*agape*),» hac definitione existimari ille potest quodammodo etiam veram caritatis navitatem suam significare statuisse.

death, for once again the reader is provided an historical marker for the context in which Ignatius lived. The second century, much like the third, was a time when Christians were a rather small group and did not fit well into the religious landscape of their day. Indeed, Ignatius' letter to the Romans (similar to his letters to other churches) was written specifically as a preparation for his own martyrdom at the hands of the beasts of the theater. Ignatius was on his way to die, and the letter is a request that the Christians in Rome not prevent his martyrdom (cf. *Ep. to the Romans* 5-6). The immediate context of the quotation used in *DCE* is the preface to the letter, in which Ignatius acknowledges the many good things he believes to be true about the Roman Christians. "[To the] church that is presiding in the land of the Romans, worthy of God, worthy of honor, worthy of blessing, worthy of praise, worthy of success, worthy of holiness, and preeminent in love, ..."331 Consequently, *DCE* makes it clear that the quotation it uses from Ignatius is not specifically addressing a particular instance of charity, nor is *DCE* even certain that Ignatius was referring to a pattern of charity for which the Roman church was renown at that time. *DCE* is only suggesting that Ignatius *may* have had such things in mind, and that it will presume, for the sake of its own argument, that he does. Rhetorically, then, *DCE* wants Ignatius to play an illustrative role much as did Tertullian and Justin Martyr; however, this is not appropriate here since, even if we give *DCE* the benefit of any doubt in its presumption, then we are left to wonder just what that practical illustration is. Ignatius, rather, is an argument from authority to support *DCE*'s point that the charity of Christian churches is old as the Church itself.

DCE called upon the previous three patristic citations to extol the Church's charity. In the next paragraph, *DCE* 23, three further patristic citations are called upon to testify to the *diaconia*, one of the earliest structures for organizing the Church's charitable work. The first reference here is a general comment about the development of the *diaconia* in Egypt from the fourth to sixth centuries. Specifically, it is written at *DCE* 23,

> Towards the middle of the fourth century we see the development in Egypt of the "*diaconia*": the institution within each monastery responsible for all works of relief, that is to say, for the service of charity.

---

331. Ignatius, *Ep. to the Romans* Preface (ed. and transl. Ehrman, *Apostolic Fathers, Vol. I*, LCL, I.269): ἥτις καὶ προκάθηται ἐν τόπῳ χωρίου Ῥωμαίων, ἀξιόθεος, ἀξιο-πρεπής, ἀξιομακάριστος, ἀξιέπαινος, ἀξιοεπίτευκτος, ἀξιόαγνος καὶ προκαθημένη τῆς ἀγάπης...

By the sixth century this institution had evolved into a corporation with full juridical standing, which the civil authorities themselves entrusted with part of the grain for public distribution. In Egypt not only each monastery, but each individual Diocese eventually had its own *diaconia*, this institution then developed in both East and West.[332]

No footnote is present to indicate from what sources the drafters of this CST document were aware of these historical facts. This reference may be a nod to Pope John Paul II's visit to Egypt in early 2000. There the pope met with Patriarch Shenouda III and toured Christian sites in Egypt, including St. Catherine's monastery, the traditional site where Moses met with God following the Hebrews' exodus from Egypt (cf. Ex 19-20). Still, the reader is bereft of source material here, and it is understandable why that is the case. The secondary literature on *diaconia* in late antique Egypt is quite small, and what has been written must draw its conclusions from meager evidence. In addition to being a term for that part of the monastery from which goods were distributed, Jean Maspero had concluded from his study of Egyptian papyri and from the discovery of two silver objects that have *diaconia* inscribed thereon that the term *diaconia* referred to the material possessions of the monastery.[333] H.-I. Marrou responded to Maspero's study arguing that to the papyri evidence must be added evidence from patristic literature, including two (passing) comments from the *Sayings of the Desert Fathers (Apophthegmata patrum)* and a passage from John Cassian's *Conferences*.[334] Upon doing so,

332. *DCE* 23 (www.vatican.va): Medio IV saeculo in Aegypto oritur «*diaconia*» uti vocant; singulis in monasteriis ipsa est institutio responsalis pro universo opere assistentiae, nempe pro caritatis ministerio. Ab his primordiis evolvitur in Aegypto usque ad VI saeculum societas quaedam omnimodo iuris potestate praedita, cui civiles auctoritates concredunt etiam partem frumenti pro publica distributione. In Aegypto non solum quodque monasterium, sed etiam omnis dioecesis habuit denique suam *diaconiam* – institutionem quae exinde evolvitur sive in oriente sive in occidente.

333. Jean Maspero, "Sur quelques objets coptes du Musée du Caire," *Annales du Service des antiquités d'Egypte* 10 (1910) 173-174. The papyri were published in J. Maspero, *Papyrus grecs d'époque byzantine*, Catalogue général des antiquités égyptiennes du Musée du Caire, Papyrus grecs d'époque byzantine, 4 volumes (Cairo: IFAO, 1911-1916). The silver objects (perhaps bowls for incense) were excavated from a small monastery in Luxor and are now at the Museum of Cairo. Cf. Josef Strzygowski, *Koptische Kunst*, Catalogue général des antiquités égyptiennes du Musée du Caire (Osnabrück: Zeller, 1904, repr. 1973) 341-344.

334. Henri-Irénée Marrou, "L'origine orientale des diaconies romaines," *Mélanges d'archéologie et d'histoire* 57 (1940) 95-142, here 121-131. Although Marrou is not cited here, his conclusions are affirmed in Ewa Wipszycka, "Diaconia" in *The Coptic Encylopedia*, Vol. 3, ed. Azis S. Atiya (New York: Macmillan, 1991) 895-867. Marrou is cited in A. Kalsbach, "Diakonie," in *Reallexikon für Antike und Christentum, Lieferung 22: Deus internus (Forts.) – Diamant*, ed. Theodor Klauser et al. (Stuttgart: Anton Hiersemann, 1957) 909-917, see esp. 916.

the term *diaconia* in the papyri points not to the material goods of the monastery, but to the goods of the monastery destined for the poor. Excavations at Christian sites in Egypt continue to turn up evidence of these *diaconia*.[335] Thus, it is possible that, in time, even greater clarity as to the role played by *diaconia* in the monasteries of late antique Egypt will be known. In sum, this reference to the *diaconia* in Egypt functions rhetorically as an opportunity for the CST document to offer a vision for organized charity by Christian churches through an examination of the practical experience of such work in the patristic period.

Furthering this rhetoric is the second patristic citation in support of the *diaconia*, this time to Gregory the Great. Here again the CST document includes no footnote making reference to a specific text by Gregory, but it points out that Gregory had "mentioned" the *diaconia* in Naples. In fact, it is in Gregory's letters that reference is made to the *diaconia* in various cities, including Naples.[336] To wit, the CST document here should have cited Gregory's letter, *To John, Praetorian Prefect of Italy*, in which may be found extended discussion of the *diaconia* in Naples.[337] In that letter, Gregory assails the prefect for having diverted

For the *Sayings*, see Elias 3 and John the Persian 2. For the Greek text, see PG 65.184 and 237, respectively. Only the second of these two was also preserved in the late fifth century re-organization of the *Sayings* into thematic chapters (as opposed to the earlier format of organizing the sayings alphabetically by author's name). [On the dating, see Jean-Claude Guy's introductory remarks in *Les Apophthegmes des pères I-IX*, SC 387, 83]. The critical edition for the thematic collection, to which one may turn for John the Persian 2, is *Les Apophthegmes des pères*, SC 387, 318-320. ET: Benedicta Ward, *The Sayings of the Desert Fathers: The Alphabetical Collection* (London: Mowbrays, 1975) 60 and 91-92, respectively.

For Cassian, see *Conferences* XXI.1-9 in which is described Theonas' encounters with John, the distributor of alms to the poor. PL 49.1169-82; the critical edition is John Cassian, *Collationes XXIII*, CSEL 13, ed. Michael Petschenig, with rev. by Gottfried Kreuz (Vienna: Österreichischen Akademie der Wissenschaften, 2004) 573-584. ET: Boniface Ramsey, *John Cassian: The Conferences*, ACW 57 (New York, NY: Newman Press, 1997) 719-727. Ramsey states in his introduction (cf. p. 2) that the edition by Petschenig has been reprinted almost verbatim in Pichery's 1959 edition for the SC series (cf. vol. 64).

335. Georges Descoeudres, "Kirche und Diakonia. Gemeinschaftsräume in den Ermitagen der Qusur el-Izeila," in *Explorations aux Qouçour el-Izeila lors des campagnes 1981, 1982, 1984, 1985, 1986, 1989 et 1990*, Mission Suisse d'archéologie copte de l'université de Genève (EK 8184, tome III), ed. Philippe Bridel et al. (Louvain: Peeters, 1999) 463-517.

336. Francis J. Niederer, "Early Medieval Charity," *Church History* 21 (1952) 285-295, here 286. Marrou, "L'origine orientale des diaconies romaines," 101-102.

337. This letter is number 21 in Register 10 of PL 77.1080-81. It is numbered 8 in Register 10 of the critical editions, including Gregory the Great, *Registrum epistolarum, tome II: Libri VIII-XIV*, ed. Paulus Ewald, MGH (Berlin: Weidmann, 1899) 242; id., *Registrum epistularum libri I-VII*, CCSL 140A, 833-834. No English translation of the letter has been published.

for other purposes the money intended for distribution to the poor through the *diaconia*. According to Marrou, it appears from Gregory's phrase *annonas et consuetudines* in reference to the funds that it was the state, and not Christian tithes, that was the source of these funds for the *diaconia*.[338] Thus, Gregory was aware of a *diaconia* system in the early seventh century that resembles what can often be found in state welfare programs today; governments distribute block grants to local organizations that are trusted with those funds to care for the needs of the poor.

The third patristic citation in *DCE* 23 is a reference to Ambrose's *On the Work of Ministry* II.28.140-143 in which he recorded the account of the martyrdom of St. Lawrence.[339] *SRS* 31 had earlier cited this same text of Ambrose, but without any reference to St. Lawrence.[340] Here, at *DCE* 23, Lawrence is offered as a great example of Christian charity. The CST document situates Lawrence historically by indicating that he died as a martyr in the year 258, that he was a deacon, and that he was responsible for the care of the poor in Rome.

> As the one responsible for the care of the poor in Rome, Lawrence had been given a period of time, after the capture of the Pope and of Lawrence's fellow deacons, to collect the treasures of the Church and hand them over to the civil authorities. He distributed to the poor whatever funds were available and then presented to the authorities the poor themselves as the real treasure of the Church.[341]

Lawrence had defied the orders of either the emperor Valerian or, more likely, of the urban prefect of Rome, P. Cornelius Saecularis.[342] Lawrence's story was a help to Ambrose who himself had recently traded sacred vessels for Christian slaves. Like the CST document, Ambrose held up Lawrence as an example of how God views people as more sacred than the sacred objects used in worship. Arguably, either Lawrence's or Ambrose's

338. Marrou, "L'origine orientale des diaconies romaines," 102.

339. PL 16:139-41; the critical edition is Ambrose, *De officiis*, CCSL 15, 148-149. ET: Davidson, *Ambrose: De officiis, Volume I*, Oxford Early Christian Studies, 347-349.

340. See above, 94-95.

341. *DCE* 23 (www.vatican.va): Ipsi, cui commissa erat cura pauperum Romae, concessum est aliquid temporis, post comprehensionem Summi Pontificis eiusque confratrum, ut thesauros Ecclesiae colligeret eosque civilibus auctoritatibus traderet. Laurentius distribuit liberam pecuniam pauperibus eosque deinde magistratibus exhibuit tamquam verum Ecclesiae thesaurum.

342. For a commentary on this part of Ambrose's text, cf. Ivor Davidson, *De officiis, Volume II: Commentary*, Oxford Early Christian Studies (Oxford: Oxford University Press, 2001) 793. For a discussion of the internal church disputes in response to which Ambrose recalled this story, cf. Richard Finn, *Almsgiving in the Later Roman Empire: Christian Promotion and Practice, 313-450*, Oxford Classical Monographs (Oxford: Oxford University Press, 2006) 63-65.

deed would have supported the general argument in the CST document about charity and compassion for the suffering. Yet *DCE* says just before its recollection of Lawrence that Christian charity had been present from the very beginning *in Rome*. Lawrence's deed, not Ambrose's, fits that context better. Besides, according to *DCE*, even if the historical reliability of the account of Lawrence's deed may be questioned, what is most important is that memory of him continues in the Church's charitable work around the world.[343]

Still another citation in support of the Church's charitable activity is a reference to Julian the Apostate at *DCE* 24. Of course, as the appellation to his name implies, Julian was not a Church Father and so may arguably have been discarded from a study such as this; however, *DCE* cites Julian's *Letter* 84[344] in which, for all his grousing about Christianity, he expressed admiration for its charitable activity. Although a voice outside the Christian realm, Julian's sheds light on the behavior of Christians during the middle of the fourth century. His specific contribution to *DCE* is outlined in the encyclical as follows:

> A mention of the emperor Julian the Apostate († 363) can also show how essential the early Church considered the organized practice of charity ... Upon becoming emperor, Julian decided to restore paganism, ... In one of his letters, he wrote that the sole aspect of Christianity which had impressed him was the Church's charitable activity ... According to him, this was the reason for the popularity of the 'Galileans'. They needed now to imitated and outdone.[345]

343. Cf. end of *DCE* 23.

344. This is *Letter* 22 in Wright's LCL edition. The critical edition is Julian the Apostate, *L'Empereur Julien. Oeuvres Complètes, tome I, 2e partie: Lettres et fragments*, ed. Joseph Bidez (Paris: Les belles lettres, 1924) 144-147. ET: William Cave Wright, *The Works of the Emperor Julian in Three Volumes, Vol. III*, LCL (Cambridge, MA: Harvard University Press, 1923) 67-73.

A check of the source for Julian's text cited by the CST document reveals one immediate problem with the reference. *DCE* cited *Letter* 83, but the proper reference is to *Letter* 84. That *DCE* gave a page reference was helpful in sorting out the confusion. Still another issue is the fact that *DCE* does not indicate an awareness of concerns about the letter's authenticity raised in Peter Van Nuffelen, "Deux fausses lettres de Julien l'Apostat (La lettre aux Juifs, *Ep.* 51 [Wright], et la lettre à Arsacius, *Ep.* 84 [Bidez])," *Vigiliae Christianae* 55 (2002) 131-150. Van Nuffelen argues the letter bears too many inconsistencies with Julian's *Letter* 89, which includes similar reflections on Christian versus pagan charity.

345. *DCE* 24 (www.vatican.va): Ex recordatione Iuliani Apostatae imperatoris († 363) iterum erui potest quam essentialis fuerit apud primorum saeculorum Ecclesiam caritas ordinate exercita ... . Imperator factus, decrevit cultum paganum restaurare, ... In quadam sua epistula scripsit hoc unum christianae religionis, quod eius permovit animum, exercitium fuisse caritatis in Ecclesia ... . "Galilaei" – ita ipse asserebat – hoc modo suam popularem consecuti erant auram. Illi itaque non tantum imitandi, immo etiam superandi erant.

DCE provides valuable historical context both for Julian and for his appeal to the priests that they construct a system of charity comparable to that of the Christians. Julian had earlier blamed the assasinations of his father and other family members on the Christian religion, so it was of little surprise that resurrected the older, pagan Roman religions. The CST document understands here that whatever Julian asked his own priests to do (i.e., they were to foster love of God and neighbor), the Christians must have already been doing them. Rhetorically, then, Julian's testimony is a practical elaboration on the importance of charity to the earliest Christians. Yet, the reader of the CST document who does not also examine Julian's letter will miss a host of the particulars. Indeed, Julian's *Letter* 84, to a priest in Galatia named Arsacius, makes a two-fold attack on the indifference of pagan priests to live in a way that honors the gods. On the personal level, Julian forbade the pagan priests to visit disreputable taverns, and he demanded that their families regularly participate with them in the worship of the gods. Equally important and interesting is that priests were to treat government officials as "private citizens" or "commoners" (ἰδιώτης)[346] when such enter the pagan temples. On the organizational level, Julian demanded that his priests supercede the charity of the Christians. Specfically, he pointed out their "benevolence to strangers, their care for the graves of the dead and the pretended holiness of their lives … I believe that we ought really and truly to practise every one of these virtues."[347] Later, he writes, "For it is disgraceful that, when no Jew ever has to beg, and the impious Galilaeans [his term for Christians] support not only their own poor but ours as well, all men see that people lack aid from us."[348] Julian even encouraged the building of hostels for foreigners and announced that his administration will provide corn and wine to Galatia, one-fifth of which should go to the priests, and four-fifths to the poor. All told, Julian's letter is more than just a testimony to the *importance* of charity

---

346. Cf. LSJ, s.v. ἰδιώτης, p. 819.

347. Julian the Apostate, *Letter* 84 (ed. Bidez, *Oeuvres Complètes, tome I, 2e partie*, 145; transl. Wright, *Works of the Emperor Julian*, LCL, 70): …ἡ περὶ τοὺς ξένους φιλανθρωπία καὶ ἡ περὶ τὰς ταφὰς τῶν νεκρῶν προμήθεια καὶ ἡ πεπλασμένη σεμνότης κατὰ τὸν βίον[.] Ὧν ἕκαστον οἴομαι χρῆναι παρ' ἡμῶν ἀληθῶς ἐπιτηδεύεσθαι.

348. Julian the Apostate, *Letter* 84 (ed. Bidez, *Oeuvres Complètes, tome I, 2e partie*, 145; transl. Wright, *Works of the Emperor Julian*, LCL, 70): Αἰσχρὸν γὰρ εἰ τῶν μὲν Ἰουδαίων οὐδὲ εἷς μεταιτεῖ, τρέφουσι δὲ οἱ δυσσεβεῖς Γαλιλαῖοι πρὸς τοῖς ἑαυτῶν καὶ τοὺς ἡμετέρους, οἱ δὲ ἡμέτεροι τῆς παρ' ἡμῶν ἐπικουρίας ἐνδεεῖς φαίνοιντο.

for the early Christians; it is a testimony to many of their concrete prac-
tices, some of which are attested in writings by the Christians themselves as the references previous to this in *DCE* demonstrate.

The next patristic citation is a quotation from Augustine's *City of God*
IV.4[349] at *DCE* 28. This is the same text to which *PT* 92 had also
referred, though not with the same general theme in mind. Although
PT relied on the Latin text of the PL, here *DCE* turned to the more
recent critical edition. Importantly as well, *DCE* retained the Latin text
for the quotation in its English translation, leaving the English reader
only with its comment introducing the quotation, "Augustine once said,
a State which is not governed according to justice would be just a bunch
of thieves."[350] Below are the Latin texts for the quotation, both from
Augustine and from *DCE*.

City of God IV.4[351]	*DCE* 28[352]
Remota itaque justitia, quid sunt regna, nisi magna latrocinia?	Remota itaque iustitia, quid sunt regna nisi magna latrocinia?

Unlike *PT*'s use of this quotation, *DCE* here retains the word *itaque*
("thus, therefore"). This means Augustine's argument in IV.3 has some
bearing on how this quotation is to be understood. As discussed above,
in IV.3 Augustine argued that good rulers have become good because
they receive from God the good gifts of rulership. The exercise of these
good gifts results in happiness; the exercise of rule by bad rulers (i.e.,
those who do not exercise the good gifts of God) yields injustice. To
connect this context to the quotation from IV.4 used in *DCE*, states led
by bad rulers are little more than bands of robbers. They are discontent
with their own resources and greedy for the goods of others. Assuming,
therefore, that states want to pursue justice, *DCE* 28 follows this quote
with an explanation of what help may be offered to it by the Church.
Whereas it is the responsibility of states to enact laws that protect the
rights and livelihood of their citizens, it is the responsibility of the
Church to help politicians think reasonably through their deliberations
over what is the path to justice in any given situation. Augustine's text

---

349. PL 41:115; the critical editions are Augustine of Hippo, *De civitate Dei, Pars I*,
CSEL 40.1, 166; id., *De civitate Dei, Libri I-X*, CCSL 47, 101. ET: Dyson, *The City of
God Against the Pagans*, Cambridge Texts in the History of Political Thought, 147-148.
350. *DCE* 28 (www.vatican.va): Civitas quae non regitur iustitia, in magnam
latronum manum redigitur, sicut dixit quondam Augustinus.
351. CCL 47, 102.
352. *DCE* 28 (www.vatican.va).

caricatures the unjust state, providing *DCE* with a foil to which its own vision for a just state may be set in contrast. The quotation is little more than a rhetorical ornament, for the Church's contribution to justice and to charity is established by different arguments later in the text.

Another quotation of an Augustine text, this time to his *Sermon LII* 16,[353] may be found at *DCE* 38. Again, the Latin text for the Augustine quotation is supplied in the English edition of the encyclical, but this time there is also an English translation of the quotation following it. Below are the Latin texts for the quotation from Augustine and from the encyclical and the English translation available in the encyclical.

Sermon LII 16[354]	*DCE* 38[355]	*DCE* 38[356]
… non est Deus:	Si comprehendis,	If you understand him,
si comprehendere potuisti	non est Deus	he is not God

The Latin text of Augustine's quote in *DCE* differs quite a bit from the PL text upon which it relied. This is because the quote is taken from two different clauses in Augustine's text, and then *DCE* has reversed their order. The clauses from Augustine from which these words are excerpted and changed read, *Si enim quod vis dicere, si cepisti, non est Deus: si comprehendere potuisti, alius pro Deo comprehendisti.* *DCE* has presented the last three words of the first clause and the first three words of the second clause in reverse order. In addition, *DCE* changed the verbal structure of the second clause; it substituted the complementary infinitive *comprehendere* with a present indicative in the second person. It is not clear what *DCE* gained by making the changes it did. The meaning would be equally clear if it simply quoted the entire second clause. As it is, the quotation of Augustine as presented in *DCE* does not exist in Augustine's text; yet the meaning is unaltered by the changes *DCE* has made. It remains, then, to consider whether or not there are contextual differences between Augustine's text and that of *DCE*.

The CST document has situated the quotation within a context of how to deal with pain and suffering in the world. The Christian response, according to *DCE*, should be one of prayer, during which the Christian asks God both how long will the suffering last and for comfort in the midst of it. "We should continue asking this question in

353. PL 38.360-361. ET: Edmund Hill, *Augustine. Sermones III (51-94)*, WSA, 57.
354. PL 38.360.
355. *DCE* 38 from www.vatican.va.
356. *DCE* 38 from www.vatican.va.

prayerful dialogue before his face: 'Lord, holy and true, how long will it be?' (Rev 6:10)."357 Following this, Augustine's quotation is introduced with these words, "It is Saint Augustine who gives us faith's answer to our sufferings."358 Thus, for the CST document, Augustine's words deflect criticism away from God and direct it instead to an acknowledgment that God is, to a certain extent, unknowable. Sometimes suffering is inexplicable. Indeed, as the CST document later says, "Our protest is not meant to challenge God, or to suggest that error, weakness or indifference can be found in him ... Instead, our crying out is ... the deepest and most radical way of affirming our faith in his sovereign power."359

For Augustine's part, the context could not be more different. Far from any concern about suffering in the world or about pleas to God for intervention in the midst of suffering, Augustine addressed those who believed their own reflections on God had led to some measure of understanding of God's nature. *Sermon LII* is an exposition of the Gospel text on the baptism of Jesus, and this lent itself to an examination of the Christian doctrine of the Trinity.360 Towards the middle of the sermon, in which this quotation is set, Augustine backed away from the details of his exposition and reminded his audience that God is, by nature, unknowable. God is beyond perfect comprehension. "This and that, whatever it is that God is, must be believed with piety."361 The

357. *DCE* 38 (www.vatican.va): Consistere nos oporteat hac cum interrogatione eius ante vultum et orantes colloqui: "Usquequo, Domine, sanctus et verus" (*Apc* 6, 10) cunctaris?

358. *DCE* 38 (www.vatican.va): Sanctus Augustinus ipse nostro huic dolori responsionem fidei praebet.

359. *DCE* 38 (www.vatican.va): Nos interpellantes, Deum lacessere nolumus, neque in eo errorem, debilitatem vel neglegentiam inesse innuere ... . Immo verum est clamorem etiam nostrum ... esse extremum et modum perquam altum ut fidem nostram de eius absoluta potestate confirmemus.

360. Augustine offered a solution to the problem the text presents. At the baptism, the Father is represented by the voice from heaven; the Son is represented by the man Jesus; the Spirit descends on Jesus in the form of the dove. The three persons of the Trinity appear to be doing different, that is to say, *separable* things, and the Nicene-Constantinopolitan creed declares the Father and Son are of the same nature (ὁμοούσιος), thus, *inseparable*. Therefore, Augustine's task was to explain that it is possible for the persons to be engaged in different activities while not being separable in terms of essence. He answered that the actions of any one person at the baptism was the work of all three of them. The exact details of how this can be possible are, admittedly, not made known to us. However, Augustine suggested a variety of corollary examples from the biblical text, including the creation of the universe which, according to Genesis, was the work of God, and according to the New Testament letter to the Colossians, was through the Son.

361. Augustine, *Sermon LII* 15 (PL 38.360): Illud et illud, quidquid est quod Deus est, pie credatur, sancte cogitetur.

quotation used in the CST document is, for Augustine, an important caveat that may be overlooked only to the detriment of one's theological vision. Turning back to the CST document, the quotation functions there also as a caveat. The Christian concerned to understand why God does not move more quickly to requite suffering and pain is reminded that God is not able to be fully understood. Rhetorically, then, Augustine's text is intended as a theological elaboration on this caveat; however, the reader of the CST document alone is left without the valuable context, biblically, that Augustine believed would put such a questioning mind at some ease.

Two final patristic citations are included near the end of this CST document in *DCE* 40. The encyclical draws to a close with a consideration of the charity demonstrated in the lives of particular saints throughout history. The first saint mentioned is Martin of Tours, whose contribution to *DCE* is explained by the events recorded in Sulpicius Severus' *Life of St. Martin* 3.1-3.[362] *DCE* writes,

> [L]et us consider the saints, who exercised charity in an exemplary way. Our thoughts turn especially to Martin of Tours († 397), the soldier who became a monk and a bishop: he is almost like an icon, illustrating the irreplaceable value of the individual testimony to charity. At the gates of Amiens, Martin gave half of his cloak to a poor man: Jesus himself, that night, appeared to him in a dream wearing that cloak, confirming the permanent validity of the Gospel saying: "I was naked and you clothed me ... as you did it to one of the least of these my brethren, you did it to me" (Mt 25:36, 40).[363]

DCE's attention to the historical setting of Martin's life and to the literary context in which this story is set by Severus is now a commonplace for this CST document. The reader is given more information about Martin's life here than what may be found at *ChP* 114, which limited itself to the historical context surrounding Martin's exodus from the military.[364] What is more, *DCE* offers a theological tribute to Martin,

362. PL 20.162; the critical edition is Sulpice Sévère, *Vie de Saint Martin,* SC 133, 256-258. ET: Peebles, *Sulpicius Severus. Writings,* FOTC 7, 106-107.

363. *DCE* 40 (www.vatican.va): Ad caelites denique convertimur ad omnesque a quibus caritas in exemplum est exercitata. Tendit cogitatio nominatim ad Martinum Turonensem († 397), prius militem, deinde monachum atque episcopum: tamquam simulacrum demonstrat ille necessarium momentum testificationis singularis caritatis. Ad urbis enim Ambianensis ianuas dimidiam pallii sui Martinus partem cum paupere homine dividit: noctu vero Iesus ipse in somnis eodem pallio vestitus ei comparet ut perpetuam efficacitatem verbi evangelici confirmet: "Eram ... nudus et operuistis me ... Quamdiu fecistis uni de his fratribus meis minimis, mihi fecistis" (Mt 25:36,40).

364. See above, 87.

suggesting his life is "almost like an icon," and suggesting by this comment that meditation on Martin's life may open up a channel through
which God's grace may be communicated to the one meditating. Turning briefly to Severus' text, the further details provided there shed only
a little more light on the event. Martin had used his sword to cut his
cloak into two pieces; subsequently, he suffered the ridicule of those
bystanders who thought his own appearance amusing wearing only half
a cloak. However, Severus adds a scornful rebuke to those who passed
by the poor man at the city gate prior to Martin's arrival. While some
had laughed at Martin, others" … of saner mind, sighed deeply. When
they, who had more to give, might have clothed the pauper without
making themselves naked, they had done nothing of the sort."³⁶⁵
Severus juxtaposed Martin's actions with the sins those who had abandoned the poor man. As a matter of pastoral care, the juxtaposition is
powerful, for the reader of Severus' text is invited not only to live like
Martin, but also to consider how his or her own life reflects the patterns of thought prevalent in those who abandon the poor. Through
the example of Martin and the other saints whose names are mentioned, the CST document has admirably encouraged its readers to
mimic their lives of charity; the CST document has, however, shied
away from directly condemning those who turn aside from the plight
of the poor.

The second citation in *DCE* 40 is a general reference to Antony and
other monastics in the patristic period. No footnote is supplied directing the reader to a source text. One is left with the comments from
DCE, which read,

> [T]he entire monastic movement, from its origins with Saint
> Anthony the Abbot († 356), expresses an immense service of charity
> towards neighbour. In his encounter "face to face" with the God who
> is Love, the monk senses the impelling need to transforrm his whole
> life into service of neighbour, in addition to God.³⁶⁶

---

365. Severus, *Life of St. Martin* 3.2 (ed. Fontaine, *Vie de Saint Martin*, SC 133, 258;
transl. Peebles, *Writings*, FOTC 7, 107): … quibus erat mens sanior, altius gemere, quod
nihil simile fecissent, cum utique plus habentes uestire pauperem sine sua nuditate
potuissent.

366. *DCE* 40 (www.vatican.va): Praesertim vero totus motus monasticus, iam inde
suis a primis initiis cum sancto Antonio abbate († 356) immensum declarat caritatis
ministerium erga proximum. In ipso congressu "facie ad faciem" illo cum Deo qui Amor
est, necessitatem animadvertit monachus instantem ut totam suam vitam in adiumen-
tum proximi praeter Deum ipsum transformet.

DCE has moved the discourse beyond its earlier focus on the soldier-turned-monk Martin to all monastics in the Church, here acknowledging the monastic movement has its roots in the patristic period. Much as Martin was revered for his care for the poor man in Amiens, so too are all monastics who offer their lives in the service of others and of God. For their selflessness, Antony and the monastics after him are the ideal models of charity. The reader of this CST document may well be left wondering how he or she, if not a monastic, may live as Antony did and as many still do. Yet, *DCE* does not enjoin its reader to the monastic life, but instead to a selfless life of charity towards God and neighbor. Indeed, *DCE* will conclude with adoration for Mary who, not being a monk, nevertheless exemplified the desired charity (made evident by her service to Elizabeth during the last months of her cousin's pregnancy, and by her willingness to be of service to God in the bearing of the Son). The exhortation to mimic the charity of monks is grounded in the behaviors of particular monks; it is not connected to Antony or the origins of monasticism, *per se*. Rhetorically, then, the reference to Antony is ornamental speech, intended to complete the picture of monasticism for the reader's understanding and imagination.

In several important ways, *DCE* represents a new direction in the CST tradition in terms of how it incorporates patristic source citations. *DCE* situated nearly every one of the sixteen citations within an historical context, and most also within their literary context. Not only were the original contexts explained, but so too did *DCE* take pains to explain exactly what is the contribution of each citation to the larger argument of the encyclical. Indeed, the discussion of Julian the Apostate's contribution comprised an entire paragraph. Consequently, more than any other encyclical, the rhetorical function of the patristic sources in *DCE* were classified as offering further practical or theological elaborations on the document's main themes. In fact, it could be argued the encyclical's understanding of the Church's mandate to engage in social charity (both in terms of defining it and practicing it) rests largely on the evidence adduced from the patristic sources. For the reader interested in a *rapprochement* between the Christian past and the Church's ministries in the present, this CST document is a welcome change.

III

Reflection

Summary of the Study's Findings

In the introduction to this study, it was said that each CST document would be treated as a separate, rhetorical *tour de force*. This was done in the course of the preceding analysis of the 110 patristic source citations. It is appropriate now to turn a corner and offer some reflections of a summary nature as to the place of those patristic sources in this body of CST literature. Several points deserve mention in this regard. Each of the points reflects the feeling that, on the whole, the patristic sources were treated rather casually and that they played a minor role in the CST documents.

First, in numerical terms, the patristic sources are hardly noticeable amidst the sea of words that comprise the CST documents. In the introduction to this study, tables one and two quantified the presence of patristic sources; they comprise less than 1% of the text for most documents. The first five documents in this study incorporated a total of eighteen patristic sources, and eight of those were found in one footnote in one document. Only five of the twenty-one CST documents in this study included more than six patristic source citations. Thirteen of the documents have three or fewer patristic citations. Simply put, there is very little recourse to patristic sources in these CST documents. However, as pointed out above, the scene changed dramatically with *DCE*, and so one hopes this portends a different future.

Second, fifteen of the seventeen CST documents that included patristic source citations avoided framing those citations within their historical or literary contexts. Only *ChP* and *DCE* made a conscious effort to do so with the patristic sources in their texts. Beyond those, this study identified historical notations only at source numbers eight and ninety-three. While one might always wish for more contextual data, the fact is *ChP* and *DCE* were careful to include both a reference to the time during which the patristic sources lived and a summary of the literary context in which the citation is found. These are critical pieces of information to help the reader assess the contribution of each patristic source to the wider argument of the CST document. For example, *DCE*'s reference to Julian the Apostate (source number 106) is a powerful testimony to the charity of Christians. Yet, most readers of the CST document probably know very little about this fourth century emperor. The poignancy of Julian's testimony is clear only after *DCE* explained that it comes from a non-Christian and that it is set within a letter urging priests of the pagan cults to be *better* than the Christians. This study regularly identified missed opportunities in the CST documents, for had they provided the relevant contextual data, the contribution of the patristic sources would have been more pronounced.

That having been said, it would be wrong to claim the patristic sources themselves were beholden to the original contexts of the documents, biblical or otherwise, that they had cited. The Church Fathers regularly extracted earlier sources from their own historical, literary, and theological contexts to create new ones. Still, the CST documents emerged in an age that paid greater attention to contextualization. Arguably, readers approach these documents expecting not to be misled by manipulated sources. A modern reader expects the CST documents to more faithfully represent the original contexts of the historical sources to which they turn.

Third, and perhaps as one explanation for the second point, the CST documents often incorporated the patristic sources into a context that did not match their own original context. Across the board, the CST documents restricted the full effect of the patristic sources by either not incorporating the fullness of their arguments or by substantially changing the arguments those patristic sources had made. Among many examples, consider source numbers twenty-seven and twenty-eight, whose ideas about what constitute threats to the Church are supplanted by the CST document's own ideas. Consider as well source numbers thirty-seven and ninety-two, whose condemnations of the wealthy are absent in the CST document in favor of focusing instead on what the wealthy can do to help the poor. Another interesting example is source number sixty-seven. Basil has actually given a good socio-ethical argument about balancing the benefits of labor that would be of benefit in many places in the CST corpus, but *SRS* overlooks the argument entirely and sees instead a concern with the Church's own financial priorities in light of international development goals. A similar problem is also seen in source numbers sixty-eight and sixty-nine. One final example: *ComCST* incorporated a text from Augustine (source number eighty) in support of the point that natural law is a building block to good societies; by contrast,

Augustine argued natural law convicts human persons of sin. Neither in the CST document nor in Augustine's text is a connection made between the value of conviction over sin and the construction of good societies. In short, the CST documents all too often misapply the original contexts of the patristic sources to their own.

Fourth, and related to the previous point, the CST documents often modified quotations of patristic sources in order that those quotations might better fit the new context. Such changes were documented in source numbers 1, 2, 6, 8, 9, 49, 56, 57 and 108. To be fair, the changes rarely altered the meaning of the patristic source, and, in some cases, the changes were honest, scribal errors. In the handful of cases where alteration of the quote did change the meaning (source numbers one and nine, perhaps also forty-nine), it is clear that the CST document did so to match the argument it had already established and was trying to avoid the larger context of the original patristic source.

Fifth, the CST documents rarely included patristic sources that were themselves interested in socio-ethical themes. This concern is a bit more difficult to tease out, for, on the one hand, many patristic sources were employed to undergird theological points (e.g., anthropology, Christology, eschatology, or ecclesiology) which, one could argue, are important to any construction of a socio-ethical argument. That is to say, the CST documents cannot encourage development efforts for the common good if they have not first taken the time to explain that every person has inherent dignity on account of the *imago Dei* within them and that Christ (the God-Man) had come to redeem them. Patristic sources are certainly helpful on these points. On the other hand, far too many of the patristic sources were used for these purposes and not for emphasizing or explaining, to keep the current example, what development for the common good looks like. In a broad sense, any biblical passage or any patristic source citation could be woven into an argument in such a way that makes it appear to be concerned with social ethics. Yet, one wonders how appropriate is, for example, Augustine's statement in *Confessions* I.1, "our hearts are restless until they rest in you" to social ethics. As well, consider Augustine's comments on the need for pastors to lead moral lives in *Sermon XLVI* 1-2 (source number thirty-seven). It is a helpful text for many reasons, but it is not, *per se*, a socio-ethical text. The same could be said for many other patristic source citations in the documents (cf. source numbers 3, 8, 11-18, 20-25, 26, 29, 30, 39, 40-41, 45-48, 49, 50-51, 52, 58, 73, 79, 94 and 99, and all the general references to the "Church Fathers"). These are not patristic texts that are themselves concerned with social ethics. They support theological points or ornament arguments, but they do not give helpful insight into what it means for the Church or its members to promote justice, peace, or economic equality. I suspect one of the main problems here is that drafters of the CST documents are not aware of appropriate patristic texts concerned with socio-ethical themes. The publication in 1967 by R. Sierra Bravo of a compendium of patristic texts on economic and political issues certainly helped the drafters of some CST documents in identifying relevant texts, as this study pointed out at the appropriate places. However, that work is dated, difficult to locate, provides little to no historical and literary context for the texts it includes, and could be expanded into other areas of social concern besides economics and politics.[1] This is a problem to which I will return later in my discussion of a vision for the use of patristic sources in CST documents of the future.

Sixth, and on a somewhat more positive note, an examination of the rhetorical function of each patristic source in the CST documents reveals that, more often than not, the CST documents used the patristic sources for theological or practical extensions of their own arguments. As the reader of the analytical portion of this study was aware, the examination of each patristic source citation included some comment on the rhetorical function of that source within the argument of the CST document. The patristic sources were able to be divided into four rhetorical categories. The first is ornamental speech, which is to say the patristic source did not add to or detract from the argument of the text, but repeated the argument in different words. The second is an appeal to authority. In this case, the patristic citation did not add to or detract from the argument of the the CST document, but was called upon to buttress the argument by showing it was not a new idea. A third rhetorical function is theological elaboration. The patristic citation extends the argument of the CST document by giving a theological defense for it or by drawing out its theological implications (e.g., Augustine's eschatology is operating behind the language of the CST

---

1. Now four decades old is R. Sierra Bravo and Florentino Del Valle (eds.), *Doctrina social y económica de los padres de la Iglesia: Colección general de documentos y textos* (Madrid: Biblioteca Fomento Social, 1967). The Greek and Latin patristic documents in Bravo's collection range in length from one-sentence excerpts to full texts that are searchable with a substantial index. However, besides the fact that it is in Spanish, a search of the major library catalog databases turned up fewer than twenty-five copies in all of continental Europe and across the United States. Second, my review of the book has turned up a number of errors in its references to the original language editions of the patristic sources it includes.

document). The fourth rhetorical category is practical or pastoral elaboration. In this case, the patristic source extends the argument of the
CST document by offering an illustration of its implications or by
explaining what may be expected of a person who agress or disagrees
with it (e.g. what rich people ought to do to care for the poor). The following table summarizes what was identified as the rhetorical function
for each patristic source citation in the preceding analysis.

Table 5: Rhetorical Function of the Patristic Sources in the CST Documents (Sorted by CST Document)

Source No.	CST Text	Patristic Source	Patristic Text	Citation Type	Rhetorical Function[2]
1	RN 19	Gregory the Great	*Homily on the Gospel* 9.7	Q	1
2	RN 24	Tertullian	*Apology* 39	Q	4
3	QA 16	Ambrose	*On the Passing of Satyrus* I.44	Q	1
4	QA 50	"Church Fathers"		R	2
5	MM 119	Gregory the Great	*Homily on the Gospel* 9.7	Q	1
6	MM 214	Augustine	*Confessions* I.1	Q	1
7	MM 235	"Ascetical tradition"		R	2
8	PT 46	John Chrysostom	*Comm. on Rom., Hom. XXIII* 13.1	Q	4
9	PT 92	Augustine	*City of God* 4.4	Q	3
10	PT 165	Augustine	*Sermon LIIIA* 12	Q	4
11	DH 10	Lactantius	*Divine Institutions* V.19	R	2
12	DH 10	Ambrose	*Letter to the Emperor Valentinian* 21	R	2
13	DH 10	Augustine	*Contra Litteras Petiliani* II.83	R	2
14	DH 10	Augustine	*Letter* 23	R	2
15	DH 10	Augustine	*Letter* 34	R	2
16	DH 10	Augustine	*Letter* 35	R	2
17	DH 10	Gregory the Great	*Letter to Virgil and Theodore*	R	2
18	DH 10	Gregory the Great	*Letter to John of Constantinople*	R	2
19	GS 21	Augustine	*Confessions* I.1	Q	1
20	GS 22	Tertullian	*The Resurrection of the Body* 6	F	3

2. This column indicates the rhetorical function for each patristic source citation.
1 = the patristic source citation is an ornament to the main argument of the document;
2 = the patristic source citation is an appeal to authority for the main argument of the
CST text;
3 = the patristic source citation is a further, theological elaboration of the document's
main point;
4 = the patristic source citation is a further, practical elaboration of the document's main
point.

Source No.	CST Text	Patristic Source	Patristic Text	Citation Type	Rhetorical Function
21	GS 22	Council – Const. II	*Canon 7*	F	3
22	GS 22	Council – Const. III		F	3
23	GS 22	Council – Chalcedon		F	3
24	GS 22	Council – Const. III		F	3
25	GS 39	Irenaeus (Lyon)	*Against Heresies* V.36	F	3
26	GS 43	Ambrose	*On Virginity* Ch. 8, Art. 48	F	3
27	GS 44	Justin Martyr	*Dialogue with Trypho* Ch. 110	F	2
28	GS 44	Tertullian	*Apology* 50.13	F	2
29	GS 48	Augustine	*On the Good of Marriage* 2-5, 23-24	F	3
30	GS 57	Irenaeus (Lyon)	*Against Heresies* III.1.2	F	3
31	GS 69	Basil (Caesarea)	*Homily VII* 2	R	4
32	GS 69	Lactantius	*Divine Institutions* V.5	R	4
33	GS 69	Augustine	*On John Ev. Tr.* 50, Art. 6	R	4
34	GS 69	Augustine	*Enarrationes in Psalmos* 147	R	4
35	GS 69	Gregory the Great	*Homily on the Gospel* 20.10-11	R	3, 4
36	GS 69	Gregory the Great	*Rules for Pastors* III.21	R	3
37	PP 23	Ambrose	*On Naboth* 12.53	Q	4
38	PP 23	"Church Fathers"		R	1
39	EN 15	Augustine	*Sermon XLVI, De Pastoribus*, 1-2	F	4
40	EN 16	Cyprian (Carthage)	*On the Unity of the Church* 14	F	2
41	EN 16	Augustine	*Enarrationes in Psalmos* 88, II.14	F	3
42	EN 16	John Chrysostom	*Homily on the Capture of Eutropius* 6	F	2
43	EN 21	Minucius Felix	*Octavius* 19 and 31	F	4
44	EN 21	Tertullian	*Apology* 39	F	4
45	EN 53	Justin Martyr	*Apology, Book I* 46.1-4	Q	2
46	EN 53	Justin Martyr	*Apology, Book II* 7.1-4; 10.1-3; 13.3-4	Q	2
47	EN 53	Clement (Alex.)	*Stromata* I.19.91, 94	Q	2
48	EN 53	Eusebius (Caesarea)	*Preparatio evangelica* I.1	Q	2
49	EN 59	Augustine	*Enarrationes in Psalmos* 44.23	Q	3
50	EN 61	Didache	*Didache* 9.1	R	1
51	EN 61	Gregory the Great	*Homily on the Gospel* 19.1	R	1
52	EN 67	Leo I	*Sermons* 69.3; 70.1-3; 94.3; 95.2	R	2
53	EN 71	John Chrysostom	*Homilies on Genesis* VI.2; VII.1	Q	2
54	Puebla II.1.1	"Church Councils"		R	2
55	Puebla II.2.4	"Church Fathers"		R	2
56	FC 6	Augustine	*City of God* 14.28	Q	3
57	FC 13	Tertullian	*Ad Uxorem* II.8.6-8	Q	4
58	FC 16	John Chrysostom	*On Virginity* 10	Q	1
59	FC 25	Ambrose	*Hexameron* V.7.19	Q	4
60	ChP 81	Augustine	*City of God* 4.15	R	2

Source No.	CST Text	Patristic Source	Patristic Text	Citation Type	Rhetorical Function
61	ChP 112	Justin Martyr	*Dialogue with Trypho* Ch. 110	Q	3
62	ChP 112	Justin Martyr	*First Apology* 14 and 39	F	3
63	ChP 113	Cyprian (Carthage)	*Letter to Cornelius* 60.2	Q	1
64	ChP 114	Sulpicius Severus	*Life of St. Martin* 4.3	Q	1
65	EJA II.34	Cyprian (Carthage)	*On Works and Almsgiving* 25	Q	3
66	EJA II.57	"Church Fathers"		R	2
67	SRS 31	Basil (Caesarea)	*Longer Rules* Q. 37, 1-2	R	4
68	SRS 31	Theodoret (Cyrus)	*Concerning Providence* Or. 7	R	3
69	SRS 31	Augustine	*City of God* 19.17	R	4
70	SRS 31	John Chrysostom	*On the Gospel of St. Matthew* 50.3-4	R	4
71	SRS 31	Ambrose	*On the Work of Ministry* II, 28.136-40	R	4
72	SRS 31	Possidius	*Life of St. Augustine* 24	R	3
73	CA 3	Irenaeus (Lyon)	*Against Heresies* I.10.1 and III.4.1	Q	1
74	SDomingo I.1.9	Epistle to Diognetus	*Epistle to Diognetus* 8	F	4
75	SDomingo II.1.4.3	Council – Const. I	Nicene-Constantinopolitan Creed	R	4
76	ComCST 53	"Church Fathers"		F	2
77	ComCST 87	"Church Fathers"		R	4
78	ComCST 114	Augustine	*Confessions* I.1	Q	1
79	ComCST 135	Gregory (Nyssa)	*Life of Moses* 2.2-3	F	3
80	ComCST 142	Augustine	*Confessions* II.4.9	F	2
81	ComCST 184	Gregory the Great	*Rules for Pastors* III.21	Q	3, 4
82	ComCST 265	John Chrysostom	*Homilies on Acts* 35.3	F	2
83	ComCST 265	Basil (Caesarea)	*Longer Rules* Q. 42	F	2
84	ComCST 265	Athanasius (Alex.)	*Life of St. Antony* 3	F	3
85	ComCST 265	Ambrose	*On the Death of Valentinus* 62	R	2
86	ComCST 266	Irenaeus (Lyon)	*Against Heresies* V.32.2	F	3, 4
87	ComCST 266	Theodoret (Cyrus)	*Concerning Providence* Ors. 5-7	F	3
88	ComCST 328	"Church Fathers"		R	2
89	ComCST 329	Hermas	*The Shepherd* III.1	F	4
90	ComCST 329	Clement (Alex.)	*Homily, Quis dives salvetur* 13	Q	4
91	ComCST 329	John Chrysostom	*21 Homilies "On the Statues"* 2.6-8	R	2
92	ComCST 329	Basil (Caesarea)	*Homily VII* 5	Q	4
93	ComCST 329	Gregory the Great	*Rules for Pastors* III.21	R	2
94	ComCST 582	John Chrysostom	*Homily on Perfect Love* 1.2	Q	3
95	DCE 7	"Church Fathers"		R	2
96	DCE 7	Gregory the Great	*Rules for Pastors* II.5	Q	4
97	DCE 9	Ps. Dionysius	*Divine Names* IV.12-14	F	2
98	DCE 17	Augustine	*Confessions* III.6.11	Q	4
99	DCE 19	Augustine	*On the Trinity* VIII.8.12	Q	3
100	DCE 22	Justin Martyr	*Apology, Book I* 67	R	4

Source No.	CST Text	Patristic Source	Patristic Text	Citation Type	Rhetorical Function
101	DCE 22	Tertullian	*Apology* 39.7	R	4
102	DCE 22	Ignatius of Antioch	*Letter to the Romans*	Q	2
103	DCE 23	4-6th centuries Egypt		R	4
104	DCE 23	Gregory the Great	*Letter to John of Italy*	R	4
105	DCE 23	Ambrose	*On the Work of Ministry* II.28.140-43	R	4
106	DCE 24	Julian the Apostate	*Letter 83*	R	4
107	DCE 28	Augustine	*City of God* 4.4	Q	1
108	DCE 38	Augustine	*Sermon LII* 16	Q	3
109	DCE 40	Sulpicius Severus	*Life of St. Martin* 3.1-3	R	4
110	DCE 40	Antony/Early monastics		R	1

In three cases, the rhetorical function of the patristic source extended the argument of the CST document both in theological and practical ways. This is reflected in the chart by the inclusion of numbers three and four in the rhetorical function column for those three citations. The data in Table 5 has been summarized in the following two tables. The first of these summarizes the number of times the different rhetorical functions are used in accordance with the three citation types (i.e., quotations, references, and footnote-only citations) identified in this study.

Table 6: Frequency of Rhetorical Function according to Citation Category

Rhetorical Function	Quotations	References	Footnote-only	TOTAL
Ornamental (1)	11	4	0	15
Historical Authority (2)	6	20	9	35
Theological (3)	9	4	15	28
Practical/Pastoral (4)	11	18	6	35

This table makes clear that the rhetorical function of a majority of the citations (63 out of 113; 56%) were to extend the argument of the CST document in theological or practical terms. The citations in these categories are evenly split as quotations (20), references (22), and footnotes-only (21). Thus, the CST documentary tradition does not privilege one form of incorporating a patristic text over another in terms of how that patristic text functions rhetorically. Arguably, the footnote-only references will escape the attention of the common reader, and this limits their effect in extending the arguments, a point the analytical portion of this study made clear where such footnote-only references are discussed. Related to this, Table 6 also makes clear that more than half the footnote-only citations are theological elaborations, and most of the theological elaborations of the CST arguments found in patristic sources are relegated to footnote-only citations. Thus, when the CST documents relied on a patristic source to explain their theological arguments, they chose not to do so in the main body of the text. This too was pointed out at various points in the analytical section above. The drafters of the CST documents did not want to take the time to explain the theological thinking behind their arguments in the main body of the text. Perhaps they concluded this would bore the reader, or that it would expose their argument to challenges from theologians and not just from politicians, economic power brokers, ethicists, and the laity.

The second summary table identifies the number of times each rhetorical function is used in the individual CST documents. For example, of the two patristic citations in *RN*, one functions in an ornamental way and the other functions as a practical elaboration of the argument.

Table 7: Frequency of Rhetorical Function according to CST document

CST Document	Ornamental (1)	Historical Authority (2)	Theological (3)	Practical/ Pastoral (4)
RN	1			1
QA	6	1	1	
MM	2	1		
PT			1	2
DH		8		
GS	1	2	11	5
PP	1			1
EN	2	8	2	3
Puebla		2		
FC	1		1	2
ChP	2	1	2	
EJA		1	1	
SRS			2	4
CA	1			
SDomingo				2
ComCST	1	8	6	6
DCE	2	3	2	9
TOTAL	15	35	28	35

In the first five CST documents, almost none of the patristic source citations extend the main arguments with which they are associated. Instead, they functioned as rhetorical ornaments or as appeals to authorities. In fact, with the exception of *GS*, this is the case for the first nine documents in the study. That one finds in *GS* so many patristic citations classified as theological elaborations is not surprising, for seven of these eleven citations are found in Part I of the document, which is its theological vision for the Church's role in the world. Thus, *GS* employed these patristic sources in a manner consistent with its own goals. From *FC* to *DCE*, there appears to have been a general tendency to use the patristic sources to a greater extent for theological or practical extensions of the arguments. This coincides with John Paul II's pontificate, so perhaps one could say this was a time during which greater sensitivity to Christian voices from the past was encouraged. However, such a generalization would have to be founded on a study of many more encyclicals from John Paul II and from additional pastoral letters prepared by the regional bishops' conferences.

With no intention of dismissing the preceding charts or associated analysis, the fact is an examination of the rhetorical function of the patristic source citations does not reveal any particularly interesting patterns or trajectories. Yet, this is a noteworthy point in and of itself. Each document truly is its own rhetorical *tour de force*. The decision to select certain patristic texts and not others, and the decision on how to incorporate those texts was the responsibility of those who drafted the CST documents. Certainly, some drafters looked back at earlier documents to mine them for patristic source material, indications of which were included in the study above where appropriate, but there is no indication they did so with an interest in correcting perceived woes or in following good examples, rhetorically.

A New Vision for CST

The preceding summary of the study data reminds one of this book's title. The patristic sources are, indeed, a forgotten dimension in CST. Their original historical and literary contexts were largely ignored, which had the concomitant effect of limiting appropriation of the fullness of their arguments. Most of the patristic citations do not reflect the socio-ethical concerns of the patristic authors themselves. Even when the patristic citations supported related, theological themes, usually they were relegated to footnotes. Consequently, any vision for the use of patristic sources in future CST documents should incorporate some understanding of what constitutes "fair use."

With that in mind, I suggest three components to a new vision. The first is a commitment to situate patristic source citations within their literary and historical contexts, or at least to acknowledge when the contexts are different. This concern emerges from a presumption that most readers of the CST documents do not know the history of early Christianity, including the names, the places, or the key events that shaped it. Devoid of context, readers may dismiss ancient source citations as quaint. Footnote-only references to patristic sources are particularly troubling in this regard. Relegating quotations or explanations of the patristic sources to footnotes makes sublime their rhetorical effect, and they are of little use to the reader in a pastoral document. Instead, incorporate the author and argument of the patristic source into the main argument of the text, and leave to footnotes only the details pertaining to references for the relevant passages. Again, *DCE* illustrates well this component to a new vision. To a certain extent, this will restrict the freedom of CST documents to use patristic texts in a merely ornamental or authoritative fashion; however, the theological and pastoral proclivities of the patristic texts may re-invigorate CST and give it a powerful, new-found voice.

A second component to this vision is a willingness to broaden the scope of interaction with patristic sources. Simply put, CST documents should emphasize patristic socio-ethical texts as much as or more than they emphasize patristic theological or pastoral texts. As it is, one does not read CST documents and come away impressed that the patristic world, or, for that matter, the medieval world, had much to say on social ethics. As discussed in the above summary, one way of facilitating this broader interaction with patristic texts is the availability of a reference work directing its user to such sources. Indeed, our research center in Leuven has already begun work to create a new compendium of patristic texts on a number of socio-ethical themes. The value of this new compendium will be found as much in its historico-critical analysis of the patristic documents as in its identification of the relevant sources. It is believed this new work will help drafters of future CST documents more readily identify appropriate patristic texts, and to be aware of the important historical and literary contexts surrounding them.

The third component to this vision, and related to the previous one, invites future CST documents to embrace even the imprecatory language directed towards the wealthy and powerful in the patristic texts. At many points in this study, it was noted that CST documents overlooked a patristic author's critique of the wealthy for their culpability in the spread of poverty. The parenetic nature of patristic teaching on social ethics is obscured in such cases. Not unlike the CST documents, many patristic texts on social ethics are pastoral in nature (e.g., homilies or letters). The patristic authors considered it their duty to chastise oppressors of the poor alongside exhortations to the poor. For example, Ambrose's exposition of the biblical story of Naboth's vineyard was not complete until he had identified the "Ahabs" and the "Naboths" in his own day. Ambrose excoriated the wealthy for their pursuit of luxury, their greed, and their discontent. Chrysostom, too, in his second homily in the series, "On the Statues," promoted hard work as a corrective to the opulent and carefree lifestyles of the wealthy. Pointed critiques towards the economic and political power brokers of our own day are missing in the CST documents of this study. In attempting to embrace too wide an audience with their teachings, these pastoral documents are too politically correct to be of much good to the average reader. My own supposition is that the world's audiences today would welcome a voice that says something unnerving and profound. Future CST documents need look no further for Christian examples of such a voice than in patristic socio-ethical texts.

One way of directing the focus of future CST documents towards this end involves a narrative approach to ethics. The Christian story of God's compassion for the poor and marginalized as expressed in various biblical pericopes (i.e., the historical narrative) demands to be told and retold in every generation. That story, when read in light of one's present situation (the present narrative) requires a response: either engage in social action or consciously decide not to do so. The patristic authors often recalled the same biblical pericopes (e.g., Matthew 25, Luke 16) in expositing their vision for Christian social justice (e.g., the poor are the ones truly rich before God; the wealthy are obliged to transfer their excess to the poor; yet, the rich are not specifically denounced for being such, and poverty is accepted as part of the necessary balance between people), and this served to preserve the historical narrative for action in the present narrative of their hearers. The same must be done in Catholic social thought of today.[3] Some have suggested such an approach will contribute (happily)

---

3. For a more full articulation of this vision, see Johan Verstraeten, "Re-Thinking Catholic Social Thought as Tradition," in *Catholic Social Thought: Twilight or Renaissance?*, ed. J. S. Boswell, F. P. McHugh, and J. Verstraeten (Leuven: Peeters, 2000) 59-77.

to a further shift away from a natural law framework[4] and, instead, towards a theological approach in which Christians share in the life of the poor Christ. It is further suggested this shift demands separate documents or arguments for the Church's two audiences (i.e., Christians and "all people of good will"). Perhaps, but particular Christian teachings need not be exclusivist. They may, in fact, help formulate new, universal ways of thinking that future societies will deem "natural."[5] What is said to Christians now may well be of value to "all people of goodwill" in the future.

In sum, the point is not to fill future CST documents with *more* references to patristic sources, but to include within them *better* references to patristic sources. The goal is to protect the freshness of pastoral teaching that is the CST documents and not to burden them with academic footnoting. They should invite the reader into the world of Christianity's past for an understanding of its contribution to the present and future. CST should unsettle its readers and disrupt society's complacent attitude towards social injustices. I believe the world wants to hear from the Church; even more importantly, it wants to see the Church draw from its unique, historical well in support of this agenda.

4. Cf. Charles Curran, *Catholic Social Teaching 1891-Present: A Historical Theological and Ethical Analysis* (Washington D.C.: Georgetown University Press, 2002). Curran points out that, beginning with Vatican II, CST has shifted from a "natural law" approach to an *attempt at* an integrated theological approach. However, he does not believe they have succeeded, in part because of the two-fold audience of Church and "people of good will" to whom the documents are addressed. In fact, the only one addressed to a Church audience only (*Evangelii nuntiandi*) is, in Curran's opinion, the most theologically integrated.

5. Johan Verstraeten, "Catholic Social Thought as Discernment," *Logos* 8 (2005) 94-111, here 103.

Bibliography

1. Primary Sources

Ambrose of Milan. *De Iacob, de Ioseph, de Patriarchis, de fuga saeculi, de inter-pretatione Iob et David, de apologia David, apologia David altera, de Helia et ieiunio, de Nabuthae, de Tobia.* Ed. Carolus Schenkl. CSEL, 32. Vienna: F. Tempsky, 1897.

—. *De obitu Satyri fratris laudation funebris.* Ed. Paulus B. Albers. FP, 15. Bonn: Sumptibus Petri Hanstein, 1921.

—. *De officiis.* Ed. Maurice Testard. CCSL, 15. Turnhout: Brepols, 2000.

—. *De virginitate liber unus.* Ed. Egnatius Cazzaniga. CSLP. Turin: In Aedibus Io. Bapt. Paraviae et Sociorum, 1954.

—. *Opera, Pars VII: Explanatio symboli, de sacramentis, de mysteriis, de paeni-tentia, de excessu fratris, de obitu Valentiniani, de obitu Theodosii.* Ed. Otto Faller. CCSL, 73. Turnhout: Brepols, 1955.

—. *Opera, Pars X: Epistula et Acta, Tome III: Epistularum liber decimus, Epistu-lae extra collectionem, Gesta concilii Aquileiensis.* Ed. Michaela Zelzer. CSEL, 82. Vienna: F. Tempsky, 1982.

—. *Opera, Pars prima qua continentur libri: Exameron, De paradiso, De Cain et Abel, De Noe, De Abraham, De Isaac, De bono mortis.* Ed. Carolus Schenkl. CSEL, 32. Part 1. Vienna: F. Tempsky, 1897.

—. *Ambrosiana scritti varii publicati nel XV centenario della morte di Sant Ambrogio.* Ed. Carolus Schenkl. Milan: L. F. Cogliati, 1897.

Athanasius of Alexandria. *Vie d'Antoine.* Ed. Gerhardus J. M. Bartelink. SC, 400. Paris: Les éditions du Cerf, 1994. Revised 2004.

Augustine of Hippo. *Confessionum libri tredecim.* Ed. Pius Knoll. CSEL, 33. Vienna: F. Tempsky, 1896.

—. *Confessionum libri XIII.* Ed. Lucas Verheijen. CCSL, 27. Turnhout: Brepols, 1990.

—. *De civitate Dei, libri I-X.* Ed. Bernardus Dombart and Alphonsus Kalb. CCSL, 47. Turnhout: Brepols, 1955.

—. *De civitate Dei, Pars I: libri I-XII.* Ed. Emanuel Hoffmann. CSEL, 40. Part 1. Vienna: F. Tempsky, 1899.

—. *De civitate Dei, libri XI-XXII.* Ed. Bernardus Dombart and Alphonsus Kalb. CCSL, 48. Turnhout: Brepols, 1955.

—. *De civitate Dei libri XXII, Vol. II: Libri XIV-XXII.* Ed. Emanuel Hoffmann. CSEL, 40. Part 2. Vienna: F. Tempsky, 1899.

—. *De fide et symbolo, de fide et operibus, de agone christiano, de continentia, de bono coniugali, de sancta virginitate.* Ed. Iosephus Zycha. CSEL, 41. Vienna: F. Tempsky, 1900.

—. *De Trinitate libri XV, Libri I-XIII.* Ed. W. J. Mountain and F. Glorie. CCSL, 50. Turnhout: Brepols, 1968.

—. *Enarrationes in Psalmos 1-50, Pars 2: Enarrationes in Psalmos 34-50.* Ed. Franco Gori and Iuliana Spaccia. CSEL, 103. Part 5. Vienna: Österreichische Akademie der Wissenschaften, 2005.

—. *Enarrationes in Psalmos I-L.* Ed. D. Eligius Dekkers and Johannes Fraipont. CCSL, 38. Turnhout: Brepols, 1956.

—. *Enarrationes in Psalmos 51-100, Pars 5: Enarrationes in Psalmos 141-150.* Ed. Franco Gori and Iuliana Spaccia. CSEL, 95. Part 5. Vienna: Österreichische Akademie der Wissenschaften, 2005.

—. *Enarrationes in Psalmos LI-C.* Ed. Eligius Dekkers and Johannes Fraipont. CCSL, 39. Turnhout: Brepols, 1956.

—. *Enarrationes in Psalmos 101-150, Pars 5: Enarrationes in Psalmos 141-150.* Ed. Franco Gori and Iuliana Spaccia. CSEL, 95. Part 5. Vienna: Österreichische Akademie der Wissenschaften, 2005.

—. *Enarrationes in Psalmos CI-CL.* Ed. Eligius Dekkers and J. Fraipont. CCSL, 40. Turnhout: Brepols, 1956.

—. *Epistulae I-LV.* Ed. Klaus D. Daur. CCSL, 31. Turnhout: Brepols, 2004.

—. *In Iohannis Evangelium, tractatus CXXIV.* Ed. Radbodus Willems. CCSL, 36. Turnhout: Brepols, 1954.

—. *Sancti Augustini sermones post Maurinos reperti. Probatae dumtaxat auctoritatis nunc primum disquisiti, in unum collecti et codicum fide instaurati studio et diligentia.* Ed. Germain Morin. Miscellanea Agostiniana: Testi e studi pubblicati a cura dell'ordine eremitano di S. Agostino nel XV centenario dalla morte del santo dottore, 1. Rome: Tipografia Poliglotta Vaticana, 1930.

—. *Scripta contra Donatistas, Pars II: Contra litteras Petiliani libri tres, Epistula ad Catholicos de secta Donatistarum, Contra Cresconium libri quattuor.* Ed. Michael Petschenig. CSEL, 52. Vienna: F. Tempsky, 1909.

—. *Sermones de Vetere Testamento, id est sermones I-L secundum ordinem Vulgatum insertis etiam novem sermonibus post Maurinos repertis.* Ed. Cyril Lambot. CCSL, 41. Turnhout: Brepols, 1961.

Basil of Caesarea. *Homélies sur la richesse.* Ed. and transl. Yves Courtonne. Collection d'études anciennes. Paris: Firm-Didot, 1935.

—. *Homilien zum Hexaemeron.* Ed. Emmanuel Amand de Mendieta. GCS, 2. Berlin: Akademie Verlag, 1997.

Vita di Cipriano, Vita di Ambrogio, Vita di Agostino. Ed. Anthony A. R. Bastiaensen. Scritti greci e latini: Vite dei santi, 3. Milan: Fondazione Lorenzo Valla, 1997.

Bihlmeyer, Karl. *Die Apostolischen Väter.* Sammlung ausgewählter kirchen- und dogmengeschichtlicher Quellenschriften. Tübingen: J. C. B. Mohr, 1924.

Clement of Alexandria. *Les Stromates: Stromata I.* Ed. Marcel Caster. SC, 30. Paris: Éditions du Cerf, 1951.

—. *Stromata: Buch I-VI.* Ed. Otto Stahlin and Ludwig Fruchtel. GCS, 52. Berlin: Akademie Verlag, 1985.

—. *Stromata: Buch VII und VIII; Excerpta ex Theodoto; Eclogae propheticae; Quis dives salvetur; Fragmente.* Ed. Otto Stählin, Ludwig Früchtel, and Ursula Treu. GCS, 17. Berlin: Akademie Verlag, 1970.

Conference of Latin American Bishops. *Puebla and Beyond: Documentation and Commentary.* Ed. John Eagleson and Philip Scharper, transl. John Drury. Maryknoll, NY: Orbis Books, 1980.

—. *Santo Domingo and Beyond: Documents and Commentaries from the Historic Meeting of the Latin American Bishops' Conference*. Ed. Alfred T. Hennelly. Maryknoll, NY: Orbis Books, 1993.

Cyprian of Carthage. *Ad Quirinum, Ad Fortunatum, De lapsis, De ecclesiae catholicae unitate*. Ed. Maurice Bévenot. CCSL, 3. Part 1. Turnhout: Brepols, 1972.

—. *Epistularium*. Ed. G. F. Diercks. CCSL, 3B. Part 3. Turnhout: Brepols, 1996.

—. *La bienfaisance et les aumônes*. Ed. Michel Poirier. SC, 440. Paris: Éditions du Cerf, 1999.

Denzinger, Heinrich and Hünermann, Peter, eds. *Enchiridion symbolorum, definitionem et declarationum de rebus fidei et morum*. Thirty-first edition. Bologna: Dehoniana, 2001.

Eusebius of Caesarea. *Die Praeparatio Evangelica: Einleitung, die Bücher I bis X*. Ed. Édouard des Places. GCS, 43. Band 2. Berlin: Akademie Verlag, 1982.

—. *La préparation évangélique, Livre I*. Ed. Jean Sirinelli. SC, 206. Paris: Éditions du Cerf, 1974.

Gregory the Great. *Homiliae in evangelia*. Ed. Raymond Étaix. CCSL, 141. Turnhout: Brepols, 1999.

—. *Homiliae in evangelia*. Ed. and transl. Michael Fiedrowicz. Fontes Christiani, 28. Part 1. Freiburg: Herder, 1997.

—. *Registre des lettres, Livres I et II*. Ed. Pierre Minard. SC, 370. Paris: Éditions du Cerf, 1991.

—. *Registrum epistolarum, tome II: Libri VIII-XIV*. Ed. Paulus Ewald. MGH. Berlin: Weidmann, 1899.

—. *Registrum epistularum libri I-VII*. Ed. Dag Norberg. CCSL, 140. Turnhout: Brepols, 1982.

—. *Règle pastorale, Tome I*. Ed. Floribert Rommel, transl. Charles Morel. SC, 381. Paris: Éditions du Cerf, 1992.

—. *Règle pastorale, Tome II*. Ed. Floribert Rommel, transl. Charles Morel. SC, 382. Paris: Éditions du Cerf, 1992.

Gregory Nazianzen. *Discours 38-41*. Ed. Claudio Moreschini, transl. Paul Gallay. SC, 358. Paris: Éditions du Cerf, 1990.

Gregory of Nyssa. *De vita Moysis*. Ed. Herbertus Musurillo. Gregorii Nysseni Opera, 7. Part 1. Leiden: E. J. Brill, 1964.

Hermas. *Le pasteur*. Ed. Robert Joly. SC, 53. Paris: Éditions du Cerf, 1958.

Irenaeus of Lyon. *Adversus haereses*. Ed. Norbert Brox. Fontes Christiani, 8. Part 3. Freiburg: Herder, 1995.

—. *Adversus haereses*. Ed. Norbert Brox. Fontes Christiani, 8. Part 5. Freiburg: Herder, 2001.

—, *Contre les hérésies*. Ed. Adelin Rousseau. SC, 153. Paris: Éditions du Cerf, 1969.

—. *Contre les hérésies, Livre I*. Ed. Adelin Rousseau and Louis Doutreleau. SC, 264. Paris: Éditions du Cerf, 1979.

—. *Contre les hérésies, Livre III*. Ed. Adelin Rousseau and Louis Doutreleau. SC, 211. Paris: Éditions du Cerf, 1974.

—. *Epideixis Adversus Haereses*. Ed. Norbert Brox. Fontes Christiani, 8. Part 1. Freiburg: Herder, 1993.

John Cassian. *Collationes XXIII*. Ed. Michael Petschenig. Rev. Gottfried Kreuz. CSEL, 13. Vienna: Österreichische Akademie der Wissenschaften, 2004.

John Chrysostom. *La virginité*. Ed. Herbert Musurillo. SC, 125. Paris: Éditions du Cerf, 1966.

—. *Sermons sur la Genèse*. Ed. Laurence Brottier. SC, 433. Paris: Éditions du Cerf, 1998.

John Paul II. "L'homme et la révolution urbaine: Citadins et ruraux devant l'urbanisation." *La Documentation Catholique* 62 (1-15 August, 1965): 1363-1366.

Julian the Apostate. *Oeuvres Complètes, tome I, 2e partie: Lettres et fragments*. Ed. Joseph Bidez. Paris: Les belles lettres, 1924.

Justin Martyr. *Apologie pour les Chrétiens*. Ed. Charles Munier. Paradosis: Études de littérature et de théologie anciennes. Fribourg, Switzerland: Éditions Universitaires, 1995.

—. *Apologiae pro Christianis*. Ed. Miroslav Marcovich. PTS, 38. Berlin: Walter de Gruyter, 1994.

—. *Dialogus cum Tryphone*. Ed. Miroslav Marcovich. PTS, 47. Berlin: Walter de Gruyter, 1997.

—. *Opera quae feruntur omnia, Tomi I Pars I: Opera Iustini indubitata*. Ed. Johan Karl Theodor von Otto. Corpus Apologeticorum Christianorum saeculi secundi. Jena: Fischer, 1876.

Lactantius. *Institutions divines*. Ed. Pierre Monat. SC, 204. Paris: Éditions du Cerf, 1973.

—. *Opera omnia, Pars I: Divinae institutiones et epitome divinarum institutionum*. Ed. Samuel Brandt. CSEL, 19. Prague: F. Tempsky, 1890.

Leo I. *Sermons, Tome IV*. Ed. René Dolle. SC, 200. Paris: Éditions du Cerf, 1973.

—. *Tractatus septem et nonaginta*. Ed. Antoine Chavasse. CCSL, 138 and 138A. Turnhout: Brepols, 1973.

Leo XIII. *L'Enciclica Rerum novarum: Testo autentico e redazioni preparatorie dai documenti originali*. Ed. Giovanni Antonazzi. Rome: Storia e letteratura, 1957.

Minucius Felix. *Octavius*. Ed. Michael Pellegrino. CSLP. Turin: G. B. Paravia and Co., 1972.

Pseudo-Dionysius Areopagita. *De divinis nominibus*. Ed. Beate Regina Suchla. PTS, 33. Berlin: Walter de Gruyter, 1990.

Sulpicius Severus. *Vie de Saint Martin, Tome I*. Ed. Jacques Fontaine. SC, 133. Paris: Éditions du Cerf, 1967.

Tanner, Norman P., ed. *Decrees of the Ecumenical Councils*. 2 Vols. Washington D.C.: Georgetown University Press, 1990.

Tertullian. *À son épouse*. Ed. Charles Munier. SC, 273. Paris: Éditions du Cerf, 1980.

—. *Apologeticum*. Ed. Heinrich Hoppe. CSEL, 69. Vienna: F. Tempsky, 1939.

—. *Opera, Pars I: Opera Catholica, Adversus Marcionem*. Ed. Eligius Dekkers, Janus G. P. Borleffs and R. Willems. CCSL, 1. Turnhout: Brepols, 1954.

—. *Opera, Pars II: Opera monastica*. Ed. Aloïs Gerlo. CCSL, 2. Turnhout: Brepols, 1954.

—. *Opera, Pars III*. Ed. Aemilii Kroymann. CSEL, 47. Vienna: F. Tempsky, 1906.

2. Translations

Abbott, Walter M., ed. *The Documents of Vatican II*. New York, NY: The America Press, 1966.

Ambrose of Milan. "Consolation on the Death of Emperor Valentinian." In *Funeral Orations by Saint Gregory Nazianzen and Saint Ambrose*. Transl. Roy J. Deferarri. FOTC, 22. Washington, D.C.: Catholic University of America Press, 1968.

—. *De officiis, Volume I: Introduction, Text, and Translation*. Transl. Ivor J. Davidson. Oxford Early Christian Studies. Oxford: Oxford University Press, 2001.

—. *Hexameron, Paradise, and Cain and Abel*. Transl. John J. Savage. FOTC, 42. New York, NY: Fathers of the Church, 1961.

—. "In Honor of His Brother Satyrus." In *Funeral Orations by Saint Gregory Nazianzen and Saint Ambrose*. Transl. John J. Sullivan and Martin R. P. McGuire. FOTC, 22. Washington, D.C.: Catholic University of America Press, 1953.

—. *Letters*. Transl. Mary Melchior Beyenka. FOTC, 26. Washington, D.C.: Catholic University of America Press, 1954.

—. *On Virginity*. Transl. Daniel Callam. Peregrina Translations Series, 7. Toronto: Peregrina Publishing Co., 1980.

Athanasius of Alexandria. *The Life of Antony and the Letter to Marcellinus*. Transl. Robert C. Gregg. CWS. New York, NY: Paulist Press, 1980.

Augustine of Hippo. "Answer to the Letters of Petilian, Bishop of Cirta." In *The Writings Against the Manichaeans and Against the Donatists*. Transl. J. R. King. NPNF. First Series, 4. Edinburgh: T. & T. Clark, 1887.

—. *Confessions*. Transl. Henry Chadwick. Oxford: Oxford University Press, 1991.

—. *De bono coniugali, De sancta virginitate*. Transl. P. G. Walsh. Oxford Early Christian Texts. Oxford: Clarendon Press, 2001.

—. *Expositions of the Psalms (Enarrationes in Psalmos) 33-50*. Transl. Maria Boulding. WSA, 16. New York, NY: New City Press, 2000.

—. *Expositions of the Psalms (Enarrationes in Psalmos) 73-98*. Transl. Maria Boulding. WSA, 18. New York, NY: New City Press, 2004.

—. *Expositions of the Psalms (Enarrationes in Psalmos) 121-150*. Transl. Maria Boulding. WSA, 20. New York, NY: New City Press, 2004.

—. *Letters 1-82*. Transl. Wilfrid Parsons. FOTC, 12. Washington, D.C.: Catholic University of America Press, 1951.

—. *Letters 1-99*. Transl. Roland Teske. WSA, 2. Part 1. New York, NY: Newman Press, 2001.

—. *On the Trinity, Books 8-15*. Transl. Stephen McKenna. Cambridge Texts in the History of Philosophy. Cambridge: Cambridge University Press, 2002.

—. *Sermones II (20-50) on the Old Testament*. Transl. Edmund Hill. WSA. Part III, II. Brooklyn, NY: New City Press, 1990.

—. *Sermones III (51-94) on the New Testament*. Transl. Edmund Hill. WSA. Brooklyn, NY: New City Press, 1991.

—. *The City of God Against the Pagans*. Transl. R. W. Dyson. Cambridge Texts in the History of Political Thought. Cambridge: Cambridge University Press, 1998.

—. *Tractates on the Gospel of John, 28-54.* Transl. John W. Rettig. FOTC, 88. Washington D.C.: Catholic University of America Press, 1993.

Basil. *Ascetical Works.* Transl. M. Monica Wagner. FOTC, 9. Washington, D.C.: Catholic University of America Press, 1950.

Bravo, R. Sierra and Florentino Del Valle, eds. *Doctrina social y económica de los padres de la Iglesia: Colección general de documentos y textos.* Madrid: Biblioteca Fomento Social, 1967.

Clement of Alexandria. *Stromateis: Books One to Three.* Transl. John Ferguson. FOTC, 85. Washington, D.C.: Catholic University of America Press, 1991.

—. *The Exhortation to the Greeks, The Rich Man's Salvation, and the fragment of an address entitled To the Newly Baptized.* Transl. G. W. Butterworth. LCL. Cambridge, MA: Harvard University Press, 1919.

Cyprian of Carthage. *De Lapsis and De Ecclesiae Catholicae Unitate.* Transl. Maurice Bévenot. Oxford Early Christian Texts. Oxford: Clarendon Press, 1971.

—. *Letters (1-81).* Transl. Rose B. Donna. FOTC, 51. Washington, D.C.: Catholic University of America Press, 1964.

—. *The Letters of St. Cyprian of Carthage: Volume III, Letters 55-66.* Transl. G. W. Clarke. ACW, 46. New York, NY: Newman Press, 1986.

—. *Treatises.* Transl. Roy J. Deferarri. FOTC, 36. Washington, D.C.: Catholic University of America Press, 1958.

Dionysius the Areopagite. *The Complete Works.* Transl. Colm Luibheid. CWS. New York, NY: Paulist Press, 1987.

Ehrman, Bart, ed., *The Apostolic Fathers, Volume I: I Clement, II Clement, Ignatius, Polycarp, Didache.* LCL. Cambridge, MA: Harvard University Press, 2003.

—. *The Apostolic Fathers, Volume II: Epistle of Barnabas, Papias and Quadratus, Epistle to Diognetus, The Shepherd of Hermas.* LCL. Cambridge, MA: Harvard University Press, 2003.

Eusebius of Caesarea. *Eusebii Pamphili Evangelicae praeparationis Libri XV. Ad codices manuscriptos denuo collatos recensuit Anglice nunc primum reddidit notis et indicibus instruxit.* Four volumes. Transl. Edwin H. Gifford. Oxford: Typographeo Academico, 1903.

Gregory of Nyssa. *The Life of Moses.* Transl. A. J. Malherbe and Everett Ferguson. CWS. New York, NY: Paulist Press, 1978.

Gregory the Great. *Forty Gospel Homilies.* Transl. David Hurst. Cistercian Studies Series, 123. Kalamazoo, MI: Cistercian Publications, 1990.

—. *Pastoral Care.* Transl. Henry Davis. ACW, 11. Westminster, MD: The Newman Press, 1950.

—. "The Book of Pastoral Rule and Selected Epistles." In *Leo the Great. Gregory the Great.* Transl. James Barmby. NPNF. Second Series, 12. Edinburgh: T. & T. Clark, 1895.

Irenaeus of Lyon. "Against Heresies." In *The Apostolic Fathers with Justin Martyr and Irenaeus.* Transl. Alexander Roberts and James Donaldson. ANF, 1. Edinburgh: T. & T. Clark, 1867.

—. *Against the Heresies, Book 1.* Transl. Dominic J. Unger and John J. Dillon. ACW, 55. Mahwah, NJ: Paulist Press, 1992.

Janis (Berzins), Hieroschemamonk. "Homily on the Words of St. Luke's Gospel: 'I will pull down my barns and build larger ones' and on Avarice." *Orthodox Life* 42 (1992): 10-17.

John Cassian. *The Conferences*. Transl. Boniface Ramsey. ACW, 57. New York, NY: Newman Press, 1997.

John Chrysostom. "Homilies on the Acts of the Apostles." In *John Chrysostom. Homilies on the Acts of the Apostles and the Epistle to the Romans*. Transl. H. Browne and G. B. Stevens. NPNF. First series, 11. Edinburgh: T. & T. Clark, 1889.

—. *Homilies on the Gospel of Saint Matthew*. Transl. George Prevost. NPNF. First series, 10. Grand Rapids, MI: William B. Eerdmans, 1991.

—. "Homilies on the Statues, to the People of Antioch." In *John Chrysostom. On the Priesthood; Ascetic Treatises; Select Homilies and Letters; Homilies on the Statues*. Transl. W. R. W. Stephens. NPNF. First series, 9. Edinburgh: T. & T. Clark, 1889.

—. *On Virginity, Against Remarriage*. Transl. Sally Rieger Shore. Studies in Women and Religion, 9. New York, NY: Mellen Press, 1983.

—. "The Homilies on the Epistle of St. Paul to the Romans." In *Saint Chrysostom: Homilies on the Acts of the Apostles and The Epistle to the Romans*. Transl. J. B. Morris and W. H. Simcox. NPNF. First series, 11. Edinburgh: T&T Clark, 1877.

—. "Two Homilies on Eutropius." In *John Chrysostom. On the Priesthood; Ascetic Treatises; Select Homilies and Letters; Homilies on the Statues*. Transl. W. R. W. Stephens. NPNF. First series, 9. Edinburgh: T. & T. Clark, 1889.

Julian the Apostate. *The Works of the Emperor Julian in Three Volumes, Vol. III*. Transl. William Cave Wright. LCL. Cambridge, MA: Harvard University Press, 1923.

Justin Martyr. *The First and Second Apologies*. Transl. Leslie William Barnard. ACW, 56. Mahwah, NJ: Paulist Press, 1997.

—. *The First Apology; The Second Apology; Dialogue with Trypho; Exhortation to the Greeks; Discourse to the Greeks; The Monarchy or the Rule of God*. Transl. Thomas B. Falls. FOTC, 6. Washington, D.C.: Catholic University of America Press, 1977.

Kelly, Thomas A. *Sancti Ambrosii Liber de consolatione Valentiniani: A Text with a Translation, Introduction and Commentary*. Patristic Studies, 58. Washington, D.C.: Catholic University of America, 1940.

Lactantius. *Divine Institutes*. Transl. Anthony Bowen and Peter Garnsey. Translated Texts for Historians, 40. Liverpool: Liverpool University Press, 2003.

Leo the Great. *Sermons*. Transl. Jane P. Freeland and Agnes J. Conway. FOTC, 93. Washington, D.C.: Catholic University of America Press, 1996.

McGuire, Martin R. P. *S. Ambrosii De Nabuthae: A Commentary, with an Introduction and Translation*. Patristic Studies, 15. Washington, D.C.: Catholic University of America Press, 1927.

Minucius Felix. *Octavius*. Transl. Rudolph Arbesmann. FOTC, 10. Washington, D.C.: Catholic University of America Press, 1950.

—. *The Octavius*. Transl. G. W. Clarke. ACW, 39. New York, NY: Newman Press, 1974.

Possidius. *The Life of Saint Augustine*. Transl. John E. Rotelle. The Augustinian
    Series, 1. Villanova, PA: The Augustinian Press, 1988.
Ramsey, Boniface. *Ambrose*. The Early Church Fathers. London and New York,
    NY: Routledge Press, 1997.
Sulpicius Severus. "Life of St. Martin." In *The Works of Sulpicius Severus*. Transl.
    Alexander Roberts. NPNF. Second series, 11. Edinburgh: T & T Clark,
    1894.
—. *Writings*. Transl. Bernard Peebles. FOTC, 7. Washington, D.C.: Catholic
    University of America Press, 1949.
Tertullian. *Apologetical Works*. Transl. Emily Joseph Daly. FOTC, 10. Washing-
    ton, D.C.: Catholic University of America Press, 1950.
—. *Treatise on the Resurrection*. Transl. Ernest Evans. London: SPCK, 1960.
—. *Treatises on Marriage and Remarriage: To His Wife, An Exhortation to
    Chastity, Monogamy*. Transl. William P. Le Saint. ACW, 13. Westminster,
    MD: Newman Press, 1951.
Theodoret of Cyrus. *On Divine Providence*. Transl. Thomas Halton. ACW, 49.
    New York, NY: Newman Press, 1988.
Toal, Martin Francis. *The Sunday Sermons of the Great Fathers*. Four Vols.
    Chicago, IL: Henry Regnery, 1957-1963.
Ward, Benedicta. *The Sayings of the Desert Fathers: The Alphabetical Collection*.
    London: Mowbrays, 1975.

3. Secondary Literature

Bainton, Roland. *Christian Attitudes Towards War and Peace*. New York: Abing-
    don Press, 1960.
Barrera, Albino. *Modern Catholic Social Documents and Political Economy*.
    Washington, D.C.: Georgetown University Press, 2001.
Boersma, Hans. "Irenaeus, Derrida and Hospitality: On the Eschatological
    Overcoming of Violence," *Modern Theology* 19 (2003) 163-180.
Bourg, Florence Caffrey. *Where Two or Three Are Gathered: Christian Families as
    Domestic Churches*. Notre Dame, IN: University of Notre Dame Press,
    2003.
Brottier, Laurence. "De l'église hors de l'église au ciel anticipé sur quelques
    paradoxes Chrysostomiens." *Revue d'histoire et de philosophie religieuses* 76
    (1996) 277-292.
Burns, Mary A. *Saint John Chrysostom's Homilies on the Statues: A Study of Their
    Rhetorical Qualities and Form*. Patristic Studies, 22. Washington, D.C.:
    Catholic University of America Press, 1930.
Cadoux, C. John. *The Early Christian Attitude Toward War*. London: Headley
    Brothers, 1919.
Cameron, Alan. "A Misidentified Homily of Chrysostom." *Nottingham Medi-
    aeval Studies* 32 (1988) 34-48.
Charles, J. Daryl. "Pacifists, Patriots or Both? Second Thoughts on Early Chris-
    tian Attitudes toward Soldiering and War." Unpublished paper delivered
    at the Annual Meeting of the Evangelical Theological Society (Philadel-
    phia, PA, 2005).

Clark, Elizabeth. *Reading Renunciation: Asceticism and Scripture in Early Christianity*. Princeton, NJ: Princeton University Press, 1999.

Curran, Charles. *Catholic Social Teaching 1891-Present: A Historical Theological and Ethical Analysis*. Washington, D.C.: Georgetown University Press, 2002.

Davidson, Ivor J. *Ambrose. De officiis, Volume II: Commentary*. Oxford Early Christian Studies. Oxford: Oxford University Press, 2001.

Davis, Leo D. *The First Seven Ecumenical Councils (325-787): Their History and Theology*. Theology and Life, 21. Wilmington, DE: Michael Glazier Press, 1987.

de Lubac, Henri. *Medieval Exegesis. Two volumes*. Transl. Mark Sebanc and E. M. Macieroweski. Grand Rapids, MI: Eerdmans, 1998, 2000.

Descoeudres, Georges. "Kirche und Diakonia: Gemeinschaftsräume in den Ermitagen der Qusur el-Izeila." In *Explorations aux Qouçour el-Izeila lors des campagnes 1981, 1982, 1984, 1985, 1986, 1989 et 1990*. Ed. Philippe Bridel et al. Mission Suisse d'archéologie copte de l'université de Genève (EK 8184, tome III). Louvain: Peeters, 1999.

Dorr, Donal. *Option for the Poor: A Hundred Years of Vatican Social Teaching*. Dublin: Gill and Macmillan, 1983. Revised 1992.

Drobner, Hubertus R. *Augustinus von Hippo: Sermones ad populum*. Supplements to Vigiliae Christianae. Leiden: E. J. Brill, 2000.

Elm, Susanna. *"Virgins of God": The Making of Asceticism in Early Christianity*. Oxford Classical Monographs. Oxford: Clarendon Press, 1996.

Finn, Richard. *Almsgiving in the Later Roman Empire: Christian Promotion and Practice, 313-450*. Oxford Classical Monographs. Oxford: Oxford University Press, 2006.

Geerard, Maurits, ed. *Ab Athanasio ad Chrysostomum*. CPG, 2. Turnhout: Brepols, 1974.

—. *A Cyrillo Alexandrino ad Iohannem Damascenum*. CPG, 3. Turnhout: Brepols, 1979.

—. *Patres Antenicaeni*. CPG, 1. Turnhout: Brepols, 1983.

—, et al. *Supplementum*. CPG. Turnhout: Brepols, 1998.

Glare, P. G. W., ed. *Oxford Latin Dictionary*. Oxford: Clarendon Press, 1982.

Gould, Graham. *The Desert Fathers on Monastic Community*. Oxford Early Christian Studies. Oxford: Clarendon Press, 1993.

Guroian, Vigen. "Family and Christian Virtue: Reflections on the Ecclesial Vision of John Chrysostom." In *Ethics after Christendom: Toward an Ecclesial Christian Ethic*. Grand Rapids, MI: William B. Eerdmans, 1994, 133-154.

Haidacher, Sebastian. "Quellen der Chrysostomus-Homilie De perfecta caritate (PG 56, 279-290)." *Zeitschrift für katholische Theologie* 19 (1895) 387-389.

Hankey, Wayne J. "Mind." In *Augustine Through the Ages: An Encyclopedia*. Ed. Allan D. Fitzgerald. Grand Rapids, MI: William B. Eerdmans, 1999, 563-567.

Hardwick, Michael E. *Josephus as an Historical Source in Patristic Literature through Eusebius*. Brown Judaic Studies, 128. Atlanta, GA: Scholars Press, 1989.

Harmless, William. *Desert Christians: An Introduction to the Literature of Early Monasticism*. New York: Oxford University Press, 2004.

Harnack, Adolf von. *Militia Christi: die christliche Religion und der Soldaten-stand in den ersten drei Jahrhunderten.* Tübingen: Mohr Siebeck, 1905. ET: David McInnis Gracie, tr. *Militia Christi: The Christian Religion and the Military in the First Three Centuries.* Philadelphia, PA: Fortress Press, 1981.

Helgeland, John. "Christians and the Roman Army A.D. 173-337." *Church History* 43 (1974): 149-163.

—. *Christians and the Roman Army from Marcus Aurelius to Constantine.* Berlin: Walter de Gruyter, 1979.

—, Robert J. Daly and J. Patout Burns. *Christians and the Military: The Early Experience.* Philadelphia, PA: Fortress Press, 1985.

—. "Time and Space: Christian and Roman." In *Religion (Vorkonstantinisches Christentum: Verhältnis zu römischem Staat und heidnischer Religion [Forts.]).* Ed. Wolfgang Haase. Aufstieg und Niedergang der römischen Welt. Series 2, 23. Part 2. Berlin: Walter de Gruyter, 1980, 724-834.

Himes, Kenneth, ed. *Modern Catholic Social Teaching: Commentaries and Interpretations.* Washington, D.C.: Georgetown University Press, 2005.

Holmes, Augustine. *A Life Pleasing to God: The Spirituality of the Rules of St. Basil.* Cistercian Studies 189. Kalamazoo, MI: Cistercian Publications, 2000.

Hornus, Jean-Michel. *Évangile et labarum: Étude sur l'attitude du christiansime primitif devant les problèmes de l'État, de la guerre et de la violence.* Nouvelle série théologique, 9. Geneva: Labor et Fides, 1960.

Johnson, James T. *The Quest for Peace: Three Moral Traditions in Western Cultural History.* Princeton, NJ: Princeton University Press, 1987.

Kalsbach, A. "Diakonie." In *Reallexikon für Antike und Christentum, Lieferung 22: Deus internus (Forts.) – Diamant.* Ed. Theodor Klauser et al. Stuttgart: Anton Hiersemann, 1957. 909-17.

Kannengiesser, Charles. *Handbook of Patristic Exegesis: The Bible in Ancient Christianity.* Two volumes. The Bible in Ancient Christianity, 1. Leiden: E. J. Brill, 2004.

Katz, Sheri. "Person." In *Augustine Through the Ages: An Encyclopedia.* Ed. Allan D. Fitzgerald. Grand Rapids, MI: William B. Eerdmans, 1999, 647-650.

Keller, Adalbert. *Translationes Patristicae Graecae et Latinae: Bibliographie der Übersetzungen altchristlicher Quellen.* 2 vols. Stuttgart: Anton Hiersemann, 1997-2004.

Marrou, Henri-Irénée. "L'origine orientale des diaconies romaines." *Mélanges d'archéologie et d'histoire* 57 (1940) 95-142.

Maspero, Jean. *Papyrus grecs d'époque byzantine.* Catalogue général des antiquités égyptiennes du Musée du Caire, Papyrus grecs d'époque byzantine. Four volumes. Cairo: IFAO, 1911-1916.

—. "Sur quelques objets coptes du Musée du Caire." *Annales du Service des antiquités d'Égypte* 10 (1910): 173-174.

Mayer, Wendy and Pauline Allen. *John Chrysostom.* The Early Church Fathers Series. New York, NY: Routledge Press, 2000.

Monfrin, Françoise. "Pauvreté et richesse: Le lexique latin de l'encyclique: inspiration classique ou inspiration patristique?" In *Rerum Novarum: Écriture, contenu et reception d'une encyclique: Actes du colloque international organize par l'École française de Rome et le Greco n 2 du CNRS (Rome, 18-20 avril 1991).* Rome: École française de Rome, 1997, 133-186.

Nell-Breuning, Oswald von. *Reorganization of Social Economy: The Social Encyclical Developed and Explained.* Transl. Bernard W. Dempsey. New York: Bruce Publishing Co., 1936.

Niederer, Francis J. "Early Medieval Charity." *Church History* 21 (1952) 285-295.

Nuffelen, Peter van. "Deux fausses lettres de Julien l'Apostat (La lettre aux Juifs, *Ep.* 51 [Wright], et la lettre à Arsacius, *Ep.* 84 [Bidez])." *Vigiliae Christianae* 55 (2002) 131-150.

O'Brien, David J. and Thomas A. Shannon. *Catholic Social Thought: The Documentary Heritage.* Maryknoll, NY: Orbis Books, 1992.

Ogilvie, R. M. *The Library of Lactantius.* Oxford: Clarendon Press, 1978.

Owen, Richard. "Analysis: Encyclical is Work of Two Popes." In *The Times Online* (London: Jan 25, 2006).

Paul VI. "L'homme et la révolution urbaine: Citadins et ruraux devant l'urbanisation." *La Documentation Catholique* 62 (1-15 August, 1965) 1362-1365.

Paverd, Frans van de. *St. John Chrysostom. The Homilies on the Statues: An Introduction.* Orientalia Christiana Analecta, 239. Rome: Pontificium Institutum Studiorum Orientalium, 1991.

Rousseau, Philip. *Pachomius: The Making of a Community in Fourth-Century Egypt.* The Transformation of the Classical Heritage, 6. Berkeley, CA: University of California Press, 1985.

Salamito, Jean-Marie. "*Rerum novarum,* une encyclique néo-scolastique? La question sociale ou le déclin de la communauté." In *Rerum Novarum: Écriture, contenu et reception d'une encyclique: Actes du colloque international organize par l'École française de Rome et le Greco n 2 du CNRS (Rome, 18-20 avril 1991).* Rome: École française de Rome, 1997, 187-206.

Strzygowski, Josef. *Koptische Kunst.* Catalogue général des antiquités égyptiennes du Musée du Caire. Osnabrück: Zeller, 1904.

Swift, Louis J. *The Early Fathers on War and Military Service.* Message of the Fathers of the Church, 19. Wilmington, DE: Michael Glazier Press, 1983.

Tanner, Norman P. *The Councils of the Church: A Short History.* New York, NY: Crossroad, 2002.

Teske, Roland J. "Soul." In *Augustine Through the Ages: An Encyclopedia.* Ed. Allan D. Fitzgerald. Grand Rapids, MI: William B. Eerdmans, 1999, 807-812.

Wipszycka, Ewa. "Diaconia." In *The Coptic Encylopedia,* 3. Ed. Azis S. Atiya. New York: Macmillan, 1991, 895-867.

Vasey, Vincent. *The Social Ideas in the Works of St. Ambrose: A Study on De Nabuthe.* Studia Ephemeridis "Augustinianum", 17. Rome: Institutum patristicum "Augustinianum", 1982.

Verstraeten, Johan. "Catholic Social Thought as Discernment." *Logos* 8 (2005): 94-111.

—. "Re-Thinking Catholic Social Thought as Tradition." In *Catholic Social Thought: Twilight or Renaissance?* Ed. J. S. Boswell, F. P. McHugh, and J. Verstraeten. Bibliotheca Ephemeridum Theologicarum Lovaniensium, 157. Leuven: Peeters Press, 2000, 59-77.

Voicu, S. "La volontà e il caso: La tipologia dei primi spuri di Crisostomo." In *Giovanni Crisostomo: Oriente e Occidente tra IV e V secolo.* Studia Ephemeridis "Augustinianum", 93. Rome: Institutum patristicum "Augustinianum", 2005, 101-118.

Yoder, John Howard. *The Original Revolution: Essays on Christian Pacifism.*
    Christian Peace Shelf Series, 3. Scottdale, PA: Herald Press, 1971.
Young, Frances M. *Biblical Exegesis and the Formation of Christian Culture.*
    Cambridge: Cambridge University Press, 1997.

PRINTED ON PERMANENT PAPER • IMPRIME SUR PAPIER PERMANENT • GEDRUKT OP DUURZAAM PAPIER - ISO 9706

N.V. PEETERS S.A., WAROTSTRAAT 50, B-3020 HERENT